Including your missing 20% by embedding web and mobile accessibility

About the author

Professor Jonathan Hassell is a thought leader in digital inclusion, with over 14 years' experience of embedding accessibility within digital production teams and sharing best practice at international conferences.

He is the lead author of BS 8878 – the British Standard on embedding accessibility within organizations' business-as-usual policies and processes – and chaired its drafting committee, IST/45.

He is the former Head of Usability & Accessibility, BBC Future Media where he combined usability and accessibility disciplines to embed inclusive user-centred design across web, mobile and IPTV product creation.

He has won awards for product managing: the accessibility features of BBC iPlayer, the accessibility personalization tool MyDisplay, the accessibility information site '*My* web *my* way', the 'uKinect' Makaton sign language games, and the 'Nepalese Necklace' mobility games for blind and partially sighted children.

Through Hassell Inclusion he provides strategic accessibility training and consultancy to organizations worldwide, undertakes inclusion research, and leads innovation projects to create breakthrough products for people with disabilities and make inclusion easier and cheaper to implement.

He and his wife, Rosnah, make their home in London, UK.

Including your missing 20% by embedding web and mobile accessibility

Professor Jonathan Hassell

bsi.

First published in the UK in 2015
by
BSI Standards Limited
389 Chiswick High Road
London W4 4AL

Typeset in Great Britain by Letterpart Limited – letterpart.com
Printed in Great Britain by Berforts, www.berforts.co.uk

British Library Cataloguing in Publication Data
A catalogue record for this book is available from the British Library

ISBN 978 0 580 81204 0

Contents

Appendix 275

Acknowledgements

A book is never the solitary work of a lone writer. I am indebted to a huge number of people who inspired me, and gave me the opportunity to build up the knowledge that I've aimed to share in this book.

Though I am sure I will forget someone, I'd like to especially thank the following people:

- God, for making it all happen.
- My wife, Rosnah, for being my best friend, inspiration, confidante and touchstone.
- My son, Robbie, for giving up being read numerous books at bedtime so that Daddy could lock himself in a room and write his own book.
- Norman and Moya, for hosting my writing retreats so graciously.
- All of my interview contributors – Andrew Arch, Graham Armfield, Jennison Asuncion, David Banes, Gavin Evans, Lainey Feingold, Judith Fellowes, Steve Green, Shawn Henry, Brian Kelly, Shannon Kelly, Jeff Kline, Axel Leblois, Sarah Lewthwaite, Cam Nicholl, Debra Ruh, Makoto Ueki and Martin Wright – for their time and insights.
- The Silverton Road 'Dream Journey' crowd in whose company the idea for the video interviews accompanying this book arrived.
- Julia Helmsley, my editor at BSI.
- My reviewers, Jennison Asuncion, Cam Nicholl and Andy Heath who provided invaluable feedback on my first draft.
- My IST/45 committee at BSI, who brought their considerable expertise, passion and stamina to our three-year journey to BS 8878.
- All the people whose valuable comments on BS 8878's second draft for public consultation improved the standard no end.
- Richard Titus, who shared my vision for bringing the usability and accessibility disciplines together, and hired me to do that at the BBC.
- My team of Usability & Accessibility specialists at the BBC for joining me on the journey with such good humour and skill.
- Anne Eastgate and Derek Butler, who gave me the time and money to research deep into the needs of disabled children and create the solutions and techniques that are still the underpinning of all my innovation work.
- Martin Wright, Richard England and Gamelab for being my partners in creation and always seeing a challenge as an opportunity.
- My Hassell Inclusion clients, whose engagement with accessibility and with BS 8878 keep me learning every day.

Foreword

There is a powerful case for ensuring that disabled and older people can participate fully online through the use of digital technologies. Giving everyone full access to technology results in a more inclusive and productive society. The digital economy depends on making sure that everyone can contribute and everyone can benefit.

However, too many people are currently excluded.

The United Kingdom has a proud history of furthering the rights of disabled people, and was one of the first countries to establish a link between those rights and the accessibility of websites, in Part III of the Disability Discrimination Act 1995, which came into force in 1999. But legislation and regulation are only part of the story. While there is the perception that accessibility is a burden on business, we believe that accessibility offers numerous opportunities for business, consumers and citizens.

Designing products for ease of use by the vast majority of people is a great opportunity, particularly keeping in mind that as we get older most of us find our eyesight is not what it was, our fingers become stiffer and we find it more difficult to absorb new information.

Accessibility helps businesses develop products that greater numbers of consumers value, therefore reducing the number of demands made on a business's customer service department. There are increasing cases of businesses finding that innovative technologies they have created to serve the specific needs of disabled people are the solutions to challenges that everyone increasingly experiences when they are using mobile technologies on the move.

Moreover, embedding accessibility as a business-as-usual practice enables businesses to employ disabled people, and draw on a larger workforce whose skills it would not otherwise have access to.

Getting the accessibility question right will ensure that the UK continues to be one of the most competitive, highly skilled and technologically advanced economies in the world.

Events like the London Paralympics 2012 helped change people's attitudes to disabled people in the UK and across the world, and we believe that businesses are also slowly developing a better understanding of the needs of disabled people from their products, and changing their attitude to supporting people with those needs.

However, while the UK is a world leader in the provision of accessible websites and services to meet the needs of disabled people, research in 2006 found that many organizations were finding it difficult to become competent and confident in accessibility – the technical standards were not sufficient.

To change this, the UK government commissioned the British Standards Institution to come up with a framework that any organization could follow to embed digital accessibility in their business-as-usual policies and web development processes. That work culminated in the publication of BS 8878 in 2010, in which much of the experience of many of the UK's top accessibility experts has been distilled.

This book by Jonathan Hassell, former Head of Usability & Accessibility at the BBC, and Lead Author of BS 8878 provides examples of best practice and a step-by-step explanation of how to use BS 8878 to accelerate your organization forward on your accessibility journey.

The book addresses all the biggest challenges to organizations wanting to embed digital accessibility as business-as-usual. It includes real-world case study interviews from experts all over the world in the various aspects of accessibility that you'll need to master as you mature in accessibility.

In government we have been working to embed accessibility into a whole range of agendas, making sure that it is part and parcel of everything we do.

In this book, Jonathan clearly articulates how businesses can do the same.

Ed Vaizey, Minister of State for Culture and the Digital Economy

Mark Harper, Minister of State for Disabled People

London, UK, May 2014

Support materials to accompany this book

This book contains many of the most important lessons learnt by some of the world's most successful website owners when they've embedded a framework for accessibility competence in their organization.

To help you put their advice into practice in your organization, I've created a whole goodie bag of free resources to help you complete the practical 'Now it's your turn' exercises, included at the end of most sections of the book:

- Tools and templates that you can use to quickly get started with:
  o generating an accessibility business case slide-deck which is appropriate for your organization;
  o creating your organizational accessibility policy;
  o documenting your web product accessibility policy; and
  o prioritizing issues that get uncovered by accessibility testing.
- Access to exclusive YouTube videos of interviews with the contributors to this book, help forums, webinars, and coaching.

This book is just the beginning. Get help for the rest of your journey from:

http://qrs.ly/3a4a6bm

Chapter 1

Introduction

Most organizations are oblivious to, or terrified about, web accessibility.

They're probably aware that up to 20% of their customers – people with disabilities – could be clicking away from their websites, or leaving their mobile apps every day without having bought anything or found the information or service they wished to find, without wishing ever to return.

They may have even heard from one of this 20%, complaining about problems they can't reproduce, talking about 'assistive technologies' they don't understand, asking for what seem like impossible fixes, when their teams are already overloaded with much needed new feature development.

They know there's the possibility of being sued if they don't do the right thing, but they don't know how far they need to go to prevent that.

They don't know if there's anything in it for them other than risk mitigation, against laws that seem to be constantly changing, that don't align internationally, and for which they can find precious little case law to constitute a credible legal threat.

So they're anxious to know what their competitors are doing, whether this is an area in which they should be a leader or follower, and what the value of accessibility would be (possibly as a 'unique selling point') if they invested in it.

Their web teams may have read the industry standard *Web Content Accessibility Guidelines* (WCAG) *2.0*, but have found them impenetrable and badly organized. Worse, when their designers have located the 'success criteria' for design, the guidelines seem like a creative straightjacket that tells them everything they can't do, but very little about why.

Accessibility it seems, is a cul-de-sac they're being legally blackmailed into spending time on, which will result in products that are better for the 20% of people with disabilities and worse for the 80% who are not disabled.

Moreover, they have no idea how many disabled people are actually using their site or app, or how many more will because they're now spending good money making it more accessible.

So, if they do make something 'accessible', it's usually only for one product, or one version of a product.

It's usually because of one committed, passionate 'accessibility superhero' on their team whose eventual departure would leave them needing to start all over again.

If this sounds like where you work, I have some comforting news; you are not alone.

Where I believe most organizations want to be I learnt directly from the heads of diversity and inclusion of the top blue-chip corporations in Europe at a meeting of the Vanguard Network, early in 2011. I was speaking for the BBC at the event on the innovation possibilities of web accessibility for inclusion, but before I could speak, the event's chairwoman did something amazing. She spent a whole hour going round the room asking each of the delegates what one thing would really make a difference to their organization's inclusion practices, if they could achieve it. When asked to vote for which of the contributions each felt was the most important, the following was the unanimous choice:

'What I want is to strategically embed inclusion into my organization's culture and business-as-usual processes, rather than just doing another inclusion project.'

If you were sitting opposite me at the event you'd have seen my mouth open wide in recognition: the standard that I and so many other people had laboured on for three years to create, was exactly what those in the room were asking for, or at least it was when it came to their organization's digital presence.

I spent much of the lunch conversations conveying the following to the people in the room:

- That they could implement a strategy that would allow them to attract and keep that 20% of their audience who are disabled, while not detracting from the user experience of those who aren't.
- That there was a way they could sleep soundly, knowing that they'd done enough to cover their 'accessibility risk', but without costing the earth.
- That through following a simple, strategic business-aligned framework, they could embed the best practice necessary to consistently achieve these aims throughout their organization and digital products.

- That the framework would allow them to align accessibility and usability within their product teams, and show them when both could be achieved together, and when differences in the user-needs of different groups would require them to add personalization to their products.
- That all of this work could benefit their organization, not just in risk mitigation, customer service and corporate social responsibility, but also in their bottom line, as benchmarked analytics show how disabled people's increased use of their sites increases their turnover and profits.

Q. What did I have that could take them from their position of pain to the place they all wanted to be?

A. BS 8878:2010, *Web Accessibility – Code of Practice*

It's not the catchiest title in the world, but the journey from pain to relief that it promises couldn't be more timely.

BS 8878 opens up in detail, the strategies, policies and processes that award-winning, best-of-breed organizations like the BBC, IBM, Vodafone, Opera, BT and Lloyds Banking Group have used to become 'accessibility competent and confident', so that they can be used by any organization, no matter how big or small.

It does this at a time when the legal imperatives behind accessibility are being strengthened internationally, and when tablet and smartphone vendors are racing to promote accessibility as a key selling point of their handsets. It also does this as we start to enter the massive demographic change that will result in the number of people who need accessibility rocketing up as our populations age and the 'missing 20%' becomes 50%.

There's never been a better time to get into web accessibility, and people who have implemented BS 8878 are increasingly telling me that incorporating its user-centred inclusive design thinking into their production processes has resulted in not only more accessible websites and apps for disabled people, but better websites and apps for everyone.

On top of that, I have numerous stories of how the inclusive design thinking in BS 8878 has helped organizations be more innovative in their product ideation too, which is why I was in the room with the organizations in the Vanguard Network in the first place.

So I'm hoping that you, like them, will want to know more.

Note on inclusion vs accessibility

You'll find that I interchange the words 'accessibility' and 'inclusion' throughout this book. I sometimes use 'accessibility' as it's the word most people know. However, I prefer 'inclusion' as it avoids one of the main pitfalls that people who care about ensuring that people with disabilities are not excluded can fall into: that they care so much about how easy it is for disabled people to use products, that they forget about the needs of non-disabled in using the same product.

For them accessibility is the most important aspect of the product, not an important aspect of the product. Accessibility advocates often sacrifice the needs of the majority non-disabled audience to uphold the needs of a much smaller minority of disabled people.

I believe this is always the wrong thing to do. It's unsustainable. It doesn't allow everyone to win, just swaps the 'people who win' from being the usual non-disabled people to being the disabled people.

That's not a good enough goal. The goal should always be to make products work for everyone rather than saying that's the goal, and then acting like disabled audiences are more important than any other audience, spurred on by guidelines that don't take the impact of each of their checkpoints on non-disabled users and project budgets adequately into account.

This 'inclusive design' goal is at the heart of BS 8878. It reminds everyone that all user groups should be considered. It benefits all user groups, because when it asks website creators to think about people with disabilities who are so different from themselves, they start becoming sensitive to the needs of people who are a little different to themselves too – the needs of their ageing parents, for example. Going the extra mile makes you more sensitive to everyone's needs which can only be a good thing.

Chapter 2

Overview of the four stages of your journey with BS 8878

Let's start with an overview of the different stages of the journey towards digital accessibility competence and confidence that most organizations could benefit from.

I like to call these the four Es of digital accessibility strategy:

1. Expanding your thinking about why inclusive design has benefits to offer your organization.
2. Embedding inclusion as a value and competence across all parts of your organization, so all your staff and policies are working together to gain you those benefits.
3. Enabling your digital production teams to create products that are inclusive by giving them a process to follow that results in inclusive products every time.
4. Measuring the Effect all of this has on your organization's users/customers, brand reputation and bottom line.

I will go into detail on each of these stages in the following chapters, but for now I want to introduce each by way of a real-world story.

Expand your thinking about why you should 'do' inclusive design

It's critical to establish the first E before you go any further in your journey towards accessibility competence and confidence. Without being clear about it, your whole organization will be unsure of the reasoning behind the training, governance, policies or processes you introduce. You'll be taking your staff on a journey that will involve them learning new skills, working in new ways and changing 'the way things are done around here' without telling them why any change is necessary, what the point of the change is and when it will be over. Even worse, without it your organization may start on a journey because 'that's what everyone else is doing' and end up in the wrong destination because your organization is actually different from 'everyone else'.

The first E is Expanding your thinking about why you should go on the journey at all – examining the reasons and motivations for doing it, to find which best fit your organization's culture, purposes and products or services.

There are lots of good reasons for behaving in a certain way, but if you're unsure of your motivation, you will be forever second-guessing how you should behave when the journey gets difficult.

Let me tell you a story.

Have you ever been in a traffic jam?

Picture yourself sitting next to me in my slightly ageing blue 2002-model Ford Focus – the most inclusively designed car of all time – at 11.15 on a crisp winter's morning in January. We're just coming out of a traffic jam that has been frustrating me for the last 30 minutes. But finally the road ahead looks clear. I should be feeling relieved.

However, today is my mother's birthday. That's the reason why my family is on this motorway, and it's the reason why I'm still frustrated, because between me and the clear road ahead is a figure that is stressing me out. The figure is one of the main reasons why I bought my satnav. It's the one thing that no satnav will ever be sold without. It's the ETA for when we will arrive.

My mother's birthday lunch is booked for 12.15. The ETA says 12.30.

So what does my right foot do?

Five minutes later you'd be able to feel the stress lifting in the car until another aspect of my satnav comes into play – the speed-camera detection, which shows me a camera is coming up.

Why is this a problem? Because I'm not going at the speed limit, like pretty much every other car I can see on the road.

So I slow down. For how long? 10 minutes? One minute? No, more like 15 seconds. Because as soon as I'm past the camera my right foot takes over again.

So why this behaviour? Why am I not going below the speed limit, when everything says that I should? The law says that I should be going slower. I also know it's the 'right thing to do' – it would be better for the environment, and safer for my wife and son sitting in the back of the car. It would even be cheaper for me, and over time help me save money which I could spend on whatever I wanted…

But no, all of these motivations are outweighed by my ETA. That's what's driving me. Anything else is a distraction I'll work around.

Compare this situation with the roads in Norway. If my colleagues at an accessibility conference in Oslo are correct, in Norway, they seem to actually understand human behaviour. In Norway, speed cameras aren't just a bad thing. In Norway, speed cameras take photos of all the cars that go past them, not just those that are speeding. Because, in Norway, you don't pay your speeding fines to a faceless bureaucrat in a government office somewhere. You pay them to the people who were going under the speed limit past the same speed camera on the same day.

In Norway, a speed camera can be your friend. It can even make you money.

In Norway, you can win!

So, where would you prefer to drive? England? Or Norway?

That's just a simple example of why it's necessary to reframe the accessibility conversation. For too long digital accessibility has been considered to be all about avoiding losing. All about getting away with as little as you absolutely have to do to avoid getting into legal trouble. Riding your luck. Because the best thing that could happen is that you can successfully get away with ignoring it, because there's nothing to win. Buying the cheapest accessibility insurance policy you can, because you're not convinced that you'll ever need it. That's not motivational to anyone other than your risk management department.

No, to be worth doing at all, accessibility needs to be considered in the right way. With 20% of your potential audience caring about how you handle the accessibility of your products, accessibility isn't about avoiding losing, it's about winning. Winning a bigger audience. Winning better brand reputation. Just plain old winning.

Now that sounds far more interesting doesn't it?

So Chapter 3 will allow you to expand the way you think about accessibility, so that you can understand its relative importance to your organization when compared with all the other aspects of product design, and so provide a much more stable, reliable motivation for spending time on it.

Embedding organizational competence and confidence

Once you've expanded your view to encompass better motivation for accessibility, the second E is critical to ensure that you can actually deliver it in the culture and structure of your business. This is about identifying all the things that need to work together to make sure you can deliver the accessibility you want efficiently, and make sure that nothing critical is able to snatch defeat from the jaws of success.

I'm talking about Embedding inclusion as a value that pervades your organization. Like a stick of seaside rock, you should be able to take a cross-section of any part of your organization and find the same values at play. Not only is there nothing there that could derail your ability to deliver to your values, but there is understanding, competence and confidence present that this is not only worth doing, but it is also achievable.

To give you an analogy from a sport I've just taken up, spurred on by Britain's successes in the 2012 London Olympics, let's consider how rowing teams win.

Firstly, everyone in the boat has the same goal – to go in the same direction, and to get there as quickly as possible. There's not much chance for an individual rower doing otherwise with only one oar in their hands, but they could turn it over and push the water the other way if they wanted to slow the whole team down. And, yes, a couple of times on my early outings in the boat a number of us novices inadvertently ended up doing just that, not because we wanted to, but because we were concentrating on another part of our stroke at the time.

Secondly, everyone in the boat is doing their job, not someone else's. There are effectively three jobs in the boat: the one 'stroke' rower is establishing the rowers' rhythm; the other seven rowers are rowing to that rhythm; and the one cox is steering and providing feedback to each rower on how they need to tweak their performance to stick to that rhythm. If two people try to steer the boat, say, by stopping rowing on one side so the boat starts turning against its rudder, it's fighting against itself. If a rower who isn't 'stroke' decides to set a rhythm that is different, say, by trying to row faster to go faster, this actually slows the boat down and confuses the whole crew. If an inexperienced or lower-skilled rower doesn't pay attention to feedback from the cox on how they are rowing, an unchecked increase in the depth their blade goes into the water could unbalance the boat and end up rocking it up and down, resulting in the other rowers needing to work to stabilize it rather than concentrating on powering forwards.

Thirdly, the equipment the team is using could sabotage the enterprise. A great crew, harmonized in purpose, rhythm and technique can be beaten by a group of novices if there's a leak in the boat.

Finally, a winning team can slowly go off the boil if they start to feel that the club they row for is beginning to take them for granted. They may feel that new club leaders are more interested in other parts of running the club, assuming that they'll always win even if they aren't given the time to practise, or feedback on any bad habits that might be creeping into their game.

The same is true for any organization – for it to succeed in its goals, all of its members need to agree on the goal; understand their role in working towards it; be trained in how to perform that role; and have someone providing feedback on how they are performing, both to correct errors or inefficiencies, and to allow them to recognize, and feel appreciated for great performance.

Traditional accessibility guidelines have concentrated almost exclusively on what developers, designers and content creators (the seven ordinary rowers in our analogy) need to do to deliver accessibility, without understanding that their work can either be facilitated or hindered by the layers of more strategic management and policy above them.

So Chapter 4 will look at ways of embedding accessibility as a value, goal and competence in all the people and policies in your organization that have an impact on whether your products are made to be accessible.

Enabling project teams to deliver through an established process

Once you've embedded accessibility as a value within your organization's staff and policies, the third E is critical to ensure that you are able to deliver it consistently for all your products whether they are similar, or vary in purpose, audience, technology or importance. This is about identifying a way of working that is *stable* enough to ensure good accessibility results every time, while being *flexible* enough to handle any type of project you can throw at it without breaking.

I'm talking about Enabling your teams to get accessibility right, and to get it right all of the time.

To be clear, I'm not talking about a checklist – something that seems to be synonymous with accessibility in many people's minds. I'm talking about a *process*. A documented, flexible, repeatable process that each member of your project team buys into, for every web project your organization runs.

As establishing a new process, or change to your current process, for the way you work is much more difficult to achieve than adding a checklist to your quality assurance testing, it's important for me to convince you why this is necessary.

On 27 January 2012, the RNIB, the UK's leading vision impairment charity, served legal papers on the airline bmibaby for their failure to ensure that blind and partially sighted customers could book flights via their website.[1]

I'd like you to put yourself in bmibaby's shoes for a moment, and consider what you would do in this circumstance...

Like most organizations, I'm guessing that, on the day the legal writ arrived, the bmibaby web team were already up to their necks in creating new website features, or new ways of beating their competition via sales funnel conversion optimization; getting the site to work better for people using it on a mobile phone; trying to maximize their search engine optimization and Google pay-per-click conversions; making sure that they were monitoring Twitter and Facebook for any mentions of their organization in the social media sphere, especially detrimental ones; or pushing out the online part of marketing campaigns to sell more flights via promotions, or link-ups with their affiliates' websites.

These are likely to have been the things on the bmibaby to-do list on the day on which they got served. Each one of these to-do list items is designed to maintain or improve the airline's visibility on the web, or improve their conversion of site visitors to customers. And each one of these to-do list items needs the investment of the web team's time and energy to bring in greater revenues and profits for the company.

Into this already busy environment the notice of legal proceedings is dropped like a bombshell. The only sensible questions to ask in response are: 'What is the minimum we need to do to make the pain go away?' and 'When do we need to do it by?' It's all hands to the pump on 'remediation' – bailing out the water in your boat, and plugging the leak, so you can get back to the important thing, which is sailing into the new waters already scheduled on your roadmap.

This makes perfect sense. However, it is also likely to create a problem as well as solve one.

To illustrate, let me tell you the story of Achilles.

As anyone who's seen Brad Pitt's impressive combat prowess in the film Troy *will be all too aware, Achilles was an incredible Greek warrior whose name struck fear into his opponents. So he would doubtless be dismayed to find that he is renowned in modern popular culture for one part of his anatomy only: his heel.[2]*

Achilles is famous because, rather than actually dealing with his one weakness, he did the first century AD equivalent of putting a Band-Aid

---

[1] http://www.hassellinclusion.com/2012/01/rnib-bmi-baby-accessibility-lawsuit/

[2] http://en.wikipedia.org/wiki/Achilles'_heel

on it. This dealt with the problem immediately, but it didn't deal with the problem long term. So Achilles has gone down in history as a cautionary tale, rather than being celebrated as a mighty warrior.

Why am I bringing ancient Greeks into a book on accessibility? Because fixing the accessibility problems of your website or mobile app, when they are pointed out to you by an audit or user complaint is just such a Band-Aid.

We want to feel that we've learnt from Achilles' unintended message to us through the years. Yet most organizations are treating accessibility just like that Band-Aid. Why else would 'accessibility remediation' still be such a core service from any accessibility agency?

I think this highlights a direct link with many organizations' limited view of the first E – Expand. If we're 'trying to get away with it', we'll only think of accessibility when we get caught, and then we'll rush to find the quickest, cheapest Band-Aid to make the pain go away, so we can forget about it again.

The quick, cheap way of dealing with pain is the patch-up pill of pain relief, not the lifestyle change that prevents the pain coming back. Yet any sensible person knows that prevention is better than cure.

The fact is that you need to fix the problem in the process not the product to prevent it reoccurring.

As we all know these days, no website or app is ever finished. Most go through content and maintenance updates every day, minor version updates weekly or monthly, and full rebuilds every couple of years. So fixing your accessibility problem in the product, rather than in the way you work, means that every time you upgrade your product you may cause new accessibility problems, especially as existing, experienced product team members move on to new challenges and new team members take their place.

BS 8878's best-practice advice is to enable your staff to get accessibility right all the time by embedding it in your standard web development process, because then you will not only uphold accessibility in every new product that you create, but also in every version of those products.

While embedding a process is more challenging than just asking one person to test the product against a checklist, and do whatever fixes are necessary, its benefits are much greater.

So Chapter 5 will introduce all the steps of the flexible process you can put in place to consistently enable your teams to prevent accessibility problems coming up in the first place. So pain relief isn't such a necessary part of the picture.

Measuring the Effect you have

The final E is the one most organizations don't think about nearly enough. Often it's only something they appreciate when they think they've done everything they were supposed to do, and yet they are still faced with an email from a disabled person accusing them of not doing the right thing. It's also the one thing that can turn accessibility from a costly drain on an organization's resources to being the very thing that has the potential to make the organization rich.

It is measuring the Effect your accessibility work achieves. After all, if accessibility is about winning, then it's fundamentally about the effect your work has on the user experience of the disabled people you're trying to help and the rest of your non-disabled users.

Unfortunately, this often gets forgotten, especially as checking compliance with guidelines is the one thing most people know about accessibility. This is like working out where you've ended up at the end of a drive by double-checking all of the turns you made on the way, rather than by looking out of the window and asking a local where you've arrived. You could have taken all the 'right' turns according to the map, but what if the map is a little out of date?

BS 8878 uses the international accessibility standard WCAG 2.0 for what it's good at, providing detailed instructions for how to make decisions on various technical design and content aspects of accessibility as you create and maintain a product.

What it doesn't use WCAG for is what it's not good at – for telling you whether or not following those guidelines has resulted in a product that disabled people can actually use to complete the tasks they came to the site to accomplish. For this is often as much about usability and learnability as accessibility.

To highlight the importance of this, let me tell you another story, of how two days in 2008 pushed me to learn which accessibility outcomes are important for users and organizations, and which are not.

Let me take you to a radio studio in BBC Broadcasting House in central London in the hot sticky summer of 2008.

If you had been sitting next to me at 2.42 in the afternoon, you'd have been sitting at a green baize table looking across at Peter White, Presenter of the BBC's long-running In Touch *radio show for people who are blind or visually impaired, and he's fascinating. So much so, that I'm not paying adequate attention to the frustrated voice coming through my headphones, which is okay until it stops and the red light goes on in front of me and I realize it's my turn to speak.*

This is what I'm here for: to defend the accessibility of the BBC's most important digital product of the early 21st century. The product that has liberated BBC programmes from being just broadcast on the TV and allowed people to watch them wherever and whenever they'd like. The coolest brand the BBC have ever had. The mighty iPlayer.

This shouldn't be a problem. I know we've already done the right thing and I've prepared notes for my response. Unfortunately, unlike the Braille notes that Peter has been stroking silently under his arm as a prompt for his flawless introduction, my notes are crisply folded on the green baize in front of me, and I'm starting to think unfolding them would create noise that would be picked up by the microphone.

So I speak from the heart: 'We really do care for blind users. We care for all our users. That's why we've found the best guidelines for how to make things work for everyone, and have followed them to the letter. We've even tested iPlayer with people with all sorts of disabilities. I even checked it with the JAWS screen reader myself this morning and...'

'So why then can I not use it? Why did you have to replace something that worked, with something that doesn't?'

It's a bit difficult to argue with a disembodied voice, especially live on BBC Radio 4. I start wondering who the complaining voice belongs to, to make them more human, to have a chance of properly empathizing with their position. I start to picture a woman in her late 40s, sitting at a computer desk somewhere in middle England – she has no discernible accent, and it doesn't sound noisy where she is – with a guide dog by her side.

But already I'm figuring that this is a stereotype. That I don't really know very much about her other than she's obviously not happy, and that much of what I've pictured may be completely wrong.

And then suddenly I get a flash of insight, a glimpse into her world. You see, that's what she is actually complaining about – we haven't given her a good enough picture of the website we've created. The way we've designed it hasn't enabled her to understand how to use the thing she cannot see.

I'm really loving this train of thought, this insight into the needs of this user. I'm starting to see all sorts of implications for how we could...

Peter coughs, and suddenly I'm back in the room. These insights are helpful. But they're not answering her question.

'I, er... er...'

Peter rescues me: 'Thankfully, not all blind users are having the same problem. Here are a number of blind people who we spoke to yesterday who say that they love the product...'

The red light turns off as altogether more friendly voices soothe my ears.

Peter gestures for me to take my headphones off. His words are for me, not our audience: 'Just a word of advice. It's not the work you do. It's whether or not it helps people that matters... Wouldn't you say...?'

He's right. I've dodged a bullet today, as the usability and accessibility of our site – the requirements of my job – seem okay. But even going beyond guidelines and accessibility conformance and doing user-testing to check the usability of our site for disabled people hasn't been enough.

For this person it seems like the learnability of our product is the problem. She had something that worked. We replaced it with a version 2 that worked in a different way, but we didn't help her move from one to the other. From the rest of what Peter had to say, it sounds like the blind people we were able to recruit for our testing may be way more confident and competent in their use of the web than the majority of blind people out there.

We may be ahead of organizations that just do 'compliance'. But, in reality, there's still a long way to go in our journey...

Back at my desk the next day, I make my next steps, as my towering American boss places a letter on my desk as he breezes past: 'Sort this out'.

Two sentences of the first paragraph of typed text are underlined in red:

'I was disgusted to hear that you only test your sites using the JAWS screen reader. How exactly do you expect a pensioner to afford £800?'

The name on the bottom of the letter is a man's, so it's certainly not the woman from yesterday.

But I have learnt from listening to her. This time I have the opportunity to engage more deeply with this user's real-world difficulties. There is more to be learnt and this time, in private. I pick up the phone and dial the number at the bottom of the page...

Two weeks later we launch the UK's first survey into which screen readers are actually being used by blind people. We've bypassed asking the screen reader manufacturer and their distributors. We're talking directly to a wider variety of blind users, partnered with the RNIB asking people on their mailing list what screen readers they actually use, and what sort of user experience they are getting from BBC websites.

The time for assumptions is over: now we are going to arm ourselves with better research on which to make our decisions. And we're going to test with people who actually make up the majority of our disabled audiences, not techies whose vision impairment isn't as key to their user experience as their amazing capability to work around problems.

WCAG? It would only be the end of our journey if we didn't care whether real people were able to use the products resulting from our hard work. As we do, it's just the start…

In summary, I believe the aim of accessibility – or inclusion, as I prefer to call it – is to build a better product, not just a compliant one; through this lies sufficient return on investment (ROI) to make the costs of accessibility worthwhile.

For that's the other effect you want to have – a positive effect on your organization's bottom line.

A positive ROI is definitely possible. To give one example of the bottom-line benefits of considering the needs of disabled and older people, take OXO Good Grips – a well-known American pioneer of inclusive design. Sam Farber's wife, a keen cook, suffered from arthritis, which caused her to ask him one challenging but inspiring question: 'Why do ordinary kitchen tools hurt your hands?' The result of his engaging fully with that question, and how to answer it, made him found OXO[3], and created the company's fortune. Their first 15 products launched in 1990. They achieved sales growth of over 35% per year from 1991 to 2002. Their line of kitchen utensils has now grown to over 500 products, and they have won over 100 design awards.

Now that sounds like winning to me!

'Start with the end in mind' is always a useful policy. So Chapter 6 helps you ensure your accessibility strategy keeps this end firmly in mind, and how to measure the impact of your strategy over time, to make sure your work is having the effects that you want.

---

[3]   http://en.wikipedia.org/wiki/Sam_Farber

BS 8878 – your shortcut to the results of many experts' journeys

'Do you want to avoid losing? Or do you want to win?'

'Embed it so that, like a stick of seaside rock, you should be able to take a cross-section of any part of your organization and find the same values at play.'

'You need to fix the problem in the process not the product to prevent it reoccurring.'

'It's not the work you do. It's whether or not it helps people that matters.'

Those were the four phrases that steered me and my Usability & Accessibility team through the years after my radio show with Peter White.

Three years later we had begun to embed many of the things necessary to make sure the benefit of the hard work we were putting in was really getting through to our users.

More importantly, the British Standards Institution had given me a chance to take that experience, enrich it by comparing it against what the heads of accessibility in other best-practice organizations had done, and create BS 8878 to show others how they could do the same thing and maybe win the awards we had won.

BS 8878 is built on the combined experience of some of the world's most capable accessibility experts; it captures the progress on the journey they've made, so you can take a shortcut.

It's based on PAS 78 – the original first attempt in 2006 to create a strategic guide to accessibility, led by Julie Howell, and commissioned by the UK Disability Rights Commission when their research in 2005 revealed that existing standards did not make it easy enough for website owners to know what to do to make their websites accessible.

It was worked on for three years by the IST/45 committee that I chaired, including: experts in creating accessible products from the BBC, IBM, Nomensa, the UK government's Central Office of Information and Lloyds Banking Group; experts in understanding disabled people's needs from the RNIB, the Royal National Institute for Deaf People (RNID) and United Response; experts in the accessibility of e-learning from The Open University, TechDis, the University of Southampton and Axelrod Access for All; an expert in accessibility law from Pinsent Masons legal practice; and representatives of the rest of the IT industry from the Chartered Institute for IT, Vodafone and Opera.

It was reviewed by 328 accessibility experts, disability organizations, academics and website owners worldwide – including input from W3C, Adobe, the UK Equality and Human Rights Commission, the Engineering Design Centre in Cambridge, Business Link and Autistic UK – via two 'drafts for public consultation'. It was launched in December 2010.

How this book expands on BS 8878

Three years have elapsed since BS 8878's launch, and the standard is holding up well in the fast-moving world of the web. This book is a guide to what's in BS 8878 and also includes my experience of user-testing its value in the real world of web product creation, not only in the UK but also internationally. I've trained over 30 organizations in using BS 8878 to set their accessibility strategy, and have refined my thinking based on that experience over the years.

So the book includes some structuring of the concepts in BS 8878 that I've found helps people get to grips with the standard. It addresses a couple of places where the standard slightly downplayed something important – planning accessibility throughout a project, and how to integrate BS 8878's process steps into your current web production process, if you have one. It expands on accessibility advice for important fast-moving aspects of the web, like mobile web and app creation, which BS 8878 anticipated but which has moved on further since its publication.

To illustrate many of the book's points, and add real-world depth, it also includes verbatim extracts from video interviews that I've conducted with some of the world's top accessibility minds on their areas of greatest expertise:

- A United Nations (UN) agency director on how accessibility laws are created.
- An expert in how people learn accessibility.
- Experts in understanding disabled and older people's use of the web.
- Experts in how to commission and carry out accessibility testing.
- The creator of the accessibility ecosystem in Qatar.
- People who've embedded accessibility in a multinational IT company, a Canadian bank, the American State of Texas, the Australian government, university document repositories, innovative e-learning games.

I've only had the space to include a fraction of the riches in these interviews in the book, so I've put the full video interviews online and included QR codes and links in each interview panel so you can delve deeper into the experience of any that particularly resonate with you as you make your journey.

I know that BS 8878 can get you from the pain of confusion about accessibility to award-winning results, because it's an expression of the journey that I, and many other accessibility specialists, have gone on before you.

So let's dive in!

Chapter 3

EXPAND – why bother?

There are a number of reasons why an organization might be interested in supporting the needs of people with disabilities and older audiences. Different organizations may have very different reasons at play behind their strategy.

Are they in it because of choice or necessity, for risk aversion, to keep up good corporate social responsibility, to maximize their products' audience reach or a combination of these? And how important are each of these to the organization, in comparison to each other?

Moreover, there can often be a real difference between the public communication of these reasons and what is communicated internally to their digital production staff. Organizations are often required to hold a particular position by their public service nature or sheer size, and publish laudable words about their commitment to accessibility publicly. However, the reality of many organizations' commitment to inclusion and accessibility often doesn't live up to their fine words, as their staff aren't trained to live out the commitment and projects fail to prioritize it consistently. Organizations need to decide how important inclusion is in comparison to other things that are important to them, to avoid 'flip-flopping' between reasons for doing accessibility depending on the situation in front of them.

This chapter will help you work out what your motivation is for inclusion, and what the goals of your accessibility strategy will be: avoiding being sued; minimizing the costs of dealing with accessibility complaints; becoming 'best practice'; ensuring you're not missing a sales feature compared with your competitors; selling more products; or gaining more customers.

This is an essential foundation as you can only build a strategic framework for how you are going to embed accessibility in your organization if you know your reasons for why you are doing it, and its priority relative to other strategies you're creating.

Meet your disabled and older audiences

Let's start off by getting a better idea of the disabled and older audiences whose access needs come under the heading of accessibility.

In most Western countries the size of the disabled population ranges between 12% and 26% of the population. To give just two examples: in the UK, that's over 11 million people; in Brazil, it's over 24 million people.

Those are big numbers and many product managers can initially be puzzled or even sceptical of their large size. How can there be 20% of the population who are disabled if you don't see them every day on the street? What does disability actually mean in the context of audience size? Who is defined as disabled?

What's interesting is that when you go deeper to answer those questions, you often find that the numbers tend to underestimate the prevalence of disability. Here in the UK, disability is defined by the Equality Act 2010[4] as:

> 'anyone with a physical or mental impairment which has a substantial long-term adverse effect on their ability to carry out normal day-to-day activities'.

So, for example, this includes people with mental health issues, or people with a long-term illness that impacts their day-to-day life. However, it doesn't include anybody who wouldn't consider themselves disabled, or be comfortable disclosing their disability to a census. So people who are dyslexic are likely to be underrepresented in these figures, because many dyslexics unfortunately regard their condition as 'their guilty secret', not something that they would wish to disclose. The number of people with disabilities who are not comfortable making such a disclosure tends to underplay these figures, both here in the UK, and more notably in those parts of the world where disability is unfortunately still seen as something to be hidden, either by the disabled person themselves or their immediate family.

Something else that tends to shock people who attend my workshops is my slide on how the disabled population breaks down into different disability groups. The one thing that most people know about accessibility is that it's important to make sure that your website works well for blind people using screen readers. Yet the proportion of blind people in the disabled population is approximately 2%. So making your website work for blind people, and blind people alone, is devoting all your time and attention to 2% of your potential audience, and neglecting the needs of the other 98%, which includes many more people with lower-level vision impairments.

---

4   https://www.gov.uk/equality-act-2010-guidance

That makes no sense from anything other than a risk-avoidance perspective.

This bias towards considering the needs of people with more extreme disabilities is not confined to vision impairment. The larger groups of disabled people are those with more minor impairments, and yet we tend to concentrate on the extremes because their need is greatest and their lobbies are strongest. For a fuller discussion of the impact of these issues on the prioritization of solutions for people with different disabilities, see Step 3 of the BS 8878 process in Chapter 5.

Older people – the statistic that is going up, fast...

One last group that are impacted by accessibility issues is the ageing population.

Most websites are created by young people. But the services that most popular websites provide may potentially appeal to older people as much as those who are younger.

As many people develop impairments through the ageing process, we should all be interested in how people with impairments are supported by digital products. For, in the future 'they' are 'we'. It's not something we necessarily like to think about, but we will all develop impairments in time. So we all have something to gain from 'designing for our future selves'.

On top of this, the statistics on population ageing are startling. Every month more than a quarter of a million Americans turn 65.[5] The population forecasts from Japan for 2050 predict a massive, ongoing demographic change:

- in 1950, over 65 year-olds made up 4.9% of the population;
- by 2006, this percentage had risen to 20.8%; and
- projections for 2050 indicate this figure will reach almost 40%.

This is one of the reasons why accessibility is so important economically. On top of the pensions 'time bomb' is the increasing need for people to be able to continue living independently in their homes as they age. The gross domestic product of a nation like Japan will nosedive if 40% of the population can no longer use digital technologies in their 70s and 80s, and will require those in the working population to spend their time helping them counter digital exclusion.

Similarly, from an individual organization perspective, it is clear that if accessibility is important today, it will only get more and more important

---

[5] http://jimtingler.com/2014/05/28/aging-baby-boomers-will-be-the-biggest-business-process-improvement-driver-since-y2k/

over the coming years as the number of people with impairments in the population who wish to use your web products grows. While you may be able to exclude older people from using your website without too much loss to your bottom-line at the moment, year on year this decision will start to cost you more and more.

So I congratulate you on having purchased this book now and started on your journey of understanding the access needs of people with impairments. The insights you'll get from taking inclusion seriously will become more and more valuable as time goes on. Act now, and over time your foresight could turn into a great advantage over your competitors who came late to the party.

So, let's look at all the reasons why the needs of disabled people should matter to your organization now. We'll look at both organizational threats and opportunities.

Interview with Makoto Ueki, Accessibility Consultant at Infoaxia and Chairman of Japan's Web Accessibility Infrastructure Committee

Makoto: Japan is the world's fastest ageing country. The original name of [the] Japanese industrial standards for web accessibility was JIS X 8341-3. It's part of a series called *Guidelines for Older Persons and Persons with Disabilities.*

Jonathan: Older people and people with disabilities? That way round? Most other countries think of accessibility as mostly for disabled people…

Makoto: We have a series of guidelines as JIS, not only web but also for many things. In 2004 we already included elderly people as intended users. When we think about accessibility it's not only about people with disabilities but also people who are ageing. If people hear about accessibility and understand the concept, they know it would be the right thing to do, but if they don't need accessibility for themselves they may not do that. 'It's my business when the issue affects myself.' But as we are ageing, many more people will think about accessibility as 'My issue. It's needed for me.' My daily life heavily relies on the web. If I can't use the web I would get lost. 'No web, no life.' Actually now I'm 46 years old and my eyesight has been already degrading. So for me web accessibility is getting to be a much more important issue.

What I'd like to emphasize is that accessibility is not just about people with disabilities and elderly people, it's about everybody. The web will be accessed by many more kinds of devices, environments and it's going to be diverse. We need to make sure that web content can be accessed by everyone. In Japan when I talk about accessibility I emphasize that it is not special. 'Accessibility is the web'. That is my company's key message and name: Infoaxia. Info means information and *axia* means value in Greek. Information cannot be valuable without accessibility.

In Japan we had a big earthquake and tsunami three years ago. The web was an essential source of urgent information. People were using mobile phones or cell phones without enough power. If the information was provided by using PDF, for example, people who are using cell phones couldn't access that information. We will have the Olympic and Paralympic Games in 2020 in Tokyo. At the final presentation, there was very famous phrase, *Omotenashi*. It means accommodation; accommodate people. When my accessibility expert friends come and experience Japan – get in a taxi, get on the train, go to a restaurant, go shopping – they say they are impressed with the accommodation. Even if we don't have a legal obligation, we accommodate people and do the right thing. Maybe it's Japanese culture. I hope that the Olympics could be a big trigger for web accessibility in Japan – Japanese websites will be accessed by many more foreigners and we will have many more visitors from many more countries. As people here know the concept of universal design, it will be not so difficult for Japanese people to understand accessibility and make it happen.

Watch the complete video interview with Makoto Ueki at:

http://qrs.ly/yc4a6c7

Find more on Infoaxia at: http://www.infoaxia.com/en/

Threat – the legal business case

The first threat is well known to most website owners, as it's the one that disabled people and accessibility advocates have used most frequently in fighting for their needs to be taken into account when digital technologies are created. It's the legal threat.

Most countries have some form of anti-discrimination legislation on their statute books. In the UK it's the Equality Act 2010. In the United States it's the Americans with Disabilities Act of 1990 (ADA),[6] together with a number of state laws. Most countries in the EU have some form of disability discrimination legislation.

Those countries that haven't yet established disability discrimination legislation are likely to soon. The UN Convention on the Rights of Persons with Disabilities[7] – which now has signatories from over 170 nation states worldwide[8] – is the driving force behind much of the creation of this legislation. Countries that sign the UN Convention commit to starting on the path towards creating disability discrimination legislation, usually establishing it within the next 10 years.

While the strength and wording of these laws differ, the purpose of most is to clearly establish that disabled people may have grounds for making a discrimination claim against the owners of a product or service if that service has not been made available and usable for them.

Most of these disability discrimination laws apply to products and services provided through websites, either mentioned explicitly in the legislation (as in the EU proposed directive on the accessibility of public bodies websites 2012[9], and the Australian Disability Discrimination Act 1992[10]), or as case law establishes that websites should be considered to be services like those traditionally offered through physical premises or phone lines (as was arguably established for the ADA by a ruling in the US National Association of the Deaf vs Netflix suit in 2012[11]).

In most cases a principle of 'reasonableness'[12] is included in the law, to differentiate between the clear need for large, important online services (such as government services or banks) to be made accessible, and the lesser need for smaller, less popular websites (such as personal blogs) to be made accessible.

---

[6] http://www.ada.gov/2010_regs.htm

[7] http://www.un.org/disabilities/default.asp?navid=14&pid=150

[8] http://www.un.org/disabilities/countries.asp?navid=12&pid=166

[9] http://www.hassellinclusion.com/2012/12/clear-eu-accessibility-law/

[10] https://www.humanrights.gov.au/our-work/disability-rights/standards/world-wide-web-access-disability-discrimination-act-advisory

[11] http://www.hassellinclusion.com/2012/06/netflix-caption-lawsuit-uk-implications/

[12] http://www.hassellinclusion.com/2013/08/web-accessibility-ruinous-obligation/

To complicate matters, disability discrimination law in some countries, such as the UK and the USA, applies to both public and privately owned websites; but in others, such as France,[13] it only applies to publicly owned sites.

On top of general disability discrimination law, some countries have also passed specific accessibility legislation for different industries, which impacts on their online presence. Two recent examples, both from the USA, are:

1. the 21st Century Video Accessibility Act of 2010 (CVAA),[14] which includes requirements that full-length programmes (and, recently, clips[15]) that have been broadcast with captions on TV are also closed-captioned when they are made available on the internet;
2. the amendment to the Air Carrier Access Act of 1986 (ACAA),[16] in which the United States Department of Transportation has taken steps to address the accessibility of air carrier websites and kiosks to persons with disabilities.

While some of these laws have been in existence for decades, the amount of case law linked to them varies from country to country. To give a few examples:

• In the UK there is no case law for web accessibility. Even though Part III of the Disability Discrimination Act[17], which protected the rights of disabled people before the Equality Act, came into being at the end of the 1990s, no cases have come to the UK court for ruling. All the cases that have been brought have been settled out of court, thus depriving organizations from the clarity of application information that comes from published rulings.

---

[13] http://www.senat.fr/leg/tas04-018.html

[14] http://transition.fcc.gov/cgb/dro/cvaa.html

[15] http://globalaccessibilitynews.com/2014/07/14/new-rules-require-closed-captioning-of-online-video-clips/

[16] http://www.deque.com/air-carrier-access-act-update

[17] http://www.legislation.gov.uk/ukpga/1995/50/part/III

- In the United States this situation is very different, with many cases being brought each year, and high-profile cases like the National Federation of the Blind vs Target case[18] being well known for its $6 million settlement in 2008, which provides an indication of how courts in the different states might rule on new cases presented to them.
- In Australia, case law stretches back to Maguire vs SOCOG[19] around the Sydney Olympics in 2000, which was the first case for web accessibility globally.

The legal situation in many countries is constantly changing, so organizations should keep themselves informed of legal cases in all of the jurisdictions in which their websites and mobile apps are available. You can keep up to date with the latest cases by subscribing to the Hassell Inclusion newsletter[20].

While disability discrimination laws help raise awareness of the access needs of disabled people, organizations that are motivated purely because of the legal business case for accessibility tend to see it as a 'necessary cost' of doing business online, like data protection or website security. As such, they naturally wish to spend as little on it as possible, for it is an insurance policy that they are not convinced they need (even the most stringent accessibility laws – like Ontario's Accessibility for Ontarians with Disabilities Act 2010 (AODA) – aren't effective without enforcement[21]). This perspective makes perfect sense, as it's very similar to how I buy my insurance, whether for my house or car. While I know the insurance is a condition of my mortgage and my ability to remain legal on the road, and while I know that it is possible that I may need to claim at some point, when I buy my insurance I go to a price comparison website and generally find the cheapest insurance available, because at that point I'm more interested in the cost than the benefits of the policies on offer.

As the large numbers of settlements in the USA show, the costs of being the target for litigation are real. However, disabled people who bring cases want action, not fines, as my interview with Lainey Feingold shows.

---

18 http://news.cnet.com/8301-1023_3-10028109-93.html

19 http://en.wikipedia.org/wiki/Maguire_v_SOCOG_2000

20 http://www.hassellinclusion.com/category/accessibility-lawsuits/

21 http://enforcement.aoda.ca/government-not-enforcing-disabilities-act-says-advocate/

Interview with Lainey Feingold, a US disability rights lawyer who works primarily with the blind and visually impaired community

Jonathan: Whenever a new law comes into being that usually spurs forward the whole industry around accessibility. Are you finding cases arising from the 21st Century Video Accessibility Act (CVAA)?

Lainey: Right now CVAA is kind of new, in terms of the regulations coming up, and individuals can't sue directly under the CVAA, they have to go to the FCC [Federal Communications Commission]. But like you said it's a huge motivator, and all the industries impacted suddenly understand, 'Wow! We have to meet the needs of this part of our customer base that we never thought of before.' My work is to take that law and say, 'Okay, it's there. How are we going to use it to make it the best motivator it can be?'

Jonathan: You've been doing that for how long now?

Lainey: We're calling this the 20th year, because in 1994 we were approached to work on the ATM issue in the United States. In 1995 we wrote to three banks in California and said, 'Your ATMs don't work for blind people. Your print material is not accessible.' We didn't even deal with websites, because it was too early. 'Rather than file a lawsuit, will you be willing to work with us?' In 1999 we got our first agreement, on talking ATMs. Since then we've done 49 agreements, on a whole host of issues, and we got into web as web became bigger, and now into mobile.

Jonathan: I like that you talk about agreements rather than cases. Agreement is important for you, isn't it? That's what your whole process aims for: 'How do we find a place where this is a good way forward for everybody?' Your 'structured negotiations' seem more collaborative. Not friendly, but...

Lainey: We try for friendly.

Jonathan: The way you work on behalf of your clients seems more beneficial, to both the client and the organization that they have the complaint against, than a lot of lawyers out there, who are maybe trying to take people to court.

Lainey: There are a lot of great lawyers in this space litigating in a traditional way, filing a lawsuit, arguing legal motions, coming up with great results. You've already mentioned Target, H&R Block. I like to talk about my work as another alternative.

We work with typically the blind community. When they come to us with a problem we work with them and accessibility experts to check whether it is an issue with their assistive technology, or is there an actual problem on the site or mobile application. If there is, we approach the company's CEO or the top lawyer we can find and say, 'This is a serious legal claim, but we would rather work with you to work it out.'

Because I personally believe that the people inside the company want to be doing the right thing. There are challenges inside these corporations to get the right thing done.

So if we can help make that easier by not bringing in a bunch of suits to fight, I think that's why we've been successful. In the 20 years we've only had one person say, 'No, we won't negotiate with you. We won't do what you're asking.' We ended up filing a lawsuit against that company.

Jonathan: I was very interested in the recent H&R Block case. They got fined $145,000. But more expensive was the long list of things that they were required to do in the settlement. They had to hire somebody to be responsible for accessibility, reporting to the Chief Information Officer. They had to train their staff. They had to get people in to audit accessibility. They had to make sure that they embedded it in their processes.

Lainey: We have most of those things in our agreements too. H&R Block had the US Department of Justice come in. As private parties we can't say, 'You need to put a person on accessibility.' We've never been able to dictate the reporting structure, because we're from the outside. But yes, we include those things. The companies don't know. They think, 'Oh, we will tell our developer to make an accessible site,' but it's the whole company. It's the content providers. It's the trainers... Otherwise similar issues can crop up again – often with huge companies, one hand doesn't really know what the other is doing.

Watch the complete video interview with Lainey Feingold at:

http://qrs.ly/hj4a6bv

Read Lainey's blogs (especially her annual legal digital accessibility update each March) at: http://lflegal.com

Threat – the regulatory business case

In some countries there are also regulations that place obligations on public organizations to promote equality of opportunity between disabled and other people when carrying out their functions. In the UK, for example, the Public Sector Equality Duty[22] requires public organizations to create their own Single Equality Scheme (which replaced the previous Disabled Equality Scheme) to explain how they will do this across all of their areas of responsibility, including their digital communications, and to publish the scheme publicly.

Statements of accessibility policy are also becoming more common elsewhere. The Canadian Province of Ontario's AODA requires all businesses to create an accessibility policy[23], and there are moves towards States in the USA requiring the companies from which they procure digital products to include these policies (see, for example, the Policy Driven Adoption for Accessibility (PDAA) pilot in the State of Texas[24]).

Any regulation that requires these policies to be drafted and published by organizations requires a deeper level of thought and engagement with accessibility than anti-discrimination laws. My own anecdotal evidence in the UK, and Jeff Kline's in the USA, has found that these 'policy-based approaches' can be very effective in motivating organizations to get serious about accessibility.[25]

---

[22] http://www.legislation.gov.uk/ukpga/2010/15/part/11/chapter/1

[23] http://www.mcss.gov.on.ca/en/mcss/publications/accessON/policies_over50/toc.aspx

[24] http://www.dir.texas.gov/SiteCollectionDocuments/IT%20Leadership/EIR%20Accessibility/PDAA_Overview_DIR_Procurements.pptx

[25] http://www.slideshare.net/jonathanhassell/policy-driven-adoption-csun-final

Threat and opportunity – the ethical business case, and its link with brand values

The second business case for accessibility is the ethical business case. The basis of this case is the assertion that it is unethical to unnecessarily exclude disabled people from the benefits of modern digital technologies.

I'll illustrate this with a story.

Midway through last year I was invited back to my alma mater – the University of York, in northern England – to present a lecture to the Human-Computer Interaction Group that I used to be part of when researching for my doctorate in the early 1990s.

After the lecture one of the researchers asked if he could buy me coffee later that afternoon to discuss some research that he had done into how well the Web Content Accessibility Guidelines 2.0 – the international standard for accessibility – predict the accessibility difficulties disabled people would have with a website.[26] We agreed to meet in two hours in the department coffee shop.

I went to the coffee shop to catch up on the latest progress on some of my projects. But when I asked if they had Wi-Fi I was told that it was only available to students and delegates attending conferences.

No problem, I thought: I'll just use 3G and tether my phone to my Mac so I can work as normal. However, the location of the department was such that not only did I not have any 3G coverage, but I also had no 2G or even 1G coverage.

As I had not taken the mobile phone number of the researcher there was no way that I could let him know that I needed to meet him in a place with internet coverage, so I had to stay in the coffee shop for two hours with no internet.

I don't know when the last time was that you suddenly became acutely aware of the level of dependence that you have on being online. This was mine. My dependence on the internet is encouraged by all of the cloud services I regularly use to run both my business and personal life. Everything from the way I listen to music using Spotify to the way I communicate with my family via text and online messaging, to the way I collaborate on projects that I manage via Dropbox and Google Docs, to the way I run my agenda via iCloud, and the way I know where I am and where I need to get to via Google Maps. Everything works better with an internet connection or absolutely demands one.

---

[26] http://www.cs.york.ac.uk/hci/publications/001/index.html

Granted, I didn't have most of these services constantly available to me until the last few years. However, now I've started using them I am both facilitated and made efficient by them, and also made dependent on them. They're just the way I work.

On that particular afternoon the support they give me was not available, which made me uncomfortable, disempowered and bored. What was worse, all around me students were lounging with their laptops with full access to all the online services they could want. Because they couldn't give me their Wi-Fi password, and because there was no way I could think of to get one for myself by any other means, I was excluded from all the benefits modern technology brings.

Everyone around me was living the great digital technology dream, and for a while at least, I wasn't allowed into the club.

Have you ever been in that situation?

The difference between my situation and that of many disabled people is that my situation was temporary, and brought about by my own choices, whereas digital exclusion for disabled people is usually permanent or fluctuating, and brought about by the choices of the owners of the websites that they are locked out of. My two hours of boredom is just the merest glimpse of the regular frustrations that many disabled people experience trying to use modern digital technologies. No wonder then that many decide not to bother, unless they have no other choice.

But if they do opt out, they are missing out on real benefits. Reports such as the *Digital Britain* report 2009[27] prove many of the benefits of being online, from being able to access cheaper products and services using price comparison websites, to accessing cheaper phone calls using services like Skype.

Moreover many organizations are increasingly encouraging their customers to interact with them online, as the cost savings that organizations can get from moving existing call-centre or high-street services online can be massive, whether passed on to customers through 'online only' deals or not. In the UK, as in many other countries, this move of services online is one of the ways that government can streamline itself and provide a more financially efficient service to its population. Private companies can create more shareholder benefits using the same strategy, and maximize the value of their customer care budgets.

But this depends on all citizens and customers being able to access and use online services.

---

[27]   http://www.official-documents.gov.uk/document/cm76/7650/7650.pdf

This march to make all services 'digital by default', to use the UK government's term, is only going to become more prevalent, and so the ethical business case that such online services must be accessible will become more and more compelling as time goes on.

Most organizations feel the potential threat from this ethical case when it comes to brand value. While they may not be aware of all the aspects of the ethical business case for accessibility, most citizens are convinced by it almost instinctively, and so when they hear of the case of an organization not allowing a disabled person to book a seat on a plane using the operator's website – as was the case in the RNIB vs bmibaby case mentioned previously – their opinion of that organization takes a battering. Whether or not the organization wins or loses the legal case, in court or behind closed doors, the brand damage has already been done. I'd argue that, in terms of brand value at least, once the press release is written by the lawyers representing the disabled complainant, the organization being sued has already lost.

Of course, promoting the steps your organization is taking to make your products accessible to disabled people can also be a brand win, as recently enjoyed by Barclays with their talking cash machines[28].

In the age of corporate social responsibility, many large organizations are already aware of these benefits. You only have to look at Apple[29] as one example of this, or the public accessibility policies or statements many organizations publish on their websites stating their commitment to accessibility.[30] While public organizations in the UK are required to do this, even outside the public sector you can find voluntary statements saying things like:

'[Our] approach is to continue to involve disabled people in our work to highlight the barriers experienced by a diverse range of disabled people, and for disabled people to assist us in identifying how to effectively remove those barriers.'

However, publishing these sorts of statements without becoming competent in how to live up to them could be a real own goal.

Opportunity – the commercial business case (reach)

The next opportunity for most organizations that create websites or mobile apps that aim for a large number of users is that making them accessible can increase the size of their user base or reach.

---

[28] https://www.youtube.com/watch?v=qSJPdVewrF8

[29] https://www.apple.com/accessibility/

[30] http://www.hassellinclusion.com/2013/08/web-accessibility-ruinous-obligation/

As discussed earlier in this chapter, if 20% of the population of most countries are disabled, and many more are older or have low literacy, making your web products accessible is a sensible way of trying to ensure that as many of your potential users can use your website as possible. While figures for the spending power of disabled people (£80 billion in the UK, $220 billion in the USA)[31] could usefully be backed up with stronger research evidence, it surely makes sense to avoid excluding 20% of your potential customers from doing business with you. Moreover, research has found that disabled people tend to be more loyal to the websites that they've taken the time to learn, rather than jumping to competitors when they win on price comparison, as Axel Leblois of G3ict talks about in his interview.

Interview with Axel Leblois, President and Executive Director at G3ict – The Global Initiative for Inclusive ICTs

Axel: There are three fundamental motivations for companies to pay attention to accessibility. One is compliance, which means risk reduction. Another is corporate social responsibility, because they realize it's a good thing to do to be involved with accessibility. And a third one is marketing opportunity.

Depending upon which industry you look at, the driver may vary between those three things. For instance, if you take air transportation and banking, today the driver is compliance. In a way it's unfortunate because, while it does help the overall population of persons with disabilities to have accessible ATMs, for instance, what's happening is that they will be operating in a market with a significant number of senior consumers – and half of the persons over 65 years of age have some form of disability – and yet they don't think about it in those terms. They think, 'Okay, we've got a document that says we need to do this... we need to ensure we are doing it.' But they don't think about how to optimize things for their consumers. In that sense compliance is good but not too good.

Japan has really shown the way. They have some mobile phone service providers who have done incredible work, without any pressure from a compliance standpoint, to create 'best in market' products for persons with disabilities and seniors, and had tremendous success in gaining new business.

Jonathan: What about maintaining customers? Is there something about accessibility that impacts on a customer's loyalty to a business?

---

31 http://businessdisabilityforum.org.uk/customer-experience/the-evidence

Axel: You are raising a very good point. What we see from the mobile or hospitality industry is that it is more complex and costly to target specifically seniors or persons with different abilities to come to your service or product. However, once you have acquired that customer and serviced them correctly, you see that the retention of the customer is much higher – there is less churn.

In some industries, such as the mobile or the airline industries, customer loyalty is a fundamental attribute of successful financial results. Every year you have got to fight against a huge proportion of your customers leaving, and having to acquire new customers. It's very costly. Yet persons with disability and seniors, once they are used to a service, they are happy with it as things are accessible and they get great customer support, they just stay with you forever.

Jonathan: So accessibility is like a loyalty programme?

Axel: Accessibility is the best loyalty programme you can have, more effective than any mileage card, any loyalty card, anything.

Watch the complete video interview with Axel Leblois at:

http://qrs.ly/km49k8l

Read G3ict's blogs on accessibility at:

http://g3ict.org/resource_center/bloggers

Of course, there are well-known site maintenance and search engine optimization (SEO) benefits to making your web content accessible.[32] Using the right semantic heading tags, writing descriptive alt-text for

---

[32] http://www.w3.org/WAI/bcase/resources#cases

images, and including captions for videos help your content be more completely indexed by what could be considered to be the 'biggest blind user in the world' – Google's (and all other) search engines.[33]

We'll come back to this essential aspect of accessibility – and how to measure the reach impact of the accessibility you decide to invest in – in Chapter 6.

Opportunity – the commercial business case (selling tools to clients)

If your organization creates web applications or browser-based tools that you sell to clients then it's important for you to be aware that increasing numbers of those clients, especially those in the public sector, may ask you to prove that your web applications are accessible or can be used to create accessible web products.

The lack of proven accessibility in your products may prevent you from being considered as a supplier to government organizations in the USA and Europe. The American federal government Section 508 guidelines[34] are currently being refreshed,[35] but are very clear: no VPAT (voluntary product accessibility template),[36] no sale. Work on Mandate/ 376[37] – which is tracking the Section 508 refresh – aims to bring the same requirements to public procurement across Europe.

Outside the public sector, accessibility could still be a contributory USP (unique selling point) to win you a tender, especially where clients indicate accessibility requirements in their invitation to tender or request for proposal documentation. BS 8878 has been designed to support project teams who are procuring web products, as well as teams building them. I am regularly called on to help my clients embed accessibility requirements into their standard procurement documentation, and anecdotal evidence indicates BS 8878 is having an impact more widely on the presence and quality of the specification of accessibility requirements in procurement documentation.[38]

So gaining proof of your products' accessibility, and knowing how to sell that to your clients, may be as important an investment to your organization as any other essential part of your tool's functionality or sales pitch.

[33]   http://www.communis.co.uk/blog/2009-08-06-seo-and-accessibility-overlap
[34]   http://www.dol.gov/oasam/ocio/ocio-508.htm
[35]   http://www.access-board.gov/guidelines-and-standards/communications-and-it/about-the-ict-refresh
[36]   http://www.state.gov/m/irm/impact/126343.htm
[37]   http://www.mandate376.eu/
[38]   http://www.hassellinclusion.com/2011/12/bs8878s-one-year-anniversary/

Opportunity – the commercial business case (minimizing complaints)

Another huge opportunity in the commercial business case for accessibility is the ability to minimize complaints from disabled customers.

Often my clients tell me they have incurred huge resource costs in dealing with complaints when they have launched internal or external web products without making sure that they were accessible. Often whole months of product management, business analysis and legal resource can be spent on dealing with the complaint of one disabled person. In this age of public consumer complaints via Twitter and Facebook, the cost to your brand of dealing with these complaints unprofessionally in public can be significant, so all complaints have to be carefully handled. What's worse is that during this time product managers may take their eye off the great majority of their audience to concentrate on the small number who complain.

As anyone who buys a printer can tell you, it's not the original cost of the printer that matters, it's the ongoing cost of the consumables on top of that initial cost – the 'total cost of ownership'.

The same is true of accessibility. Money spent on making a web product accessible during its development can save you lots of money once it's launched, in terms of minimizing complaints, and the lower cost of building in accessibility rather than retro-fitting it in response to customer feedback.

The benefits also apply if you have considered accessibility properly when developing your product but haven't been able to deliver an accessible user experience for all disabled users for some reason. In Step 15 of the BS 8878 process in Chapter 5, we'll discuss how to communicate what accessibility you have and haven't been able to deliver in such a way as to minimize business risk, and pre-empt and channel any accessibility complaints so you can deal with them in a way that is efficient and effective. We'll also look at a few cases of what can happen if you don't get that communication right.

Opportunity – the commercial business case (creativity and innovation)

The final opportunity in the commercial business case is one that is rarely communicated – that encouraging your product team to support real audience diversity encourages them to be more, not less, creative.

Innovation is the lifeblood of most companies, so all of the companies I've worked with are trying to make innovative products that their competitors don't have. I've found that challenging them to think inclusively can be really helpful. My experience is that product teams can initially be a little intimidated when they are asked to design products for people with disabilities. Yet, when I've been able to get them past that, getting them thinking of the sorts of different needs that people have tends to make them change the way they think about technology. That makes them more innovative. Because, if you're stuck in a way of thinking about your product, which is probably very similar to all of your competitors, if someone comes in with a really challenging question – for example, 'How would that work for someone who can't see or who can't read...' – then you have to start thinking differently as you can't just get away with the sort of step-by-step product iterations you usually do.

In ideation circles, this is called 'getting over design fixation'[39]. In general, what people who invent new products find is that everyone, all over the world, including all of their competitors, comes up with the same initial seven ideas for the next version of a product. It's so difficult to get out of your fixation with what already exists that you make one step in each direction but don't really get anywhere.

The usual practice for getting over fixation at this point would be to do something like drop everything for five minutes and draw an alien – anything to get you thinking differently. That works, but I find the real-world challenge of designing for people with different needs from your own can work even better.

I once did some brainstorming with a major electrical company in Germany – they make lots of white goods, fridges, that sort of thing – and we were looking at ovens. I suggested 'How about this for getting past fixation? I want you to come up with an oven that would support the needs of someone who's older, who can't physically hold up the thing they are trying to put into the oven – the casserole dish or whatever... They just don't have the strength in their arms.'

One question and suddenly they are in a completely different space in terms of their imagination. And what we came up with, pretty quickly after, was the idea of an oven that was actually in your work surface. That you pressed a button, and the oven came up out of your work surface until the shelf that you wanted to put things onto was at the right level. So the older person could then just slide the dish from the work surface onto the shelf. They'd then press a button and the oven would go down until everything was cooked, at which time it would rise up and they'd be able to slide the dish out again.

Whether or not that could get to market, that was one of the most innovative ideas they'd ever had for what to do next for an oven. It wasn't 'lowest common denominator'. It was an idea worthy of their

---

[39] http://web.mit.edu/~mcyang/www/papers/2014-morenoEtalb.pdf

concept kitchen. That's how taking challenges from a wider community can lead to better products for everyone.

I firmly believe that some of the next big innovations in technology could come from people using this sort of thinking. Why? Because many of the products we take for granted these days were originally created specifically for disabled people.

The first typewriter proven to have worked was built by the Italian, Pellegrino Turri, in 1808 for his blind friend Countess Carolina Fantoni da Fivizzano[40] to solve the problem of how she was going to be able to write. This innovative solution to a problem 'no one else had' has now changed the world, with typewriter keyboards appearing on everything from tablet computers to TV screens to interactive kiosks.

Alexander Graham Bell was partly trying to help people with hearing impairments when he invented the telephone[41].

Ray Kurzweil – now Google's Director of Engineering – was trying to help people with a visual impairment to access books more easily when he came up with the first 'omni font' optical character recognition and text-to-speech synthesizers to create print-to-speech reading in 1975.[42]

Closer to the web, to give an example from my own experience at the BBC, back in 2005 I was tasked with creating an online game to help blind children improve their maths skills through play. Our research found that few 5 year-olds in the UK can master the complexity of the screen readers that most blind adults use (mastering elementary maths, in comparison, is easy). Playing a game purely through the synthesized speech of screen readers didn't exactly sound exciting. So my team came up with three-dimensional audio-games that kids could play purely using the keyboard and their ears, inspired by the games blind people were creating for themselves. Fast forward to 2012 and mobile games like Zombies Run![43] are using the same innovative audio technologies and audio-gameplay ideas to help motivate people to exercise:

How do you make jogging interesting? Well, the guys behind Zombies Run! came up with the idea that you're being chased by zombies. How's that for motivation for you? They wanted to make sure that the experience – the narrative experience of being chased by zombies – was available to you when you were jogging. But there's a problem with the idea, because you really shouldn't be looking at a screen when you're jogging. If you do, you're not jogging for that much longer. You're bumping into people around you, falling into holes... To all intents and purposes, when you are jogging you are 'situationally blind' with respect

---

[40] http://site.xavier.edu/polt/typewriters/tw-history.html

[41] http://en.wikipedia.org/wiki/Alexander_Graham_Bell

[42] http://www.kurzweiltech.com/kcp.html

[43] https://www.youtube.com/watch?v=GyFqZtKvya0 and https://www.zombiesrungame.com/

to the screen on your phone. So they couldn't put zombies on the screen. They thought about what people do when they're jogging, which is put their ear-buds in to keep them going via their favourite tunes. And thought: 'Why not do this via sound?' The game's output is sound going into your ears: if you're not jogging fast enough, the zombies sound like they're getting close, and you might get eaten. And the game's input is what you are doing with your body; where you are in terms of your 'GPS'. The rest is narrative and atmosphere.

That's one example of somebody taking something that came out of the blind audio-games community and finding that it is the solution to a mainstream need. The result was fundamentally so innovative and fresh that lots of people fell in love with it.

So, while it's likely that you're not making ovens, typewriters, phones or jogging apps, the same innovation principles apply for the creation of any website or app. Why not use my CSUN-14 SlideShare on 'Accessibility and Innovation'[44] to inspire you to think more deeply about your wider audience's needs? And see what innovative ideas arrive... If you need more help, check out the Royal London Society for Blind People's Everybody Technology website[45] to join a community going on the same journey.

Keeping up with the competition

When presented with these business cases, many organizations have one final question before being able to arrive at a sensible position on accessibility: what are our competitors doing?

While this question is reasonable – benchmarking your policies and product decisions against those of your competitors is a sensible thing to do for any organization – the frequent problem with applying this logic to web accessibility is that most organizations are necessarily private about the actual lengths they are going to, to take accessibility into account. There are many more organizations using BS 8878 to help them set their accessibility strategy than say so in public – publishing vague commitments on your website seems sufficient to ward off accusations of negligence. If an organization includes an accessibility conformance badge on their website, that seems like further evidence that their commitment is actually impacting their products. But, in reality, these badges – even VPATs (Voluntary Product Accessibility Templates) – are a poor indicator of accessibility in the long term, as discussed in Step 14.

[44] http://www.slideshare.net/jonathanhassell/accessibility-innovation-through-gestural-and-signlanguage-interfaces-32684441

[45] http://www.rlsb.org.uk/everybody-technology

It is relatively expensive to benchmark the accessibility of a competitor's products (as it requires some form of accessibility testing), let alone gain an understanding of the process behind how they delivered them (which is discussed in Chapter 4).

Nonetheless, it's worth at least checking to see if your competitors are showing visible signs of pulling ahead in the accessibility race. Even then, putting off making an investment decision until you see those signs may cost you – as it may take a while for investment in accessibility to show visible effects, by the time you notice your competitors may be well ahead of you.

Now it's your turn

Discuss and agree, at the highest appropriate level of your organization, which combination of the accessibility business cases presented in this chapter are the most aligned to your organization's values and priorities. The accessibility strategies of most mature organizations draw from all of the business cases, to ensure they don't miss out on gaining the best return from their accessibility investment. If you miss considering any of the cases you risk undervaluing accessibility to your business. Accessibility is so much more than legal risk insurance.

To help you facilitate this discussion, use the Accessibility Business Case Generator in this book's support materials (see page x) to quickly and easily generate a compelling and informative slide-deck detailing the business cases that are appropriate to an organization in your nation, of your size, ownership and field of business.

Will your organization aim to be a leader or a follower in accessibility? How should accessibility be balanced with your other organizational and project priorities and audiences?

Once you've made these decisions, you'll need somewhere to write them down so you can base your decisions on them later in the book, or revisit them if further investigation prompts you to.

BS 8878 advises you to do this in a document called an organizational web accessibility policy. Chapter 4 goes into detail about this policy. But, for now, I'd suggest downloading the organizational web accessibility policy template in the book's support materials, which is designed to lead you through your considerations, to capture your decisions and the reasoning behind them.

Chapter 4

EMBED – how to embed accessibility in an organization

Now you've got your motivation for doing accessibility agreed, it's important to work out how to do it right in your organization, and how to do it right all of the time.

If organizations want to embed inclusion into their culture and business-as-usual processes, the accessibility world's solutions unfortunately seem piecemeal and tactical, not strategic. Accessibility is portrayed as something complex, which requires continual advice, even dependency on, expert accessibility specialists, often from external suppliers.

While it is true that accessibility is complex – and it would be untrue to say otherwise – it is possible for organizations to become competent in handling accessibility across all of their web products, both internal-facing and external-facing. After all, complexity is not something that organizations are scared of. All product creation is complex. Most things worth doing are complex.

You've already come up with your organization's answer to whether this complex thing is worth gaining competency in.

So the remaining question is: can gaining competency in accessibility be broken down into manageable action steps for you to implement within your organization?

Examples of how not to do it

Think back to the RNIB vs bmibaby example in the overview of BS 8878, and you'll see one way organizations handle accessibility: they ignore it, and then it's all hands to the pump on remediation if anyone complains. As we saw there, you need to fix the problem in the process, not the product, to prevent it reoccurring. Otherwise you, like Achilles, will have placed a Band-Aid on your exposed heel, rather than had it seen-to properly.

Or maybe your organization is doing 'well' with accessibility. This is likely to be because you are lucky enough to have what I term an 'accessibility superhero' on your staff. Such a superhero is likely to be passionate, committed and energetic. They may have hidden everyone's mice on Global Accessibility Awareness Day[46] to force people to have a day of keyboard-only computing to get across their message. They may have even succeeded in getting accessibility on the organization's agenda by doing this. As a result, you're likely to have promoted them to being your 'accessibility champion' and made them the person loosely responsible for making all of your products accessible.

Unfortunately, this is another Band-Aid. For, in any large organization, your accessibility superhero is likely to burn out as they try to make all of your products accessible. Furthermore, either through this burn-out, or because they want to see if their successful practices will work elsewhere, at some point they may leave your organization for another in which they can 'save the day' again.

Depending on one person for any competency of your organization is foolhardy. No organization that considers a competency essential allows that competency to reside in a single point of failure. Even if that single point of failure works well, it doesn't scale.

Similarly, outsourcing the accessibility superhero position may also turn out to be a Band-Aid. It may solve the scalability problem, but dependency on an outside agency is rarely an economically efficient course of action, and so the 'solution' will be jettisoned whenever budgets get tight.

These aren't the behaviours of an organization that considers accessibility as valuable. They're behaviours of expediency.

To achieve efficiency and scalability, you need to embed competence throughout your organization – in your policies, processes and staff.

The challenge – which job roles impact on the accessibility of products?

To embed competence throughout your staff, you first need to look at what job roles within your organization have an impact on the creation of your web products. Every person who has an impact on your web products could be making decisions every day that will include or exclude disabled and older audiences from being able to use the product that you are creating. There are more people whose job roles impact on your web products than you might immediately think.

---

46   http://www.globalaccessibilityawarenessday.org/gaad.html

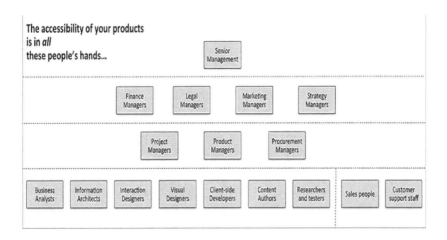

Figure 1 – The job roles that impact digital product accessibility

Let's start at the coalface, with the people who actually create the product – its design, coding and content – and those who test the product as it evolves, and handle interaction with the community of people using it after launch.

Team members with all of these job roles need to be competent and confident about doing their bit to make sure they don't drop the baton of accessibility in the relay race that is the creation of the product.

In a relay, each runner needs to do their job right for the baton to successfully reach the end of the race.

The baton can be passed on in a bad state, with poor decisions having been taken, so subsequent work is based on incorrect or incomplete decisions. Business analysts can specify the requirements for how accessibility will be handled in the product based on bad assumptions from incomplete accessibility user research. Developers can develop perfectly accessible code to implement designs that themselves aren't accessible.

Moreover, the baton can be dropped. A team member can do their job well but fumble the handover of the baton, failing to communicate some aspect of the accessibility decisions embedded in their work to the next team member, so the next person doesn't understand its importance and misses it in their implementation. An interaction designer could design the page- or screen-layout to clearly segment the product's functionality into different navigational areas, but could fail to communicate to a developer the hierarchy behind those segments, so the developer codes them all on the same level. In this case, the WAI-ARIA guidelines[47] can be useful notation for interaction designers to clearly and unambiguously communicate these structural semantics of the segments of their design,[48] as well as where the segments should appear on the screen in responsive layouts for different device screens. A sales person could fail to understand the value of mentioning the product's VPAT in its sales materials so potential licensees don't realise it's been created to support accessibility and don't buy it.

So each interaction designer, visual designer, content author, developer, researcher or tester needs not only to know what they need to achieve (how to run well), but how to communicate it to the next person in the team who'll work from that to advance the product's creation (how to handle the transitions well).

These people, in my experience, are the ones in most organizations who know most about accessibility. After all, these are the people who almost all accessibility guidelines have been created for. So often they already know what they need to do, and almost wear their ability to code, design or write content in an accessible way as a badge of competence.

The impact on accessibility of the 'forgotten' management layers

However, their time, as a resource, is manipulated by those one level above them:

- the *project manager,* who tells them whether or not there is time and money for them to do their jobs in a way that upholds accessibility, amongst all of the other quality measures that are important to the project;
- and the *product manager*, who tells them what audiences and functionalities the product must support to be successful and deliver the business value of the project.

I don't want to play down how important it is for accessibility technology pioneers (like Rich Schwerdtfeger,[49] Steve Faulkner[50] and Bruce Lawson[51]) to get WAI-ARIA and HTML 5 into shape to give us the right technical framework on which to build accessible code. Their work is essential and necessary to enable accessibility. But it's not sufficient to make people actually implement it in their products.

---

[47] http://www.w3.org/TR/wai-aria/
[48] http://www.spotless.co.uk/insights/accessibility-information-architects
[49] http://www-03.ibm.com/able/news/rich_schwerdtfeger.html
[50] https://twitter.com/stevefaulkner
[51] http://www.brucelawson.co.uk/

Here's Rob Sinclair, Chief Accessibility Officer for Microsoft, talking about how the new Indie UI accessibility standards effort might affect the development of mobile applications, at the CSUN accessibility conference in 2013[52]:

> 'I actually think the real test and the real key to success is going to be understanding how we get developers to use the standard and technologies in the intended way... Many of you may know [UI Automation] released six or seven years ago. We actually had the ability to describe the user interface...
>
> The problem is virtually no developers have used that functionality. We evangelized it, tried to promote it. The problem is it requires them to think differently about how they design their application...'

Rob makes a great point. But I think he's missed mentioning the key person who could get those developers to use the 'new UI Automation standard'. Accessibility is facilitated or constrained by many people in web production teams, but most notably by the team's product manager.[53] Put it this way, who do you think had more impact on whether Apple products include accessibility features: Steve Jobs, or the developers who implemented iOS and OS X? As Walter Isaacson's fascinating biography of Steve Jobs makes clear,[54] he dictated most of the functionality and look and feel of Apple products; the developers just had to make happen what he wanted.

While both of these 'PMs' can either encourage or inhibit the desires of their teams to deliver an accessible product, most accessibility guidelines are not written in a language that will appeal to them. BS 8878 has been designed to plug this gap, enabling product managers to understand how to balance the costs and benefits of supporting the needs of the product's disabled users with all its other users, and enabling project managers to understand how to get the team to deliver on the resulting accessibility priorities that the product manager sets.

[52] http://www-03.ibm.com/able/news/downloads/IBM_CSUN_2013_Mobile_Panel_1_Transcript_022713_final.pdf

[53] http://mindtheproduct.com/2011/10/what-exactly-is-a-product-manager/

[54] http://techcrunch.com/2011/12/16/keen-on-walter-isaacson-was-steve-jobs-a-tyrant-tctv/

Another key manager, whose importance has often been overlooked, is the organization's Procurement Manager, as many products are now 'mashed together' from web tools or commercial off-the-shelf software (COTS)[55] or components. And, if you're the product manager of a COTS product, you'll only prioritize accessibility over other possible features if you know that procurement managers are going to require this in deciding whether to purchase your software. That's why web procurement standards, like the forthcoming Mandate/376[56] in Europe and the updated Section 508[57] in the States, may be as essential to accessibility's future as technical standards like WAI-ARIA and HTML 5.

Above the project, product and procurement managers we have the middle management layer of finance managers, legal managers, marketing managers and strategy managers. Each of these, similarly, can encourage or inhibit the project, product and procurement managers below them from taking accessibility seriously. Finance managers can approve or deny budgets for accessibility. Legal managers can require that accessibility be taken seriously as a legal risk, or recommend that the risk is too low to bother with. Marketing managers may dictate major components of how websites look by setting the brand guidelines for the organization and its products, and can include or exclude accessibility criteria from the creation of these guidelines. And strategy managers can accept or downplay the relative importance of accessibility against a whole host of other harmonizing or competing concerns across the organization's overarching product strategy.

Finally, above all of these people sits a CEO, MD, or other executive manager. They will set the tone for how accessibility is considered by all those underneath them.

Obviously, in smaller organizations and start-ups, people will play multiple roles or even all of the roles in the chart, but the roles are still the same.

For a product to be accessible, all of these people need to consistently make decisions that recognize accessibility as an important quality of the organization's products, at all points of each product's development.

---

55 http://en.wikipedia.org/wiki/Commercial_off-the-shelf
56 http://www.mandate376.eu/
57 http://www.dol.gov/oasam/ocio/ocio-508.htm

Interview with David Banes, Chief Executive, MADA, Qatar

David: I think you need the champions and you need the people who can say, 'Okay I've got depth of knowledge.' But for an internal ecosystem you need lots of people with bits of knowledge who can draw upon the depth. So you're adding breadth to that.

I think the critical bit is it's not about saying, 'Okay this person's at the centre of the network and connects to each of those.' Somehow there is an interdependency. So the web designer connects to the guys producing the video, who connects to...

It's a network as opposed to a hub and spoke model. And maybe the job of the champion is to try and get that network functioning in a way where it doesn't all need to flow through the expert.

Jonathan: Absolutely... The baton may start off with a requirements person understanding what a disabled person might need from the product.

There may be some planning and budgeting, which needs to be handled by the project manager. Then it may need to be handed to interaction designers to do wireframes, and then to the visual designers, developers and the QA people. It ends up, after launch, with content people who hopefully keep the product at the same level of accessibility over its life cycle. Then generally what we find, certainly in the UK, is that it just tends to cycle around. Everything goes through versions and often the team that created version 1 is not the same team that creates version 2. You put your best team on version 1 because it's a new thing.

When it comes to the maintenance it's the guys who aren't quite so ninja. And because it's a different team, all of the expertise there drains away...

David: It's almost like a football match being played with five footballs. You've got something which is moving ahead quickly, but you've got five different activities going on at once. Then you start the second one and whilst you're doing that, the first one's come back at you again. You've got this constant flow. I think very few projects can say, 'Finished!' for accessibility. Even if you've scored the goal it's come back to the centre spot and start again.

Watch the complete video interview with David Banes at:
http://qrs.ly/s14a6bs

Read MADA's blogs on accessibility in the Middle East at:
http://www.mada.org.qa/eAccessibility/EN/blog/

The recipe for success in embedding accessibility in your organization

Embedding accessibility into the way all these people work can be daunting, because what we are talking about here is organizational change, and organizational change is one of the most difficult things to do in any organization.

We need a way of diffusing this anxiety and making embedding more manageable.

The first aspect of this is to break the task down into its component parts – the components of accessibility maturity:

- embedding *motivation and responsibility* – setting your commitment and budget, then making sure you break down responsibility for accessibility so everyone knows who should do what;
- embedding *competence and confidence* (training) – making sure everyone knows how to do the things that are their responsibility via provision of training and guidelines;
- embedding *support* – making sure your staff have a source of expertise to which they can take questions when their training or guidelines aren't enough;
- embedding *policy* – making sure you embed in policy, not just people, or your policies may hinder rather than help your progress;
- embedding *governance* – making sure you set and regularly benchmark progress against inclusion goals.

The final component is embedding process – making sure you embed a process to ensure consistency of accessibility practice across all projects. This is so important that the whole of Chapter 5 is devoted to it.

How to benchmark your level of maturity and create a plan to improve it

The second aspect of making embedding more manageable is to see where you already have some competence in the organization, and build from there. Benchmarking your organization's current level of maturity against each component is a great way to start. I regularly benchmark my clients' competence against all these components to give them an idea of where their strengths and weaknesses lie (their score), where their competitors in the market may score, and what might be necessary to raise their score to a level they are more comfortable with.

Briefly, this is the benchmarking process I take organizations through:

- introducing the different components to measure their maturity against;
- introducing a simple scale from 1 to 10 for each component, starting from what is required for conformity (score 1 to 3), through what is needed for competitiveness (score 4 to 7), to what is needed for out-performance (score 8 to 10);
- analysing and scoring the organization's maturity out of 10 on each component, by reviewing documentation (policies, processes and guidelines), interviewing staff to see how that documentation impacts their day-to-day practices, and spot-checking the accessibility of the products that those practices are delivering;
- estimating where their competitors might score for each component;
- working with the organization on where they should aim to score for each component – which components are most important to them, whether they are looking for safety from prosecution, gaining new customers, finding the lowest hanging fruit, or drawing a line in the sand to buy them time while they figure out how to resource a better strategy;
- working with them to discuss what sort of return on investment they wish to achieve, and how we'll measure that;
- creating a range of work packages that would move the organization's scores up to the levels they aspire to for each component, with cost-benefits analysis for each; and
- agreeing an action plan for which work packages will be done, and in what order.

The third aspect of making embedding more manageable is to understand that, while all the components are necessary, the order in which your organization prioritises them in their planning is flexible.

Often, the benchmarking will suggest a way forwards – building on areas where you already have some level of maturity, and moving out from there to the other components. Alternatively, the two main ways organizations tend to make the necessary changes to become more mature in accessibility are:

- top down: board decision => responsibilities => policies => standards => governance => process => products; or
- bottom up: applying accessibility process and guidelines on one project; if it's useful then doing it on all projects; summarizing what has been proven to work in policies; then getting the board buy-in to make it official.

I don't have the space here to go deeper into this accessibility embedding benchmarking and planning process – the support materials for this book include much more information.

Let's look more closely at each component.

Embedding motivation and responsibility

For an organization to embed the right practices to ensure that all of its web products are made accessible, staff performing each of the job roles that impact accessibility need to be *motivated* to accept accessibility as something that concerns them.

There are two ways of doing this:

1. motivating staff directly by providing accessibility awareness training for staff performing each of the job roles, using a version of the slide-deck you created in Chapter 3 to share why your organization cares about accessibility, and what priority it has with all your staff; or
2. motivating those high up in the business; getting them to set accessibility priorities and commission an accessibility policy; and then requiring all staff to comply with that policy, with less understanding of the reasons why.

While the first of these ways of embedding motivation for accessibility within an organization gains a greater and deeper level of buy-in, I've rarely seen it attempted. For most organizations, even achieving the second way of doing things is a massive accomplishment, as many organizations do not consider accessibility seriously at any level other than the web practitioners at the coalface. This is the reason why most web products fail on accessibility, because no strategy or structure was put in place to assure it is a value consistently delivered in all the organization's products.

Hand in hand with motivation should go *responsibility*. Ask who is responsible for accessibility in many organizations and you may get a multitude of different responses from different people – even if people may feel that accessibility is part of their job, they may not be sure who is actually responsible for ensuring it is actually delivered in products.

Creating a clear responsibility structure

A good structure for clarifying and embedding responsibility for accessibility within an organization starts with establishing an 'accessibility champion' who will be ultimately responsible for the accessibility of all the organization's products and practices. They need to be empowered and resourced to delegate this responsibility down through the ranks of the organization. They need to make sure that those delegated to are aware of, and trained in, their responsibilities. They need to make sure they are monitoring and governing how well staff are fulfilling their responsibilities.

This accessibility champion is very different from the sort of 'accessibility superhero' role mentioned earlier. Accessibility superheroes, even departments of superheroes, are usually tasked with all the responsibility for accessibility for an organization, but given very little of the power, resources or structure needed to let them safely delegate that responsibility to the people around them. So they end up racing around the organization trying to influence all the people who actually make decisions that impact product accessibility. And they do this without any ability to get those people to buy in to living up to their responsibility, without any budget to get them the training they need, without any governance mechanisms to check how accessibility is happening across the organization, or any measures to enforce accessibility 'compliance' in the products they are finally asked to test.

In my experience, organizations that handle accessibility well are those with the combination of:

- an *accessibility champion* on the organization's executive board, gaining top level buy-in for why accessibility is important for the organization, and securing a budget for making it happen, using the business cases in the previous chapter and benchmarking against best-practice organizations that have made their accessibility strategies available (via the *OneVoice Accessible ICT: Benefits to Business and Society* report[58]);
- an *accessibility programme manager* strategically planning and delivering the embedding for which the champion has secured that buy-in – organizing training for staff, providing subject-matter

---

[58] http://www.onevoiceict.org/sites/default/files/Accessible%20ICT%20-%20Benefits%20to%20 Business%20and%20Society.pdf

expertise and support for those staff, driving embedding into policies, and managing ongoing governance; and

- individual *product managers* accepting that the accessibility of the product they manage is fundamentally their responsibility, even though they delegate the details of that responsibility to the individual members of their team.

Location of the accessibility programme manager role

The best location for the accessibility programme manager role in the organization's org-chart can be a matter of some debate. Depending on the size of the organization, and the type of web products that it creates, I've seen the role located in development, in quality assurance or standards compliance, in user experience or HR. To give some examples: at the BBC the role is located in User-Experience, having moved from Editorial Compliance previously. IBM's workplace accessibility strategy worldwide lead reports into the Chief Information Officer, and they also have a Chief Technology Officer for accessibility. At Comcast there's a Vice President of Accessibility.

The important thing to be aware of is that the position of the accessibility programme manager role – or the job role of the person who is given responsibility for it as part of their role – may fundamentally impact the way accessibility is viewed in the organization. If accessibility is assigned to governance, they are likely to have a 'stick' approach to embedding it in the organization, with an emphasis on creating unambiguous, prescriptive standards to which they hold staff and suppliers accountable. If it's assigned to user experience, they are likely to take a less formal view, viewing success in accessibility more in terms of whether disabled users can use each product. If accessibility is assigned to technology, they may be most interested in embedding accessibility in code libraries. Biases will also come into play if the role is located in corporate social responsibility, HR or marketing.

Each possible location of the role brings its own flavour or bias to how accessibility is seen, and each has strengths and potential blind spots. Accessibility encompasses all of these flavours, and all bases need to be covered to fully impact the organization. The accessibility programme manager can be successful whatever their bias, as long as they acknowledge it, and balance it with an appreciation and commitment to the other ways of looking at accessibility.

Continuity of the accessibility programme manager role

In practice, the location of the role may be less important than its continuity, its empowerment and ability to flex to survive organizational restructures, including the arrival of new middle managers who may need to be introduced to why accessibility is being taken seriously in the organization. The direct link with the executive accessibility champion is the key to the organization's ability to maintain a consistently high level of accessibility embedding, and not do what so many organizations have done in the past, which is to yo-yo between times where accessibility is well supported and times where it is badly supported.

To give an example: the Ford Focus 2002 that I drive is one of the most inclusively designed cars in history. However, the current 2014 model isn't, as a change of line-management of the Inclusive Design Lead in the 1990s saw the new boss emphasize form over function, and the guy who established the competence left the company.

So make sure your organization's accessibility competency is able to withstand changes at the top, and the possibility of your accessibility programme manager leaving, through having embedded accessibility into your organization's standards, training, policies and processes.

Now it's your turn

Ask people in your organization who create your websites and mobile apps whose responsibility accessibility is, and see if you like what you hear back. If you don't have a board-level accessibility champion, consider how you might go about inspiring one of the board members to take on the role. Also consider who could take on the role of accessibility programme manager, and where the role should be best located. Use the accessibility champion to find the money and buy-in to empower the accessibility programme manager to drive forwards your accessibility strategy.

For those wanting more detail in this area, especially for larger corporations, Jeff Kline provides this in his excellent book *Strategic IT Accessibility*,[59] which I highly recommend.

---

[59] http://www.strategicaccessibility.com/

Interview with Jeff Kline, State-wide Accessibility Coordinator for Texas, author of *Strategic IT Accessibility*

Jonathan: Your take on accessibility is rather different from most people's, Jeff. Your book is all about the strategy of getting it into an organization...

Jeff: Yes. When I took up my accessibility job at IBM, after numerous other development jobs, we had an idea of what needed to be done, but we didn't really understand the magnitude of it. When I was getting ready to take the job, I asked my boss, 'How long will this mission last?' He said, 'Probably about three to four years.' I was in the job six and a half years, before leaving IBM three and a half years ago, and the end is still nowhere in sight.

What we did at IBM was focused on everything that we sold externally, and then turned around and got involved in more of the things that everybody uses inside the company. IBM have a pretty diverse population, a lot of users with disabilities, and employees with disabilities. Once you start down that path, you realize that it's very complex as you go through it.

Then once we were starting to make some inroads, IBM got on this big acquisition binge. They started acquiring all these different companies, most of whom never even knew how to spell the word 'accessibility'. Now all of a sudden they're selling products that are going to be under the IBM umbrella, and you've got to figure out a way to bring them up to speed...

Jonathan: So you wrote your book to share the knowledge and see how organizations could use what you'd learnt and apply it in their circumstances...

Jeff: I was drawing from my time in industrial design, because industrial design was an area that IBM always located in different places. If you were put into an engineering function then you had, at least in my experience and other people's experience, a lot less flexibility...

At IBM they moved the industrial design function into many different areas, and I saw how it worked in some places and how it didn't work well in other places. I also saw, when I moved over to accessibility, where they would locate accessibility in the different business units. There's no drawn conclusion; it really is about whatever the place is that works the best within an organization; where you're going to be the most effective. That's the whole key to the exercise that I illustrate in the book: figure that out.

Jonathan: And sell it to the execs?

Jeff: That can always be challenging. If you sell it as something that's very glamorous and interesting to do, some executive could latch on to that and say, 'Yes, I'm going to take that, because I can really do something with it.' You want to make sure that whoever does it really wants to champion it.

Jonathan: I think from both of our points of view that's even more important than the HTML coding – how you make sure that a business says, 'Yes, why would we do this, and then how do we do this all the way through the business?' You're now State-wide Accessibility Coordinator for Texas. How is the experience that you had at IBM now helping you with your current job?

Jeff: They had laws passed in statute for government, 2006 I think, and there were a lot of different agencies that were doing pieces of it, but they didn't have strong leadership in accessibility – that is , they didn't have anybody that understood that big picture or experience on the business side.

Having gone through all that for IBM, [I knew] how to take on challenges and just share the vision, start to communicate it out. Look for the pain points and then start to help everybody else; think about it not just in terms of fixing their webpages but how they implement it holistically across their organization.

Jonathan: We got in touch because your book is a validation that some of the things that we were talking about in our British Standard aren't just a British thing. We've talked a lot about BS 8878. What do you think of it?

Jeff: I think there's a lot of crossover points between what I had in my book and BS 8878. It goes down to that next level of detail.

In my book I touch on a lot of topics, but I try not to go too deep in it, because everybody is going to want to implement things a different way, whatever's natural for their organization. The two documents really complement each other in a lot of ways.

Watch the complete video interview with Jeff Kline at:
http://qrs.ly/tz4a6c1

Read Jeff's blogs on strategic accessibility at:
http://strategicaccessibility.wordpress.com/

Embedding competence and confidence

Having learnt that the only way to sustainably embed accessibility competence throughout the organization is to delegate and empower product team members to make competent accessibility decisions, the accessibility programme manager will wish to source the best accessibility training and guidance for product staff.

Unfortunately, most current accessibility training, like most accessibility guidelines, has one major fault: it is too general, and heaps together accessibility issues that concern designers with those that concern developers or writers or testers. And rarely does accessibility training address what project managers or product managers need to know to fulfil their responsibilities at all.

This is one of the reasons why accessibility is considered by many to be over-complex. While it is exceptionally useful and comprehensive, the international standard on technical web accessibility – WCAG 2.0 – unfortunately structures its large number of success criteria around technical categories rather than the job roles of the people who need to work with them.

Interview with Makoto Ueki, Accessibility Consultant at Infoaxia and Chairman of Japan's Web Accessibility Infrastructure Committee

Makoto: In Japan I've met many people who are sharing the same issue. WCAG 2.0 are well-designed standards. But, they're not always well designed for web designers, developers, web masters, who are actually using the standards' guidelines, to make their web content accessible.

This has been my biggest challenge as a consultant, as Chairman (of the committee that translated WCAG 2.0 into Japanese) – to make accessibility more understandable

Our standards are not easy to understand even for accessibility experts like me. What I'd like to do is to provide a plain language version of the success criteria, to bridge between standardization and web development. Maybe when we update to JIS in 2015 it might be possible for us to modify the words, phrases, language of the requirements.

Jonathan: I agree. I've just created some guidelines in the UK for one of my clients and there were two things that we knew we needed. One was that WCAG is great but it doesn't really say very much about mobile, and my client does a lot of mobile. So, we handled that. The second thing was that we needed to separate the standards and guidelines into job roles.

So, these are the six things that you have to think about if you are a visual designer. These are the 20 things if you're an interaction designer. These are the 12 things for content authors. That is so much easier for people to digest. If there were five things in WCAG that are relevant to your job, you don't want to have to look for them in an 80-page document. You want somebody to say, 'Here are the five things'. It could be a two-page document for some roles. Is that the sort of thing that you think you might be doing?

Makoto: Yes, web designers and developers are required to conform to, let's say, Level A success criteria. It is not so difficult to do that. But when they read the success criteria and try to understand them it's not so easy. They would think that conforming to WCAG is something confusing or time consuming.

When I talk about accessibility I don't talk about success criteria. I say 'Okay, here are ten points, ten topics you should follow. Provide a descriptive page title, mark up headings and describe links, you know.' After showing the points I ask them, 'Hey, do you usually do these things? This is not special, right?' And I often get 'Yes, yes. We do.' So this is not something special. This is not time-consuming. Just don't read success criteria first.

Jonathan: I use the same principle myself. When a new client has brought me in to improve their organization's accessibility, I always ask to spend a day with their team before training them. I ask them what they do; what time pressures they're under to achieve what they do; what they know about accessibility already; and if there are any particular questions that they have. We then focus on those when I do my training, to make sure it's appropriate to their needs.

And I've found the same thing you have. There are a lot of people who are doing the right thing already; they don't know it's called accessibility, they just think it's called good web design. So it's best to be able to start off by saying: 'If there is a nought to 100% to get to perfect accessibility, you're already maybe 50% there. So, this is doable because you're already doing some of it.'

Watch the complete video interview with Makoto Ueki at: http://qrs.ly/yc4a6c7

Find more on Infoaxia at: http://www.infoaxia.com/en/

To efficiently and effectively embed the right competence in your staff, I'd recommend the following course of action...

Start by giving all of your product creation staff 'accessibility awareness training' to make accessibility about real people, not guidelines. Find any way of getting your staff the most vivid, compelling experience of how different disabled people actually use your website to give them a 'voila' moment, like Peter White gave me on *In Touch* in 2008 (see section 'The effect you have' in Chapter 2), when they come face to face with people using (or not being able to use) the products they've created in ways they might never have thought of. It's much easier to motivate yourself for the journey if you feel the tension between the poor results from your current level of knowledge and the potential that you could realize if you started building your expertise.

Then find a way of getting your product creation teams accessibility guidelines that are easy for them to digest and follow – that break down the WCAG 2.0 success criteria by job role, and cover all the types of web product you create. The W3C-WAI have now created the (work in progress) WAI 'Accessibility Responsibility Breakdown'.[60] I also recommend the latest iteration of the BBC accessibility guidelines that I started creating years ago – the BBC 'Mobile Accessibility Standards and Guidelines'[61] – which are a much more complete, freely available, model for how to do this breakdown, as well as handling accessibility across mobile and web superbly.

Even better, integrate these job-specific accessibility success criteria into the other guidelines you may already have for each job on the production team. For example: integrate criteria for 'accessible design' as one aspect of 'good design', alongside other criteria like: design for readability, to be memorable and 'on brand' in your organization's web style guide.

As a quick way of getting your staff to the level of competence they need, by all means give them accessibility training. But do not send your staff on general accessibility courses. Segment your staff by job role, and send them on more specific 'accessibility for client-side developers', 'accessibility for content producers' or 'accessibility for visual designers' courses (like John Corcoran's stunning 'Beyond Big Type'[62]). Make sure the training gives them all the things they need to do to uphold *their responsibility* for accessibility on projects, and nothing more.

Finally, make sure the training gives your staff the *confidence* to know:

- when they can make decisions safely themselves – for example, by applying your guidelines to produce the accessible result they want; and
- when they should call for support from the accessibility programme manager – to help them deal with situations they feel may need to go outside or beyond your guidelines.

---

[60] http://www.w3.org/community/wai-engage/wiki/Accessibility_Responsibility_Breakdown

[61] http://www.bbc.co.uk/guidelines/futuremedia/accessibility/mobile_access.shtml

[62] http://www.wiredesign.com/page/selected_projects/beyond_big_type/13,0,0,0.html

Now it's your turn

Think about how you can most efficiently and cost-effectively provide competence-raising resources for your staff.

This is the approach I'd suggest you take to commissioning your training:

- First audit your staff by job role, considering the level of each role's impact on the accessibility of your products, and their current level of competence in upholding that responsibility. This will enable you to prioritise which of your staff need training most urgently (e.g. those with the biggest impact and least competence), and how much it is worth spending on that training.
- Adopt a user-centred approach to your training design, ensuring that all your staff accessibility training is relevant to their needs by asking them about any particular accessibility challenges that come up time and again on the sorts of products they create. Use that information, along with your understanding of their current level of accessibility knowledge and the level that you need them to achieve, to specify the training they need.
- Find a trainer who not only understands accessibility, but can meet the specification of training you've set – it's cheaper to pay for bespoke training that gives your team members what they need, than waste their precious time with cheaper training that doesn't.
- And get your staff into applying their training in real projects as soon as possible after their training – this not only embeds any guidelines they learnt in the training in their minds, it also enables them to start turning those guidelines into practical expertise as Sarah Lewthwaite describes in her interview.

To give you a start, I've included an index to the parts of this book that are most useful for people with different job roles in the Appendix. A fuller version is in the book's support materials.

> **Interview with Sarah Lewthwaite, Research Associate in Education at King's College London**
>
> **Jonathan:** You're an expert in how people learn, Sarah. I'm interested in what the best way of training people in accessibility is. My understanding is it is usually best to get people doing stuff, to really engage them in a subject. So learning a set of rules, like WCAG 2.0, especially without necessarily knowing why those rules are so important, seems to miss the mark. Is BS 8878 a better way of introducing people to accessibility than what we've had in the past?

Sarah: I think what it does very helpfully is it allows you, as a user, to develop your expertise, rather than hit a checklist. I think one of the problems with WCAG potentially can be that you learn to do a checklist rather than learning to create accessible experiences for disabled people and users in general. Learning WCAG can be a very rote process, which can be quite a turn-off particularly, I would say, for adult learners. So the question is: do you have to learn basic accessibility principles before you do accessibility work? I think what's very interesting coming out of some of David Hay's research into expertise and neuroscience – and I'd say this is quite cutting-edge stuff – is that you don't necessarily have to start learners with the rote basics. You can start in a far more critical space and people will create knowledge at a high level from the start. So if we think about BS 8878 not just as learning accessibility but actively researching accessibility, and creating knowledge from the start, it's a very strong way of engaging learners. I think, as an educational tool, BS 8878 is potentially a lot more interesting and useful than WCAG in terms of developing expertise, because instead of learning by rote, you're actually 'doing accessibility'. In that sense you're moving from a kind of technician level to a kind of expert level. When you see debates over WCAG you can often see that these are expert debates because people are using it and then they move beyond it. They recognize the weaknesses and the strengths, and there are debates about 'grey areas'. But once you move beyond WCAG, it becomes potentially quite inflexible – there become a lot of tensions and arguments over what rules should be applied when and how; that kind of minutiae. Whereas BS 8878 has a certain amount of flex that means expertise could be drawn into it more readily and actively from the start.

Watch the complete video interview with Sarah Lewthwaite at: http://qrs.ly/kk4a6c2

Read Sarah's blogs on Social Media, Disability and Higher Education at: http://slewth.co.uk

Embedding a support resource

The availability of a support resource to help your staff deal with those 'grey area' situations, where they feel they may need to go outside or beyond your accessibility guidelines is very useful. For efficiency, you need to separate the level of accessibility knowledge you should require from your designers, coders, testers and content creators, from the level of accessibility knowledge you'd require from an accessibility specialist helping them, when needed.

My experience is that most large organizations do best when they train all their staff in the basics of accessibility, and train them to identify the circumstances where they should call for support. This second aspect is as much part of their competence in making good justifiable accessibility decisions (as will be discussed in the next chapter) as understanding how to best apply accessibility guidelines.

Ideally, you should set up a hierarchy of accessibility support for your staff. They should know:

- when applying WCAG 2.0 or other accessibility guidelines is *enough* to make good decisions;
- when they need to temper accessibility guidelines with *their* existing experience – things that have worked for them on previous projects;
- when they should look for expertise (or resources such as reusable accessible code libraries) from *colleagues* in the organization who have worked on similar projects;
- when decisions are so difficult, complex or risky they would benefit from bringing in an accessibility *specialist* for their advice; and
- when they need to commission further *research* to be able to make a justifiable decision.

The sorts of difficult decisions for which your staff may need specialist support include:

- where the application of the standard accessibility guidelines for part of the product 'just doesn't feel right' for some reason (see Step 13 of Chapter 5 for example);
- where the amount of work needed to implement accessibility for a feature becomes onerous or burdensome – where the cost is a disproportionally large percentage of the total cost of implementing the feature;
- where it's not possible – due to lack of time or resource – to do all the necessary accessibility work, and so you need to prioritize work to minimize the *accessibility risk*, within the constraints you are working within, quantify the risk, and put in place any measures you can to mitigate it (see Step 15 for examples).

It is the accessibility programme manager's job to identify whether the organization should recruit accessibility specialists as an internal resource, which can be nurtured and built up over time, or to subcontract this support to a network of external accessibility support partners (including accessibility trainers, accessibility specialists, and suppliers of different types of accessibility testing). Either way, it's important that these support staff don't 'do' the accessibility work on products (they're not 'accessibility superheroes'), but they advise and support the project staff who do that accessibility work, when they need it, so competence is built-up, not dependence.

Now it's your turn

As a consultant, I have been the external accessibility support for many organizations, providing support either on an ad-hoc basis, via a retainer for a certain number of hours of on-call email response over the course of a project, or via regular on-site accessibility surgeries for staff to drop in and talk through new issues with me.

So consider if you need to recruit an external accessibility support resource for your product teams, and consider which combination of those options would work best for their needs.

I don't have space in this book to go deeper into the best ways of finding the right accessibility support service in a cost-efficient way. I'd recommend you follow my 'Finding an Accessibility Support Resource' blogs[63] to do this. These are based on my experience as the BBC's accessibility programme manager recruiting internal teams of accessibility (and usability) specialists, and external accessibility (and usability) support partners, to provide support services to the product teams in charge of the BBC's 400 products. Olivier Nourry's *Get the most out of your accessibility expert* advice from CSUN-13[64] is another good resource in this area.

---

[63] http://www.hassellinclusion.com/2013/01/accessibility-accreditation-value/
[64] http://www.slideshare.net/OlivierNourry/get-the-most-out-of-your-accessibility-expert

Interview with David Banes, Chief Executive, MADA, Qatar

Jonathan: So, David, your job at MADA was to create a whole accessibility ecosystem for the nation state of Qatar from scratch. How did you go about it?

David: One of the main things I've been really pleased about at MADA is, yes, we brought in people with a lot of experience in a range of needs over many years. But we didn't just lift the model from the US or the UK and do it here.

We tried to blend that with local knowledge, experience and commitment, and it is that blending that needs to be done. That's not always easy, it's not always straightforward, but I think without it the chances of successful implementation are really small.

Jonathan: It's fascinating what you're saying, because I think you're talking about embedding, but on a national level. That you don't want people coming in maybe in a piecemeal fashion every now and again, bringing their expertise, sharing it, and leaving, only for you to realize that actually you need them to come back over again in six months' time because everything's broken again. What you need to do is embed it in the organization…

David: Or what's even worse is you keep changing your consultant. Your first consultant comes in and says, 'Okay, this is how you should do it, this is the answer.' That's great. Then you get a couple of problems. So it's 'we'll get another consultant.' For most consultants the first part of any consultancy is to rubbish the consultancy that was done before and to start again. So the danger is you're never building one upon the other, so you don't build a sustainable, long-term vision and action plan. What you're basically doing is the same piece of development over and over again.

This is why I think that bringing people who will then make a personal long-term commitment to a business or a country is really important.

You do need to employ people. Yes, you can work with consultants. Yes you can outsource. But somebody somewhere needs to have that commitment, that vision within the organization or within a State. Because they will think, 'I'm going to bind these elements together and make sure there is a consistent development.'

Watch the complete video interview with David Banes at:
http://qrs.ly/s14a6bs

Read MADA's blogs on accessibility in the Middle East at:
http://www.mada.org.qa/eAccessibility/EN/blog/ .

Embedding in policy

Ensuring that all your staff are motivated and competent to make the right accessibility decisions at each step of the creation of a product is a great start to embedding accessibility best practice in your organization. But you need to make sure that their best endeavours are supported and not overridden by another inhibitor or facilitator: your organization's established policies, standards and guidelines.

To illustrate the importance of embedding accessibility criteria in the generation of guidelines, let me give you an example of the most common and difficult accessibility problem that organizations face.

It's the problem of inaccessible branding and colours.

An organization's brand is exceptionally valuable, and brand usage guidelines are normally one of the first sets of guidelines that any organization creates. Depending on the size of the organization, the amount of money spent on the exact shade of blue or pink used in the company's logo and brand colours is often unappreciated and ridiculed by those outside the branding world. There are good reasons for these costs, as the logo and colours will be used in thousands of different circumstances, across growing numbers of media channels – everything from radio and TV adverts, to printed collateral, billboards, websites and apps. It needs to represent the organization's values to the minds of the public, and get the right balance of distinctiveness from competitors, and familiar. It's a huge challenge and expense to get right.

So how then should a web manager respond to this very common finding from an accessibility audit?

'There is not enough contrast between the text and background colours...this can be fixed by changing the text colour to #DE0079?'

If the original colour is specified in the organization's branding guidelines, the web manager cannot achieve conformance with WCAG 2.0 AA and keep 'on brand'. They have the unenviable choice of annoying potential disabled users or their branding colleagues.

I've lost count of the number of occasions when the brand colours of a client's website have fallen foul of the colour contrast checkpoints of accessibility guidelines. And, of course, the 'simple solution' that the accessibility testers (or disabled people who write in to complain) suggest is not simple in the slightest, as a change in the colours might require much of the expensive branding work to be redone.

I'll cover *restylethis*[65] – an accessibility personalization solution to the colour contrast needs of disabled people that does not require expensive branding changes or deviation of a website from brand guidelines – later on in this book. But the point here is that these difficulties could have been averted if accessibility colour contrast constraints had been included in the brief for the creation of the organization's branding in the first place.

This is just one example of how your organization's policies, standards and guidelines – whether written or unwritten – can either facilitate or inhibit your aim of making accessible products, and how including accessibility criteria within the creation of those policies can prevent real and expensive accessibility problems occurring every time they are used.

Embed accessibility into existing policies, don't ghettoize them in a new one

A common approach to embedding accessibility in your organization's policies is to create an accessibility policy for your organization. I've read and written many such accessibility policies, especially here in the UK where the Public Sector Equality Duty requires public bodies to create, publish and update Single Equality Schemes every few years.

Unfortunately, I've also found discrepancies between the wording of such policies and what actually happens, day in day out, in the organizations that have them. Or to give a wider, multi-agency example, a survey of the Accessibility of Federal Electronic and Information Technology (US) in 2012[66] found that, despite Section 508 of the US Rehabilitation Act

---

[65] http://www.restylethis.com
[66] http://www.ada.gov/508/508_Report.htm

requiring it, 'less than 50% of agency components incorporated specific applicable Section 508 Accessibility Standards as requirements in each procurement solicitation'.

I believe one of the main reasons for these discrepancies is that this accessibility policy information is confined to one document, which is reasonably easy to overlook. Creating a central organizational accessibility policy may backfire – it puts everything in one place so people can ignore it.

For your organization to take most notice of accessibility across its functions and policies a more effective approach is to embed accessibility criteria across all the policies that are important in your business – one paragraph here, a couple of metrics there...

It is not wrong to want a central accessibility policy, so BS 8878 advises you to create an 'organizational web accessibility policy' where you summarize what your organization does in this area – most likely because you are required to have one by a set of regulations that cover your organization. However, it advises you to make this a list of links to the accessibility criteria that are distributed and embedded across your organization's policies.

You can find an example of such a policy in Annex E of BS 8878.

Which policies should have accessibility baked in?

With that approach established, you need to consider what the best strategy is for identifying which policies impact accessibility, and then how to embed accessibility criteria in them.

Identifying which policies impact accessibility is facilitated if you have an organizational policy repository from which to work. If you don't have such a repository, this could be because they are scattered throughout your organization's departments, or because you don't have any written policies at all.

Whichever of these is the case, here's a quick list of some common policies, standards and guidelines that impact the accessibility of an organization's web products, and their ability to support those products' disabled and older users:

- their design guidelines, such as:
  - o brand usage guidelines,
  - o web style guides, and design pattern libraries they have built up,
- their technology policies, such as:

     o   technology strategy – whether they have standardised on using particular web technologies to create their products (for example, whether they create native or hybrid mobile apps),
     o   browser support policy and assistive technology support policies,
     o   any code libraries they have built up,

- their procurement policies, such as:
  - o   how accessibility is mentioned in their standard templates for requests for proposals or invitations to tender, and procurement contracts,
- their standard product launch checklist;
- their support centre standards, such as:
  - o   their standard script for dealing with calls to their support centre,
  - o   their 'Frequently Asked Questions' document that they publish on their website so users can find their own answers to their questions,
- their social media guidelines.

Once you've identified which policies affect accessibility, prioritize those that have the most impact, identify who owns or is responsible for those policies, and use the support of your executive accessibility champion to approach the policy owners about how accessibility criteria could be incorporated in their next revision.

Now it's your turn

Auditing your organization's policies for whether they need to mention accessibility may seem daunting in any large organization that has large numbers of departments with large numbers of policies.

So, my recommendation is that you start your work in those digital policies that most directly impact the creation of your organization's recent web products, and work back from there into the underlying policies that impacted the creation of those digital policies.

For most of my clients, the best place to start is with establishing:

- A top-level business case and resulting organizational accessibility strategy (as discussed earlier in this chapter).
- A default degree of accessibility that you will aim to achieve for all your web products (see Step 7 of the BS 8878 process in Chapter 5). This should be:
  - o   easily specifiable and understandable inside and outside your organization, including to your suppliers and users;
  - o   flexible and scalable (to make sense across all the different platforms and product-types you expect to create);
  - o   measurable;
  - o   able to predict the quality of customer experience;

    o   achievable (there's no point in reaching for the moon if you don't have the resources to leave the ground);

    o   able to facilitate discussion around exceptions; and

    o   justifiable (to your senior management and users).

- A standard accessibility section to be added to your organization's invitation to tender or request for proposals procurement documentation, and their counterpart procurement or outsourcing contracts (see Step 11).
- A standard form of words to use in explaining your organization's accessibility commitment to your users in the web accessibility statement of each of your products (see Step 15).
- Policies documenting the organization's position on some of the key decisions made in the BS 8878 process in Chapter 5 – the default degree of accessibility you will aim for (see Step 7), the default assistive technologies and browsers you will aim to support (see Step 10), the default position on accessibility support across platforms (see Step 9).

Further guidance and examples of embedding accessibility criteria into organizational policies can be found in the support materials for this book (see page x).

Embedding governance

Most organizations currently equate accessibility governance with automated tools that constantly check the organization's website against a large number of accessibility checkpoints. Many accessibility service companies have such a tool – usually a costly one – that you can procure and use for checking millions of pages for minor slips.

But that 'minor' is the thing. While I don't want to downplay the importance of getting accessibility consistently right on a detailed heading-by-heading, image-by-image basis, many organizations get so obsessed with this that they neglect more fundamental, strategic aspects of governance, such as doing user-testing to make sure disabled people are actually able to use the site when the headings and alt-text are in place, and doing this checking over all of your sites, mobile apps and social media channels.

While smaller organizations with one small website and few social media channels may be able to get away with simple accessibility governance strategies, larger organizations should consider:

- what web products to monitor;
- what criteria to monitor for – accessibility metrics;
- how often to monitor them;
- how well to monitor them;

- how much it costs to monitor them;
- what to do with the results – do you use a carrot, stick or is no action at all taken when issues are found?

What web products to monitor – your digital portfolio

Start by enumerating all of the different web projects that your organization is currently working on, whether new versions of current products, redesigns of current websites or mobile apps, or wholly new ventures. Then add all of the web products that your administration teams are currently maintaining. Add all of your external channels – for example, your YouTube and SoundCloud channels, your Facebook page or pages, your Twitter and Flickr accounts, and any blogs or other off-site mechanisms that you use to communicate with your users.

This is your Digital Portfolio, and you should consider the accessibility of every product in it, and user journeys that cut across multiple products. For example: you may create a blog to provide the details of a new competition; you may promote that via Twitter and Facebook; and you may require users to enter the competition on your main website. Ensuring that your disabled users are able to complete that full journey, through the different levels of accessibility provided by each of the sites and services they will need to navigate, is so much more important than whether one image is missing alternative text.

You should also consider in this digital portfolio all web products you host, whether external or internal. You should make sure you don't miss products that non-technical parts of your organization manage like job application systems procured by HR departments. Otherwise you may find that you receive complaints about the accessibility of parts of your digital portfolio that users really value, but often get overlooked as they don't generate revenue – for example, anything to do with customer service or employment opportunities.

Categorizing products and degree of accessibility required

It is very likely that some of your products are more important than others, both to you as an organization, and to your users. To give an example from my time at the BBC, over 90% of the accessibility complaints that we received were for the video-on-demand service iPlayer. This does not mean that iPlayer was an unsuccessful product. The converse was true – the product was so successful that it became an overwhelming reason why most people came to the BBC website. As such it became a *pillar* for the BBC – a popular product that brought people to the BBC site, and gave the BBC the freedom to do other, riskier products and promote them to the stream of people visiting the pillar.

Other products may be thought of as *enablers* – pieces of underlying technology, such as sign-on systems and global page templating systems that are needed to provide core functionality across the whole of the website or websites, or make them run more efficiently. Yet other products may be *innovations* – punts or hunches that could turn out to be ill-conceived, one-off award winners, or the future pillars that your organization will depend on for your revenues or audience reach going forwards (most mobile sites are a good example of this, as they started as innovations, but are now becoming pillars due to mass audience take-up). Then you have your *standard websites* in the middle ground – using established enabler technologies to support common, if not glamorous, user goals, such as finding company information, help or careers information. Finally, you may have *short-term 'campaign' sites* that are designed to do a clearly defined task (such as promoting a new product or service) for a short time and then be removed from the portfolio.

Each of these different types of product has a different purpose and life cycle, and so may reasonably need to adopt a slightly different approach to accessibility (as we'll discuss in Chapter 5).

This is what you should do if you want to consider accessibility across the entirety of your portfolio:

- prioritize accessibility for enablers, as accessibility deficiencies there will be felt across all your products;
- then look to make pillars accessible, as you are likely to get the most return on your accessibility investment here;
- ensure your standard websites aren't letting you down;
- and give less attention to short-term campaign sites, unless ensuring 100% of your users can respond to the campaign is key to its business aims.

You may need to make innovations an exception case for accessibility. They may require cutting-edge technologies to be used that by definition are less likely to be supported by accessibility guidelines and assistive technologies, and, in the final analysis, may not connect with any of your audience at all. However, you will need to explain this to your audience, and make sure accessibility is 'added in' as soon as the product starts to find its audience (for example, the team behind the award-winning gov.uk site sensibly but controversially held back accessibility work[67] until the ideas behind the site had coalesced, then implemented accessibility brilliantly when the full site was built,[68] based on the lessons learnt from the alpha.gov.uk prototype).

---

[67]   https://gds.blog.gov.uk/2011/05/06/accessibility/
[68]   https://gds.blog.gov.uk/accessibility/

Multi-national organizations that create specific web products for different countries may also wish to segment their web products by territory, as they may wish to reflect the level of legal requirement for accessibility for the territory in its required degree of accessibility. For example, products designed for territories with strong accessibility legislation (such as the United States, the UK or Australia) may require stronger accessibility than products designed for territories with weaker accessibility legislation (such as Brazil, Hong Kong or France).

So your governance strategy should include the full scope of your digital portfolio, and may require different degrees of accessibility from your products in different categories, to contribute to the overall accessibility score for the whole portfolio.

Accessibility assurance metrics

The next question of course is how to measure that accessibility. I won't go into detail here because Step 14 of the BS 8878 process described in Chapter 5 will provide all of the strategic information you need. Suffice to say at this point that the metrics that you choose to measure are likely to have a massive impact on the behaviour of your staff, who will generally work to meet your metrics rather than meet your audiences' needs, unless these two things are linked by your metrics-setting process.

Level of assurance vs the costs of 'how often?' and 'how well?'

Two other important aspects of monitoring are 'how often' you monitor against your metrics and 'how well' you monitor against them. These two aspects, together with the metrics you've chosen, will dictate how much it will cost to do this accessibility governance monitoring. A balance needs to be struck: to achieve total assurance that your organization's products are consistently accessible costs a lot of money; whereas lower levels of assurance can be bought more cheaply. So you will need some way of deciding and justifying the level of money that you wish to spend to buy this assurance. And, of course, the decisions that you made on your organization's motivation for accessibility (in Chapter 3) will help you to make these new accessibility governance investment decisions based on well-considered business cases that you've created for your organization.

All data, no action?

Finally, all of this governance can be robbed of its value if you have not established what you will do with the results of your monitoring. Will the results be a carrot or a stick to those parts of your organization developing or procuring the products, or will you take no action at all based on your monitoring results? Accessibility monitoring tools can create impressive looking accessibility dashboards that enable senior management to get a handle on how well different parts of their organization are upholding their accessibility responsibilities. But these are worthless if management aren't sufficiently bought-in to the importance of accessibility to hold their staff accountable when they neglect to deliver the right degree of accessibility quality, and potentially deny a product's sign-off for launch if their accessibility is deficient.

This again is why it is so important to properly establish your organization's motivation for accessibility before you start embedding or governing accessibility. An organization's real values are not those things that they say in their policy documents, or even those things that they regularly measure. Their real values can be seen in the things that they actually deliver, and how they treat their audiences.

Now it's your turn

Use the accessibility governance spreadsheet in the support materials for this book (see page x) to guide you through documenting:

- all the products in your digital portfolio;
- each product's category (and, thus, its relative importance);
- the degree of accessibility that you expect each to contribute to the accessibility score for the whole portfolio; and
- the type of testing needed to measure that accessibility across the different stages in the lifestyle of the product, and the budget you will allocate to that testing.

Chapter 5

ENABLE – how to embed via the RuDDeR process

This quote, from Rob Wemyss, Head of Accessibility for Royal Mail Group in the UK, usefully summarizes what organizations have got to gain from using BS 8878:

> 'BS 8878 has given us a framework to help reduce costs and improve our quality when delivering accessible web products for our customers.[69]'

You've already seen how BS 8878 helps make accessibility understandable and strategic by providing a framework for how to embed accessibility strategically within an organization.

It also provides a user-centred inclusive design process that identifies the key decisions that impact whether the product will include or exclude disabled and older people across the whole of its life cycle. Importantly, it also provides an informed way of making these decisions, and a way of documenting them to capture your best practice.

In this chapter we will look at the process at the heart of BS 8878, step by step. The process is based on best accessibility practice taken from many of the top websites in the world, including the BBC.

The process is also based on similar processes from the related fields of user-centred and inclusive design, both for digital products and non-digital products. It is the missing link that enables product creators from these related fields to understand how accessibility works for websites, mobile apps and more.

To give you an example, in 2010–11 I represented the BBC as part of a European consortium of organizations exploring how to gain competitive advantage by making their products inclusive, led by the Engineering Design Centre (EDC) at Cambridge University. I found that the processes, methodologies and tools that EDC had created – the Inclusive Design Toolkit[70] – related closely to much of what my team of digital usability and accessibility specialists were already doing at the BBC. Over the

---

[69] http://www.slideshare.net/jonathanhassell/case-studies-of-implementing-bs-8878-csun-2012-12145101/31

[70] http://www.inclusivedesigntoolkit.com/

course of the year we proved that EDC's processes could be usefully applied across products ranging from confectionery wrappers to bank branches; from personal medical equipment to consumer white goods. What was interesting was that organizations that created both non-digital and digital products could not understand how accessibility guidelines in the web space were a technical checklist, when everything that they had learnt about inclusive design was about understanding user needs, encapsulating them in personas (see Step 3), and using those personas to inform all stages of an iterative design process.

I used these insights to ensure that BS 8878's process – which we created specifically for the production of web products – was designed to harmonize completely with the wider inclusive design processes that EDC use, and the ISO Standards for Human-Centred Design of Interactive Systems – ISO/FDIS 9241-210.[71]

BS 8878's process also includes user-personalization concepts that are unique to the adaptable, customizable nature of software. These add a useful flexibility to product development where the needs of one or more sets of users diverge from the needs of the majority of users.

Aligned with business intelligence for building a better product

Many people have noted that much of the guidance in BS 8878's process often reflects mantras promoted by digital web experts from outside the accessibility field for how to build an effective website.[72]

Neil Collard, Strategy and Planning Director for e3, in his great seminar 'How shopping for shoes helped change the way we sell financial products',[73] says the things a website needs to be effective are:

- to be easily found by its target audiences;
- to represent and develop your brand and its values online;
- to maximize conversion (by ensuring all your visitors find what they need and become a customer);
- to retain customers and drive value (by keeping the site fresh and responsive to the growing needs of your customers, as your business grows).

BS 8878's process maps very well to this list, and its user-centred way of thinking about accessibility provides a great way of focusing website creation around those important things. It's based on a lot of business intelligence which, when followed, should deliver a *better* product, not

---

[71]   http://www.iso.org/iso/catalogue_detail.htm?csnumber=52075

[72]   http://www.hassellinclusion.com/2012/04/effective-websites-bs-8878-website-in-1-day/

[73]   http://ll1.workcast.net/10221/4212940387039631/Documents/Nicola%20and%20James.pdf

just an *accessible* one. And this is slowly opening up organizations to accessibility that have been resistant in the past.

It's important to say here that BS 8878 does not require you to throw out your current web production process if you already have one. BS 8878's steps can be integrated with the existing process that you have. In fact this gap analysis is exactly what I have done successfully with a number of different organizations. The full BS 8878 process is really there for organizations that have yet to establish a production process into which these steps can be integrated. For information on how to integrate the process into your organization, see the section later in the chapter.

Interview with Debra Ruh, Director of Ruh Global, USA

Jonathan: How would you characterize the American market at the moment?

Debra: The good news is that American companies, government agencies, universities are spending money to become accessible. They're trying to comply, trying to reduce their risk of litigation. They understand, 'This issue is not going to go away, so we'd better do something about it.' They're actually spending good solid money on accessibility – even over the last six months, the amount of money people are spending on accessibility has risen to the point that we're having problems finding qualified people to actually do the work.

But the bad news is, the reason there's not enough qualified people to do the work is because we have really complicated things. With TecAccess – the company I built – we would go into corporations and we would test and tell them what was wrong with their accessibility. We'd help them fix it, we would encourage them to put it in their processes, but they didn't. Then as soon as we left they would have complaints again that they weren't accessible. That was discouraging because, of course it's great that they're spending money, but it was becoming apparent that the way that we were doing it was not sustainable.

Jonathan: What's missing, if you like, is that ability to embed the right practices, the right processes within those organizations?

Debra: Right, while corporations are spending money, the bad news is that I personally believe that a lot of that money is being wasted. If a company spends $250,000 to be accessible and they get accessible, then the next month they're not accessible any more, I believe that's a failure for our accessibility community. We've found that our federal agencies were making good traction, and then the stakeholders started retiring from those agencies and we lost all of it, because it has not been embedded at process level.

Jonathan: That's why I'm here, in San Diego – to bring across the process-driven approach that I created in British Standard BS 8878. What is it about that Standard that you think is going to be of value to industry here?

Debra: The thing that is exciting is that it encourages blending the change at the process level. If we do not embed accessibility at the process level we will keep trying but failing. However, if we encourage accessibility as part of the design process we can be successful. Accessibility must be built into the development life cycle. We build privacy and security in at the process level, so should manage accessibility the same way.

You've got to change the conversation. And that's why I like the British Standard because you can actually do that. It gives corporations something that they could actually implement, and make accessibility part of the process.

Watch the complete video interview with Debra Ruh at:
http://qrs.ly/tq4a6c6

Read Debra's blogs on accessibility and disability at:
http://www.ruhglobal.com/category/blog/

Web products

Before we start talking about the specifics of the process, it's important to mention what types of digital product the process can help you create.

Throughout BS 8878 we use the term 'web product' rather than website to denote the product being created. This is to make sure that people are aware that the process applies:

- for different product-types:
    - intranet and extranet websites, as well as external internet websites and workplace apps;
    - Rich internet Applications (RIAs), and 'Software as a Service' cloud services, as well as static information sites;
    - user-generated content websites (blogs and social sharing sites like Facebook and YouTube) as well as curated information websites;
    - games websites as well as company 'brochureware' websites;
- for different delivery platforms and technologies:
    - mobile websites and apps, as well as desktop websites.

While the accessibility of software is officially outside the scope of BS 8878, its harmonization with more general inclusive design processes enables BS 8878's approach to work across any digital product, and across most non-digital products too.

I've even used it to help an advertising agency think about the accessibility of motor show stands.

Making good decisions

Another essential aspect of BS 8878's contribution to accessibility best practice is its requirement for organizations to make decisions at each of the steps of the process in a way that is informed, justifiable and transparent.

A huge number of decisions are made across the team of people working on a web product every day. While BS 8878's process highlights the key decisions made in web production projects that have most impact on accessibility, all decisions, to a greater or lesser extent, may have an impact. So it's important for each member of the web production team to be empowered to make decisions, to know how to make them well, and to know when they should ask for decision support from accessibility specialists (as discussed in Chapter 4).

This may seem like teaching your grandmother to suck eggs, but my experience has found that it's essential grounding for understanding how to get the best out of the BS 8878 process. It replaces the rigidity of most accessibility guidelines with permission for team members to use their brains in working out how to make a good decision.

BS 8878 encourages team members to be aware that every decision should:

- be recognized as a decision;
- have all options and their implications considered;
- be made based on justifiable reasoning; and
- be noted in the 'Web Product's Accessibility Policy' for transparency.

And it requires that team members should do this at every step of the process.

This is essentially a democratic, empowering way of working. It encourages staff to think carefully about why they are about to do the things they are about to do, whether there is another way of doing things, and what the implications are of each. As Sarah Lewthwaite describes in her interview in Step 13, it encourages staff to make decisions based on their own understanding of the product, and the best available research on its users' needs, in the country or culture in which they will be using it.

Fundamentally, it places accessibility back in the sphere of cost-benefits like all other decisions made on a project. It understands that accessibility isn't the only important quality that teams are trying to embed in their product. It enables team members to 'listen to their gut' in dealing with situations where blindly following accessibility standards feels like 'the tail is wagging the dog' – where the amount of work necessary to make some functionality work for a particular group of disabled people is overwhelming the rest of the work on the project. It also handles situations where meeting WCAG 2.0 AA is actually unfeasible or unreasonable to implement for a particular web product.

An example of the importance of this thinking is to consider the accessibility of YouTube. The purpose of YouTube is to allow the general public to upload their own videos to share them with anyone who would want to watch them.

Two aspects of this purpose provide real challenges to making it conform to WCAG 2.0 AA. For a video to be fully accessible it needs to include captions, audio-description (AD), and even interpretation into sign language. However, as it is very unlikely that users will include such access services with the videos that they upload, video on YouTube can only be made accessible by YouTube themselves. But the massive amount of videos being uploaded to YouTube every minute of every day makes it both technically unfeasible and economically unreasonable for YouTube to be required to provide access services for all of its videos.

To give a benchmark comparison, the BBC's 'gold standard' is to provide AD on 20% of all its broadcast programming. And yet, for YouTube to reach WCAG 2.0 AA it would need to audio to describe 100% of its videos. That makes no commercial sense.

The important thing here is the *competence* to be able to justify your decisions, and the *discipline* to always write that reasoning down. You'll see lots of examples of this as we go through the steps of the process.

Interview with Brian Kelly, author of the UK Web Focus Blog and Innovation Advocate based at CETIS, University of Bolton, UK

Brian: In 2004, I ran an event for people working in public libraries. We heard a great story about a game that was developed for young children who were visiting the library and how much they enjoyed it. So I asked the question, 'What about forthcoming disability legislation?' that was going to come in a few months after that. The response was, 'Oh yes, we realize it was Flash; it doesn't conform. We'll have to get rid of the game.' I said, 'You said children like it.' They said, 'Yes, it's great; they really love it.' So I asked the sensible question: 'What's the purpose of the game? Give me the context.'

The context was the parents arrive with the children, they want to put the kids somewhere for a couple of minutes while they choose some books and come back. So the point was to entertain children for a few minutes. That was fine. If they can't use the computer game, they might have some bouncy castle or something to play with. That might be the equivalent experience. When I mentioned this to somebody, it was, 'Well, maybe you could provide chess, because you could provide an accessible version of chess.' But that was missing the point. You need to go beyond the constraints of a computer screen and think about the user and what are they looking for.

So it's perfectly appropriate to say there's a real-world equivalent in that context.

Jonathan: Sure. I'm using words from one of your papers here: 'Web accessibility is not an intrinsic characteristic of a digital resource but this is determined by complex political, social and other contextual factors.' You're expanding the whole idea of the purpose of a product into how it's used and all of the environments it's used in.

Brian: What we're talking about is really a user-centred approach to providing services. What we're saying is, you look at the users, and you look at their requirements and the challenges in providing these. The difficulty we have is a set of technical guidelines that are great, and over time they've evolved. But unfortunately they've been treated as if they've been enshrined in legislation. 'We feel we have to do this.' Suddenly the user isn't there any longer. It's not about the user. Strict conformance with treating those guidelines as mandatory requirements means services are lost. The Flash game; the kids who enjoyed it. Or within a university context, imagine all of those peer-reviewed papers in institutional repositories which are in PDF format, and typically do not have alt-tags in their images. What should you do? Do you help to enrich the accessibility of those resources by removing them? That's quite clearly preposterous.

So what we're saying is we need to have an approach which is pragmatic, which is enshrined in real-world practices.

It's not about slavishly following the guidelines. It's about thinking about them in the context you're in.

Watch the complete video interview with Brian Kelly at: http://qrs.ly/4d4a6by

Read Brian's blogs on Accessibility and Web 2.0 at: http://ukwebfocus.wordpress.com/author/ukwebfocus/

Documenting your decisions

BS 8878 requires you to document these justifiable reasons in a live document called a web product accessibility policy. This is useful for five reasons...

Firstly, the web product accessibility policy is like the Captain's Log in *Star Trek*.

You know the drill. Captain Kirk talks into his Captain's Log before going down to the surface of the planet, most likely to find some sort of crystal that the Enterprise needs to continue 'boldly going where no one has gone before'. He takes down two red-shirted men to the surface, alongside more recognizable crew members. And anyone who's seen the programme knows what regularly happens: when they beam back onto the ship, the two red-shirted men have not made it back.

I like to think that my ideal James T Kirk at this point goes back into his cabin, listens to the reasons for going to the planet surface that he dictated into his Captain's Log, and considers whether the expedition was worth losing two members of his crew for. The Captain's Log enables him to revisit the reasons for his decisions after he has got a better understanding of the implications of those decisions. Being a Captain is not easy, and part of the job is to make complex decisions based on incomplete knowledge of what the consequences will be. But a good Captain improves the odds in the long term by using his log to learn from his mistakes, whether they were hot-headed, ill-judged, naive or unavoidable.

The same reflective learning is possible, and the maturity of an organization's approach to accessibility can be easily examined, by reviewing the decisions in their web product accessibility policies. While BS 8878 does not place such an emphasis on conformance as WCAG 2.0, it requires organizations wishing to claim conformity with BS 8878 to:

- address all of the recommendations of the standard;
- be able to justify any course of action that deviates from the standard's recommendations; and
- document their decision processes in the web product accessibility policy (in hard copy or electronic media) to provide evidence of following the recommendations and guidance in the standard.

Secondly, the web product accessibility policy is like a 'black box' flight recorder.

If the worst-case scenario happens and the plane goes down, the reason crash investigators always look for the black box is because it contains a recording of the decisions made on the flight-deck in the vital last few minutes before the crash happened. Most of the breakthroughs in flight safety have come from analyses of such recordings (read Malcolm Gladwell's fabulous Outliers book[74] to see him prove that).

---

[74] http://en.wikipedia.org/wiki/Outliers_(book)

The worst-case scenario for web accessibility is complaints from users that turn litigious. Here, BS 8878's concept of 'justifiable reasoning' links with the concept of 'reasonableness' that is part of many nations' disability discrimination laws: such as the 'reasonable adjustments' required in the UK Equality Act 2010; and the phrase 'reasonable accommodation' which is included as a general principle under the Americans with Disabilities Act.[75] Lawyers on BS 8878's writing team considered the link between its principle of 'justifiable reasoning' and 'reasonableness' to be sound, and following BS 8878's advice in noting the justification for your decisions may help present a case for 'reasonableness' if you need it in legal proceedings. However, until case law is established that tests the link, the two terms cannot be considered to be synonymous.

More concretely, my experience in dealing with accessibility complaints is that most disabled people dislike website owners' failure to *consider* accessibility much more than being given a *reason* why the accessibility feature they needed wasn't included, even if they disagree with that reason.

Thirdly, the web product accessibility policy is also very useful while the project is running, as it allows the team – and especially its product manager – to keep track of the research conducted and accessibility decisions made on the project. The product manager needs to be able to review quickly whether decisions being made are sensible and justifiable, not just individually (does the decision chime with the accessibility goals of the product?), but also cumulatively (does it make sense in the context of other decisions already made?) They need to be able to see any relationships between decisions – how one decision has prompted others, or where a decision has been made that undercuts previous decisions (for example, where a project has already created or procured a media player that can play captioned video, but then a decision is made to not caption any of the video being delivered by the project). They need to be able to quickly review how each decision impacts the whole project's level of cost, benefits and accessibility risk, as this is the key way of assessing the justification of each decision, and tracking the Accessibility Risk Profile of the product as it evolves.

Fourthly, the web product accessibility policy is also essential where you are outsourcing or procuring the product externally. It becomes the set of written accessibility requirements that you need to place in your invitation to tender (ITT) or request for proposals (RFP) document to ensure potential suppliers know what you expect. It gives you something to measure suppliers' tenders against, when making procurement decisions, as it requires suppliers to say how they will 'do' accessibility on your project, rather than allowing them to trot out the 'right answer' which most know is WCAG 2.0 AA, without understanding what that means for this project. It is a great help when suppliers or product

---

[75] http://www.eeoc.gov/policy/docs/accommodation.html#general

vendors cannot deliver all of your accessibility requirements and you need to prioritize them to meet project budgets.

Rarely does a product come to market that is perfectly accessible – these are the realities of modern product development. The web product accessibility policy will detail all those pragmatic decisions made where the constraints of budget, resource or launch date have justifiably overridden the accessibility risk of not making all aspects of the product accessible.

So the fifth use of the web product accessibility policy is in helping to create the web product's 'Accessibility Statement', which you should publish as part of the product to inform its users of the reasoning behind decisions that you have made that may detrimentally or positively impact their ability to use the product. Step 15 of the BS 8878 process details how to create this accessibility statement.

A fully complete specimen web product accessibility policy is available in Annex E of BS 8878.

Integrating the BS 8878 process into your organization

Integrating the BS 8878 process into your organization may initially seem daunting, but I've done this with organizations large and small; with multinational corporations with large numbers of geographically dispersed, siloed production teams and external suppliers, and digital agencies with a staff of two; with long-established companies with well-embedded production processes, and start-ups with no written production process at all.

The process is flexible enough to handle all of these cases, and you should feel free to impose a structure on it that makes it easier for you to adopt. I created the RuDDeR acronym to do just that. But the BBC, for example, now structure many of its steps into their 'Discover, Define, Design and Deploy'[76] design framework to achieve many similar effects.

To embed the process in organizations with an existing process, I recommend the following:

- Perform a gap analysis between your existing web production process and the BS 8878 process to identify where in your process you should place the 16 steps of the BS 8878 process – this will get you to an updated 'first cut' process for your organization.
- Test out your updated process on one non-mission critical web project to check its fit with your company's culture and products.

---

[76] http://www.bbc.co.uk/rd/blog/2014/05/irfs-weeknotes-178

- Analyse how well the new process supported you in delivering the desired degree of accessibility in the product.
- Make any tweaks to the process to optimize its fit with your culture.
- Create a case study about anything that was useful, if you have time.
- And, if the process brought benefits to the project, create a plan to roll it out to your other web projects and monitor its impact there.

To embed the process in smaller organizations without a process, I recommend the following:

- Follow my 'Implementing BS 8878 for SMEs'[77] blogs to see if this process gives you a useful, lean way of focusing you on your users and what they need, and can help drive you quickly to delivering a site that you know is good enough to get you started online.
- Adopt anything that works, and use the BS 8878 communities[78] to ask questions or feed back on anything that doesn't.

Interview with Jennison Asuncion, IT Accessibility Consultant, Royal Bank of Canada; now Senior Staff Technical Program Manager, LinkedIn

Jonathan: You mentioned that accessibility is important for your bank. Can you say why?

Jennison: It's important because first of all we want to be able – like any company – to serve and attract both customers and potentially qualified employees with different disabilities. Because we want to be reflective of the communities that we do work in. So at the bank that I work for, we have executive level buy-in. We're embedded in the processes, the culture, technology-wise, all of that stuff. Is it perfect? No company is. But I am so proud of where we are.

I've been at the company now – I'm just starting year seven. To have people like project managers now reaching out to us early in the game to come get our assistance so that they can plan for accessibility in their projects... We get developers coming to us early, because they're thinking of using a particular widget in a project and they just want to make sure it's accessible. They want to make sure they have enough time that if it's not, they can work to make it accessible so that it can be brought in when the thing goes live.

---

[77] http://www.hassellinclusion.com/2011/09/ready-to-launch-how-bs8878-helped-this-sme-website-get-off-the-ground/
[78] http://www.meetup.com/bs8878-web-accessibility/

To think we actually have procurement people now picking up the phone and calling us to say, 'Hey, we're just about to start a request for proposals. We want accessibility brought in.' Just that whole thing. I know different companies are at different places, and we didn't get there overnight. The team's been around for at least 10 to 12 years, so it's taken time. But since I've been there, it's just been amazing to watch how accessibility is really baked into what we do.

Jonathan: So what's your approach at the bank?

Jennison: It breaks accessibility into a shared responsibility. It would be so easy for everyone just to dump all that work on the accessibility team – you could just get bogged down serving one project. We see over 300 projects a year so we cannot be involved at the granular level with every single project. So what we've done is we've said, 'Project managers, you have a role to play. QA testers, you have a role to play. Developers, you have a role to play. Designers,' etc., etc. 'We will be there to train you on what your role is, we will give you the documentation you need in your role, we'll consult and do all that kind of stuff. But as a project, you are ultimately responsible for delivering on accessibility.' Our job as the accessibility team is to be your centre of excellence, but what we want to continue to do is build that culture where it's a shared responsibility. And as people move on, those are skills they can take wherever they go.

Jonathan: So it's that combination of executive buy-in and education of people?

Jennison: And being built into the process so it stares them in the face. They know, as the project is building, they need to include accessibility in testing, so that means QA. They need to include accessibility in the design, so that means the business systems people and the UI designers. They need to know that they need to budget for it, so then that means the PM has to play their role. The PM also has to schedule the time for the testing. Maybe any extra time in development if a widget needs to have more time spent on it to be made accessible. So that's how all the different roles and the responsibilities end up naturally having accessibility pieces because we're baked into the process.

Jonathan: That is key to what we did at the BBC as well. That's why I was trying to build that framework for how organizations could do that with BS 8878.

Jennison: Because it's one thing to have something like the Web Content Accessibility Guidelines – which is amazing and important. That's the anchor; that's the standard. You need something like the BS 8878 standard you built, to open it up and to help people understand, 'So, what are we supposed to do? Who's going to educate people on the guidelines? Who's going to make sure people are implementing them? Who's going to teach the developers how to do that?'

What's neat about the standard that you built and why I was happy to get on board is that you understood that accessibility is more than just the guidelines. Naturally and necessarily there's a wrapper around the guidelines. The wrapper can include who's responsible for what. What about the people with disabilities? What do we need to think about for them?

So what I liked about it, and why I was so enthusiastic when you were kind enough to ask for my opinion on it, was that you're not just pointing people to the guidelines. You're actually talking about the processes that are necessary in order to execute accessibility and achieve value from people's best efforts.

Jonathan: That was born out of the same sort of experience as you had, and the same impulses that you have. We had something that worked; we had something that we wanted to share. So rather than creating the Global Accessibility Awareness Day that you did, I sat in a room with 20 people for three years trying to codify this. So that other organizations that maybe weren't quite so aware, didn't have anything baked into the process, could do that.

Watch the complete video interview with Jennison Asuncion at: http://qrs.ly/rd49k5o

Read about Jennison's Global Accessibility Awareness Day at: http://www.globalaccessibilityawarenessday.org

Overview of the four parts of the RuDDeR – to keep you on course for success

Let's be frank. For most organizations, accessibility isn't really embedded in their current web production process. It's an addition, tacked on at the end, if you're lucky.

While everyone in the accessibility community agrees that 'you should take accessibility into consideration right from the start of creating your website', for most organizations this only extends as far as making sure designers and developers blindly follow WCAG in their work, and doing some 'accessibility testing' to prove they've 'done it right' just before launch.

The problem is that people are finding this isn't working so well.

Where the current process isn't working

There are numerous places where people have found the 'current process' isn't working:

- The current process doesn't allow you to 'validate' accessibility requirements for how they will contribute to the 'levers' of the product's success and growth (acquisition, activation, retention, referral and revenue[79]). Without this, sensible modern product management processes won't even allow accessibility requirements onto the roadmap, let alone prioritize them against all the other validated requirements.
- Different types of web product may benefit from different approaches to accessibility. However, the current process doesn't take anything about the specific product you're making into account. The way you should handle accessibility on a games app is different from the way you should do it for a static information website for older people. Your process needs to take differences between products into account, not ignore them.
- The current process doesn't help when you're faced with any guideline that you feel isn't going to be appropriate or achievable for your product – you can't argue with WCAG, you're just supposed to conform to it.
- Accessibility guidelines for creating mobile apps and other new web product types exist. How do these relate to WCAG, and when should you use which?
- The current process doesn't tell you how best to test for accessibility, or when (when the design's ready, or a prototype's ready, or when it has been fully coded?)

---

[79] http://blog.trak.io/growth-hacking-like-a-pirate-a-beginners-guide-to-pirate-metrics/

- The current process doesn't help when you've followed the guidelines, and yet your user-testing has found disabled people still can't use what you've created.
- The current process allows you to choose from three WCAG 2.0 levels of accessibility to aim for, but these are still crude devices for helping you quickly identify the highest priority accessibility requirements on projects with constrained budgets, resources and time.
- The current process misses out how to consider accessibility over the entire life cycle of the project – from the original idea for the product, through development, launch and post-launch versioning, to final decommissioning.

BS 8878's process needs to cover all those issues for it to be something you can reliably follow 'to get accessibility right' on every different product you'd like.

How BS 8878's RuDDeR addresses these issues

Let's start with the end in mind. I'd like you to consider what 'success' means with respect to accessibility, for the product you are about to start working on – what you'd actually like to have achieved at the end of the project in an ideal world.

I'm assuming you're not thinking of success as a one-off, you're thinking about success in the long term. Products these days go through versions every day. So you need something that is *continually* successful; that builds huge numbers of users, because it lets them do what they came to the product to do, and does it in a way that gives them all a good user experience; and that doesn't lose any of those users as it moves forwards, adding more content and functionality through new versions and redesigns.

So the BS 8878 process needs to include the practices you need to put in place to keep your product successful, in terms of accessibility and other qualities, in the long term as you Repeat everything that's gone before to create new versions.

Obviously you've got to start off with a version 1. You've got to create a great initial version of your product. How do you do that? You need to Do – to develop the product, making tactical decisions every day on the specifics of how it should look and feel, how it should be coded, how it should be tested, how to decide when it's ready to launch. This is the point where you'd be using the WCAG guidelines, if they are appropriate for your product-type and delivery platform. But you'd also need to know: when and how best you should test the product's accessibility; what to do in those situations where your gut is telling you that you need to break or modify the 'rules' for the good of the product; and what to do if you don't have the resource, budget or time to do everything 'best practice' and you only can prioritize the essential things.

So you're going to need a firm basis on which to make your calls on prioritization and rule-breaking. You'll want to be doing everything in a justifiable way, based on good strategic Decisions that you've made before you start development: what the product needs to include; on what devices people should be able to use it; what level of user experience you're going to aim to deliver; and for whom.

And you'll need to base these decisions on solid Research, because success comes from knowing: what target audiences (if any) need your product; what your product needs to give them to satisfy their requirements; and understanding how disabled people will use your product, so you can understand how your following of accessibility guidelines will help them.

These are the four parts of BS 8878's RuDDeR:

Research – Decide – Do – Repeat.

If you follow the BS 8878 process, by the time you arrive at the guidance WCAG gives, you've already gained a lot of understanding about the accessibility you want for your product, and also learnt how to make decisions based on justifiable reasoning. So you'll be able to get the best out of WCAG, using WCAG in an informed, pragmatic way, rather than as a strait-jacket, because you've already established the strategic decisions you need to make about accessibility, before going into the details of how you're going to deliver it.

Now it's your turn

To get the most out of the rest of the book, I'd encourage you to come on the journey with me by thinking of one particular product that you're involved with, and how you'd complete each step of the process for that product. The product can be any web product: whether you're just starting out on its creation, or are already at version 5; whether the product is one in a large portfolio that you oversee, it's the single product that you own, or you're one part of the team creating the product for a product manager.

So download a copy of the web product accessibility policy template from the book's follow-up materials (see the information on support materials on page x for details), if you haven't done so already, and fill it in for your product at the end of each step. That way you'll be building a useful record of your thinking as you work through the steps: capturing your initial thoughts on the product and understanding of its audiences' needs, and using these to inform you in making each decision later in the process, as you aim to balance costs with benefits and accessibility risk.

Even better, if you have the time, integrate the questions in the template into your existing project documentation system to start embedding the process into your team's culture of decision-making.

Where you find you have more questions than answers, in applying insights from a step to your product, write the questions down and take them to your product team to engage them with your thinking. As my workshops have found, in many organizations, it's this sort of practical, real-world discussion that has the greatest impact on product teams and the accessibility of the products they are creating. And if you don't have a team to discuss them with, use the WebAIM list[80] or BS 8878 community of practice[81] meetup as your sounding-board, as many accessibility experts hang out there and give free advice.

Ready? Okay, let's start the process...

Part 1 of the RuDDeR: Research – doing the right research and thinking before you start

As your accessibility approach for the product is going to depend on its purpose and audiences, you need to research those audiences and what they want from your product, right from the start. Then you can use this information to inform your strategic and tactical decisions when you are creating the product.

Time spent getting this established now will pay off in spades later on, as this research will ensure that your decisions aren't based on wrong assumptions that might fail to connect your product with its target audiences.

This is broken down into six steps:

1. Define the purpose of the product
2. Define the target audiences for the product
3. Analyse the needs of the target audiences for the product
4. Note any platform and technology preferences and restrictions of the product's target audiences
5. Define the relationship the product will have with its audiences
6. Define the user goals and tasks the product needs to provide

---

[80] http://webaim.org/discussion/
[81] http://www.meetup.com/bs8878-web-accessibility/

Step 1: Define the purpose of the product

Step 1 ensures you start well. Without knowing this you won't have a basis for making sensible decisions at any point in the process of creating your web product. It's the one thing that changes least about a product during its creation, but impacts it most.

Step 1 is to define the 'purpose' of the web product.

You can't move forwards in the process without this, as you need to know the purpose of your product to quickly anticipate the biggest challenges to making it accessible.

The accessibility challenges inherent in products with different purposes

While the WAI team who created WCAG 2.0 intended it to address all types of web technology – all good standards try to cover the future, as BS 8878 does itself – much of WCAG 2.0 was written in the pre-Web 2.0, pre-mobile-apps, pre-responsive-design world. It was an easier time to create web products that were accessible.

That is not the world we live in any more. Web 2.0 brought in much wider purposes for websites and apps:

* the move from 'the web as information' to 'the web as video portal, games portal, replacement desktop, window on interactive experiences';
* the move from 'the web as information to be consumed' to 'the web as a place to create my own content'.

While each of these wider purposes brings with it significant challenges for accessibility, I would argue it is as essential for YouTube or Facebook to be accessible as your local council's information website. And try telling my 4 year-old son that games aren't an important part of the web.

So it's essential to note the purpose of your product immediately, and check to see if any element of that purpose is going to have any big implications for the decisions you'll need to make around accessibility.

Let's take two examples of different types of website to see how important defining the purpose of a web product is right from the start.

We've already touched on the particular challenges of making YouTube accessible:

> Its purpose is to allow people who have videos to upload and share them with everyone else.

> So, immediately from that purpose, we can guarantee that it will not be feasible for the site to be fully accessible, unless we can create systems that automatically generate captions for every second of video that our potentially unlimited number of users upload. YouTube are working on it, but the speaker-independent voice-recognition that this requires is one of the 'Holy Grails' of computing, so we shouldn't expect them to deliver quality automatic captioning any day soon.

Wikipedia's purpose is challenging, but more manageable:

> The purpose of Wikipedia is to allow people to create and share an encyclopaedia of knowledge collaboratively online.

> There's one aspect to that purpose that immediately will be key to the accessibility of the product:

> • The people who own the website – Wikipedia – do not create the content on it. Their users do. So the first question that comes up is: whose responsibility is it to make sure that the content is accessible?

> Immediately we can guarantee that it will be a real challenge for Wikipedia to keep the website accessible, unless they can ensure their content authoring system enables users to create accessible content, and persuade them to take the responsibility; or Wikipedia commit to editing user content to add accessibility themselves. That has big intellectual property and copyright implications, as well as resourcing implications for Wikipedia.

Products with some purposes may not be able to be made fully accessible at all. Can 3D experiential games really be made accessible for people who are blind, or an e-learning module on melody made accessible for people who are Deaf? You need to know these things on 'day one' of your project, as they will fundamentally impact your accessibility strategy.

Annex G of BS 8878 lists the accessibility challenges inherent in many different types of web product: social networking sites allowing users to generate their own web content; video-based sites; cloud computing 'Software as a Service' sites; online games and 3D exploratory interfaces; and e-learning platforms.

Now it's your turn

Use the web product accessibility policy template to guide you through noting your product's purpose, and any immediate accessibility implications arising from it.

Step 2: Define the target audiences for the product

Your audiences are the people who will make your web product successful or not. They are your most important stakeholders, and your only way of managing them is to try to understand their needs and desires and find some way of meeting them through your product.

That's a tall order, if you're trying to do everything for everyone.

Trying to be all things to all people can cause you to fail to do anything well for anyone. As most coaches will tell you, it's best to try to find your niche and devote yourself to serving the people in it.

It's likely that your web product won't have universal appeal, but will appeal to a certain set of people who are interested in what your site is all about – its purpose (that was Step 1).

Unfortunately, in their rush to enable universal accessibility, most accessibility guidelines fail to acknowledge that not all web products are intended for all audiences. But knowing who your web product is and isn't for is essential for you to be able to make sure that the accessibility decisions you make in its creation are right for those users.

That's why BS 8878's Step 2 is define the product's 'target audiences'.

The key distinction between target audiences, which fundamentally impacts on accessibility, is whether your web product is designed:

- to appeal to everyone (or, at least, a range of audiences);
- for a restricted and known audience you can predict or control;
- to appeal to a particular part of a public audience.

Designed to appeal to everyone

At one extreme, are websites that are intended to be used by the widest range of audiences. You may be creating a Google, a BBC, or an Amazon.

This is the biggest challenge for accessibility, as you will need to design for the widest possible audience, and may not be able to find out information about your users other than through the use of analytics or sign-on mechanisms that encourage your users to give you this information for a more personal user-experience (see Step 8).

Designed for a restricted and known audience

At the other extreme, it is possible that your web product is designed for a very restricted audience that you are completely in control of. If it's an intranet or extranet, or even a client area of your public site, you can predict and control exactly who will use it because every single user must be logged in to gain access to it. So no one will be using your site unless they have signed up and answered whatever questions you required for access, and logged in so you know exactly who is using the site at any time.

That information can be exceptionally useful to help you minimize the cost of unnecessary accessibility work. If you have no current staff with learning difficulties, it is much easier to make a case for the reasonableness of not doing everything you can to make your Intranet give people with that disability an optimal user experience. Of course, that situation may change if you recruit someone with that disability, and retro-fitting accessibility for them will be more costly than building it in from the start. However, de-prioritizing that aspect of accessibility until that point seems reasonable, if you do not have the resources to do it earlier.

Similarly, if you are providing the assistive technology that disabled members of your staff will use to access your intranet, you only need to ensure that the intranet is accessible using that assistive technology. This removes the requirement to give all users a similarly accessible experience on all the other alternative assistive technologies they could have chosen (see Step 10).

Enabling the web product to know information about the person using it, because they're logged in, also gives you the possibility of giving them a user experience that is tailored to their individual accessibility needs (see Step 5).

Designed to appeal to a particular audience

If your web product is public-facing, it may still be designed to appeal to a particular part of the public audience. It may be for silver surfers; it may be to help young children with their learning; it may be for people living in your town; it may even be designed specifically to support a particular disabled group. All of those things are fine. It is okay for you to design a website for a particular audience.

Being clear on who your target audiences are can enable you to make decisions to optimize the user experience of your product for their needs and preferences, and target the accessibility decisions you make. Knowing whether you have a wide or a narrow target audience is essential to understanding how to apply accessibility guidelines on the use of Plain English, and how to write for the reading age of your audience, and the vocabulary you can assume they will have. If you're creating a site whose purpose is to teach people how to understand Shakespeare, it's likely to be for a wider audience than a site for Shakespeare scholars, and the level of language you'll need to use will also be very different.

Primary and secondary target audiences

Once you've made that key distinction, it's useful to segment your audience into groups with similar needs. A simple way of doing this is to define some primary and secondary target audiences for your site, based on the people you believe will be interested in it, and with an idea of what they'll come to your website to find.

For example, the Primary Audience for a restaurant website would be people who want to decide whether to eat at your restaurant or one of your competitors. They are the people you need to give the right messages (information and feel) to, so they'll do the 'call to action' you want, which is to book a table.

Secondary Audiences might include people who are interested in a more general way about the restaurants in an area that they are thinking of moving to. These secondary audiences may bring you custom in the future, but appealing to your primary audience could affect your bottom line right now.

So what's all this got to do with inclusion and accessibility?

Accessibility is all about another dimension to those audiences – whether some groups of people in your target audiences have particular needs, perspectives and capabilities that should impact how you create your website.

While it makes sense to focus your site on people with particular interests, it also makes sense to try to appeal to as many people with those interests as you can, unless there's a good reason not to. To continue the restaurant example, you'd choose to focus on serving food in your restaurant that is on your menu rather than trying to serve anything people might want to order. But, if the costs weren't prohibitive, you'd also aim to serve that menu to as many people as you can, even if it meant redesigning the layout of your premises, rather than blocking some people from becoming paying customers.

Similarly, on your restaurant website, you should look at what might block people becoming customers. For example, you should consider providing information on how people who use wheelchairs will be able to get into your restaurant and use its facilities. If you don't have this information on your site, they may go elsewhere. If visually impaired people can find enough information on your site to decide to visit, but can't manage to book a table due to accessibility limitations in the technology you use for handling online bookings, you've lost another group of customers.

Ensuring that as many people in your primary and secondary audiences can use your website, whatever their abilities or disabilities, is a great way of maximizing your customer base – and that's what inclusive design is all about.

Trade-offs and conflicting needs

However, it's worth not forgetting 'reasonableness'. It's not possible to create a website that includes everybody – 'universal design' is an ideal, not something that is actually deliverable. Rather, the art of inclusion is to balance that ideal situation with what's practical.

On every website I've worked on, there have been times when we have not been able to create something which will appeal to all the audiences we've wanted. Interaction designers are usually up to the challenge of designing site navigation to meet slight variations in the user goals of your target audiences. However, it can sometimes be impossible to cater for everyone's needs, as people with different types of disability can have contradictory needs from each other and those with no disabilities. And sometimes the costs of catering for the needs of one disabled group can be prohibitively high.

To give an example from the world of e-learning: many people, including those with learning and literacy difficulties, might best learn about sustainability by playing a game where they can quickly see the environmental impact of the choices they make. However, as games are very visual and highly interactive, this choice might make it impossible for a person who is blind to play the game to access the learning, without a huge amount of extra work and expense.

While user-personalized approaches can help go beyond 'design for all' to 'design for me' – see Step 8 of the process – if you have the time and resource to include them, for most products you're likely to have to make trade-offs on whose needs you are going to concentrate on catering for, and whose maybe you are not.

It's best to acknowledge early on that you are going to have to make these trade-offs over the course of the creation of your web product, and to concentrate on how to do this in a way that is justifiable. And your justifications, as I hope you're beginning to agree with by now, should depend on cold, hard facts as the basis on which to make decisions.

That's why, while I believe that there are very few good reasons for why you could justifiably say that your website 'isn't for disabled people', it makes perfect sense to look further into *how many* people with different types of disability, or who are older, will be likely to use your site.

Now it's your turn

So, to summarize Step 2, you should carefully consider the target audiences (both primary and secondary) you'll want to attract and retain on your site, so you can go on to consider those audiences' needs, preferences and capabilities.

You'll want to base your understanding of these needs, preferences and capabilities on the best research you can afford, rather than make uneducated guesses. Which is Step 3 of the BS 8878 process – your options for doing that research, even for those with no research budget or time.

Use the questions in the web product accessibility policy template to guide you in thinking about who your product's primary and secondary audiences are.

Case study – SME consultancy site – hassellinclusion.com

Steps 1 and 2

Here are the purpose and target audiences for v1 of my own Hassell Inclusion site. This took me less than an hour of clear thinking to create. That's good value for something that kept me focused on my audiences at a time when I couldn't afford distractions, and continues to do so years later.

Step 1 – Purpose (v.1)

- To promote Hassell Inclusion Ltd.
- A shop front for potential clients: information on my services; showcase for my experience (CV, presentations, videos, academic papers) and thought-leadership (blog, tweets).
- How to get in touch with me.
- An added-value resource for clients (access to support, tools and FAQs).

Step 2 – Target audiences and what they are looking for

Segmentation by interest

- Potential clients looking for accessibility expertise or consultancy.
- Current clients looking for follow-up (e.g. after one of my courses).
- People interested in the latest information on accessibility and inclusion, or in me and what I'm doing.

Segmentation by capability

- **Primary audience** – my ideal clients: technology-aware, business-focused web professionals who are digital policy makers, or who own or manage websites. That's a niche audience of people who are interested in my services and have the ability to pay for them. So I'm looking at senior management, at a high enough level in their organization to be able to make commissioning decisions on training, research etc. In many businesses this would tend to make my likely clients older, as people gain seniority with age. However, in digital media, a CEO can just as easily be 22 years old as 62. So my primary audience is likely to be across a large age range. Looking at disability, a quick check of government stats reveals the scandalous figure (from 2005's *Improving the Life Chances of Disabled People* report) that 50% of disabled people are not in employment. But that still leaves 50% who are.
  And there is no good reason why blind and visually impaired people, people with dyslexia or hearing impairments, ADHD or on the autistic spectrum wouldn't be doing those jobs. It is, however, unlikely that someone with a learning disability would be, so if there are circumstances where it's too difficult to cater for this audience because I am giving advice on technical issues, it will be important to use Plain English, but not over-simplify issues.
- **Secondary audience** – people with less technology knowledge who are more generally interested in digital inclusion, which is likely to include everyone who is personally affected by inclusion issues because of their age or disability.

Thinking about this secondary audience uncovered a third purpose of my site – to be an example of best practice in web accessibility and the use of BS 8878. That gives me more reason to work harder to make the site work for everyone, whatever their disability, where I can. This sort of rewriting regularly happens as you move through BS 8878's steps. Like many aspects of web production, iteration is key – often you'll get insights at later steps that will help you improve and clarify your original answers.

Step 3: Analyse the needs of the target audiences for the product

'By far the most common mistake startups make is to solve problems no one has.' [Y Combinator co-founder Paul Graham[82]]

Step 3 is essential in making sure that you are not making any assumptions about how your users will use your product that are not true. Get this wrong and you may create a product that people don't want, can't use, requires assistive technologies that they don't have, or doesn't make sense in the context in which they wish to use it. Get this right and you have a chance that your product will be a lucrative success.

What do you know about your web product's target audiences? About how they use the web, and what they might want from your product? Are they like you or very different?

Isn't it a good idea to spend some time and effort working that out before you start creating something for them? Because if you don't understand the users you are creating the site for, even if you create a usable product, it may not be one they actually want.

Your product may be a solution to a problem they don't have. Or it may be a solution to a problem they do have but that doesn't fit into their lifestyle. And you really don't want to find that out when you user-test the product two weeks from launch, when it's too late and costly to do much about it.

That's why Step 3 of the BS 8878 production process advises you to do some user research early, to find out more about your audiences. It's about making sure you don't base decisions on assumptions about your audiences that may not be true. It's about letting your audiences help you decide what the product should be, so when you user-test it later it really connects with them, delights them, and keeps them coming back for more.

User research – what you need to know to delight your audiences

By now you've defined the target audiences for the product – both the primary and secondary audiences. So now it's time to look deeper at who they are, and what they may need from your product.

It's useful to break this down into three aspects:

1. How many people are we talking about in each target audience, and do the audiences have subgroups within them (for instance people with different types of disability)?

---

[82] http://www.paulgraham.com/startupideas.html

2. What are each audience's *general* needs from the user experience of any website or mobile app, and are there subgroups in the audience who have different needs from each other?
3. What are their *specific needs* from your product?

The first of these aspects is essentially quantitative – all about numbers – and the second and third are qualitative – about more detailed characteristics and opinions. But for each, you effectively have two different ways of finding out the information you need, depending on the resources you have available to you:

- to do some general desk research, collating information that is already available freely to the public or can be bought from research agencies; or
- to commission or conduct your own user research.

Finding the number of people in your potential target audiences

Finding the best research you can on how many people are in your primary and secondary audiences is essential. If you don't know this:

- how do you know whether or not the audience is big enough to warrant the time and money you'd need to invest to create a site for them?
- how do you know how much of your total potential audience your site is appealing to when you review your site-use statistics after launch?

Here's an example from my time at the BBC. BBC iPlayer was one of the first online video-on-demand services in the world. Its purpose is to enable online audiences to catch up on TV and radio programmes they may have missed. This makes the primary audience for the service pretty much everyone in the UK who is online, as almost everyone watches BBC TV.

As 77% of households are now online,[83] the BBC's huge investment in iPlayer makes very good sense. And the result is their impressive monthly performance pack figures[84]: 153 million TV and radio programmes were watched and listened to in September 2011; and their unique users are in excess of 6.3 million users.

However, if we take into account their huge potential target audience of around 48 million people, those figures don't look quite so impressive. Their audience figures could potentially be much higher if they found new ways of enabling people who don't use iPlayer to find out about it

---

[83] http://www.ons.gov.uk/ons/rel/rdit2/internet-access---households-and-individuals/2011/stb-internet-access-2011.html

[84] http://www.bbc.co.uk/mediacentre/latestnews/171011iplayer.html

and get a great user experience from it. I know they are constantly working on that because the potential prize is worth a lot of investment.

You may not be the BBC and may not have a product that everyone wants to use. But the same principles apply – find out as much as you can about the potential size of your audience, and use that information to inform you on how much to invest in your product, and to monitor how well you are doing compared to how well you could be doing. If you are reaching 10% of your potential audience you've got lots of work to do. If you're reaching 90%, growth is going to be hard, and you may also need to ensure no competitor is just about to steal your audience.

While there are many sources of statistics available on general use of the internet, the cheapest and easiest way of getting a flavour for the potential audience size for your website is to use Google Adwords Keyword Planner[85] to see if anyone is searching for what your website aims to deliver – its purpose. This also tells you *which* words they are using for their searches so you can put those words in your site's titles and headings to attract the audience to your site. More information on this is available in any number of search engine optimization blogs.[86]

What proportion of your potential target audience may be disabled or older people?

So what about disabled or older audiences? How much of your potential target audience might these subgroups make up? Are your audience likely to be experiencing the multiple minor impairments of ageing? That's why Ferraris have doors that are now easier to get into for older people – because Ferrari worked out that most of the people who could afford one of their cars were ageing. It's why the page on cold winter payments on a government website should probably pay more attention to the needs of older people than a site promoting holidays in Ibiza.

As I touched on in Step 2, it makes perfect sense to look further into how many people with different types of disability, or who are older, will be likely to use your site. If these numbers are high, it makes sense to do a lot to try to make sure these audiences (like all your others) get hooked on your site's user experience. If these numbers are low, the benefit you could gain from spending time and money trying to appeal to these audiences may not give you a good return on your investment, unless that investment is low.

So how do you find these figures? Well, if you are redesigning an existing site, you could count the number of people visiting any pages of your site that are targeted at disabled people – your accessibility

---

[85]   https://adwords.google.co.uk/KeywordPlanner
[86]   http://www.problogger.net/archives/2005/08/15/search-engine-optimization-for-blogs/

statement, for example. Unfortunately, this really only counts the number of disabled people using your site who find problems with it (see Step 15 for the reasons why). Even though web analytics systems can now tell you how many male or female users you have, they cannot tell you how many disabled people are using your site. However, the accessibility personalization and analytics solution, *restylethis*,[87] does enable you to inject this information into your analytics, enabling you to track the size and activity of anonymized disabled audiences on your site (see Step 8).

Short of having these analytics, the best information you have to go on is:

- the best figures you can find of the population of people with various types of disability; and
- the best figures you can find of how many of those people in general are using the internet.

The total disabled population and how it breaks down into different groups of people with disabilities

The best figures I've been able to find of the potential disabled audience in the UK are:

- total population of the UK: 62.2 million (from Google Public Data explorer[88]);
- total disabled people in the UK: 11 million (from the Department of Work and Pensions *Improving the Life Chances of Disabled People* Report 2005[89]);
- that's approximately 18% of the population.

As mentioned previously, knowing the *prevalence* of different disabilities can be very useful later for understanding how many people may benefit from following accessibility guidelines that are designed to help a particular disabled group or groups.

Different organizations will quote you different numbers for this (I use a combination of these with the UK Disability prevalence estimates 2009/10 from the Office for Disability Issues[90]) but these are a reasonable approximation:

- about 7 million people have a physical impairment, of which 2.6 million have difficulties using their hands which may impact their use of computer keyboards and mice;

---

87   http://www.restylethis.com
88   http://www.google.co.uk/publicdata/explore?ds=d5bncppjof8f9_&met_y=sp_pop_totl&idim=country:GBR&dl=en&hl=en&q=total+population+of+the+united+kingdom
89   http://www.disability.co.uk/sites/default/files/resources/Improving%20Life%20Chances.pdf
90   http://odi.dwp.gov.uk/docs/res/factsheets/disability-prevalence.pdf

- 2.2 million people have difficulty with memory, concentration or learning, of which about 1 million have a learning difficulty;
- 2.1 million people have some form of communication difficulty;
- almost 2 million people have a hearing impairment which is disruptive to their life style, of which 50,000 use British Sign Language to communicate
- approximately 2 million people are dyslexic;
- 1.8 million people have a vision impairment which is disruptive to their life style, ranging from those who may have difficulty reading text without it being enlarged through to those who may need to zoom the display of their computer up to 16 or 32 times;
- 180,000 are registered severely sight impaired (blind);
- over 1 million people have a progressive, cyclical or fluctuating condition such as multiple sclerosis;
- over 1 million have mental health conditions, most of which are unlikely to affect their use of the internet.

The relative size of each audience may be a real surprise to you. Most people's assumption is that accessibility is just about people who are blind, due to the success of their lobby in getting the needs of this audience known, but they make up under 2% of that population of 11 million.

While it is true that making your website work well for people with a visual impairment also tends to help those with other disabilities too, this isn't always the case. To give one example: making your site work well for blind people will do very little to help the 4–5 million people who can see your site but need the colours changed for comfortable reading because they are dyslexic or have lower-level vision impairments. I'll come back to talking about these people's needs later in the BS 8878 process where we talk about personalization.

Impact of age on impairment

If your web product is for a primary audience of older people, or children and teenagers, it's important to realise that these figures may also change with age, as the prevalence of some impairments increases with age, and others do not.

To give an example, the UK's statistics for prevalence of disability in children of school age[91] (gathered as part of the 'statementing' process that children go through to be recognized as having special educational needs) are at large variance with the statistics of the adult population. Children are less likely to have vision impairments or hearing impairments, and are much more likely to have learning difficulties, dyslexia, behavioural or social difficulties, or communication difficulties.

---

[91] http://data.gov.uk/dataset/children_with_special_educational_needs-an_analysis

The lower figures for vision and hearing impairments make sense as these impairments tend to develop or worsen as people grow older. The figures for learning difficulties and dyslexia show how society, and education, are growing in understanding of these particular conditions and disabilities. A dyslexic child in the education system 30 years ago may not have been picked up as dyslexic, and so may still be covering up this aspect of themselves as an adult. This is less likely these days.

Interview with Sarah Lewthwaite, Research Associate in Education at King's College London

Sarah: In your own work, Jonathan, you've talked about something like 'alternative video'. WCAG tends to be very keen on text and text-based representations of information for screen reader users. Which isn't to say video shouldn't be used. But we know that, in the real world, providing captions for video and that kind of accessibility work can be very expensive, very time-consuming. Practically, that means to hit particular accessibility checkpoints, people just don't use video. But more globally, literacy levels and other factors may mean that people would prefer video to text-based alternatives. I think that's one of those spaces where we can see that WCAG as a set of guidelines creates a hierarchy of impairment. The term is an academic one; it was coined by Mark Deal.

He identifies, on the basis of his own and other previous research, how types of disability are arranged in society; and how these vary across different cultures. I think it's quite important for us as accessibility practitioners to recognize how particular disabilities are conceived of, grouped, and then hierarchized within standards. Again, I think where BS 8878 has a strength is that because you're drawing on the particular expertise of somebody in a context, they can understand and look at the hierarchies that may be in play, and address them. Whereas, somebody who is stuck, potentially, with a checklist just isn't going to have that space to re-represent under-represented groups. In disability studies there's an attention to 'who is disabled?,' 'who isn't?', and 'what are the grey areas?' For example, dyslexia was relatively unknown in the 70s, but now we know what it means for schooling – our notions of disability change.

Jonathan: That was exactly what was in our mind when we were creating BS 8878 – the critique that had been made of WCAG about the skew towards those politicized, lobbyist areas for disability. People who are blind will have a dreadful experience of the web if they don't lobby to make sure that the standards uphold their particular requirements. Someone who is dyslexic may not lobby because they would prefer not to champion their needs in public. That's actually how I use the stats – I'm forever showing a pie chart to organizations, saying, 'If you think that accessibility is just about blind people, you're looking at pretty much about 2% of the disabled population. If that is where all of your work is going, your return on investment is going to be dreadful, because if you do it brilliantly you've just added another 2% of 20% to your audience, rather than adding 20%.'

Watch the complete video interview here with Sarah Lewthwaite at: http://qrs.ly/kk4a6c2.

Read Sarah's blogs at: http://slewth.co.uk

Demographically, what are disabled people like?

Extensive market research that I commissioned in 2007 when I was at the BBC looked into the demographics of disability more closely and found out the following:

- Disabled people are more likely to be older – 47% of disabled people in the UK are over the age of 65, compared to 20% of the general population.
- Disabled people are less likely to be working – 50% of disabled people in the UK who are of working age are employed, compared to 74% of the general population. This helps to explain the lack of visibility of disabled people to the rest of the population.
- Disabled people are more likely to remain at home than non-disabled people. They are less likely to be people's colleagues at

work. They are less likely to eat in restaurants, or go to cinemas or theatres, than non-disabled people, because of their lower incomes.

- Disabled people tend to be heavy media consumers, particularly of TV and radio, possibly because they are more likely to be at home than non-disabled people.
- Whatever the official disability definition states, only half see themselves as 'disabled'. The name of their particular disability is something that they would relate to, but the label 'disabled' is not one that all would own.

Interview with Debra Ruh, Global ICT Accessibility and Digital Marketing Consultant

Debra: One thing I noticed with TecAccess which was troubling to me... I did all this amazing work, I won all these awards. But after it was all said and done, except for the people I employed myself, did I change the world or the needle? Did the needle move to help more people with disabilities get employment because we were making websites accessible? The troubling answer was no.

Jonathan: The employment of disabled people is a big, hidden issue. I'm sure the situation here in the US is similar to the UK. It's a real scandal – in the UK only 45% of disabled people are in employment.

Debra: Ours is in the 70s. We define [disability] broadly...

Jonathan: Even just in terms of simple web accessibility, most organizations haven't really followed through the policies they have about recruitment. I've reviewed employers' websites where there were videos about how diverse a workforce they want to attract; how they will value everybody's differences. And are there any captions or audio-description on the video? Well no. So what they're effectively saying is – without meaning to – 'We do want a diverse workforce, we just don't want those of you who have a hearing or a vision impairment.'

When I've highlighted that to those organizations, they kind of take a step back in horror.... 'We didn't realize that.'

Debra: They're not doing it on purpose, and I will say to them, 'If I'm blind, can I send in a résumé through your online career centre?' 'Erm...' 'Well if I need an accommodation for the interview, can I get an accommodation and hope that you won't just cancel the interview?'

There's a big conversation happening on social media right now, when should a person with a disability disclose that disability? Because for most people with severe disabilities, if you disclose it you're not going to get the interview. Of course that is against the law...

Jonathan: The law is one of those things where there's no win for the employer. All you can do is avoid losing. So what seems to happen is that organizations act accordingly. If they think they can get away with it then why not do that? Because they don't see anything in it for them.

No one talks about the up-side. You've employed disabled people, Debra, so you know that there is an up-side, if people can get over their worries of 'What will it be like to employ a disabled person?'

Debra: I got very creative, very loyal, very innovative employees. Was every single person that I hired with a disability excellent? No, there were some really terrible employees. So guess what? The employees that didn't do their job that had disabilities, I fired them. I followed all the laws, gave them many opportunities... What you would with any other employee. That's equality.

Watch the complete video interview with Debra Ruh at: http://qrs.ly/tq4a6c6

Read Debra's blogs on accessibility and disability at: http://www.ruhglobal.com/category/blog/

Disabled and older people's use of the internet – one last sobering statistic

There is one last statistic which currently constrains the value of the time you put into making your products include disabled and older audiences: the number of them who currently use the internet.

Statistics on disabled people's use of the internet[92] (from the then Minister for Disabled People, Maria Miller, in 2010) in the UK found that 41% of disabled people use the internet, compared to 75% of non-disabled people.

This figure is puzzling and disappointing because people with disabilities have as much, if not more, to benefit from the internet than the general population. To give one example, people with physical or vision impairments are likely to benefit from shopping via websites, rather than having to get to shops on the high street. To understand why the figure is low, and what is being done about it, we'll need to dig deeper into why the statistics are like this. We need to look into qualitative research of disabled people's use of the internet – what they say about the experience they find, and whether they'd want to repeat it.

What are your audiences' general needs from the user experience of any website or mobile app? Qualitative desk research for those on a budget

There are research agencies all over the world that can help you do qualitative user research. Most of them are incredibly good at what they do, having evolved ways of working that go beyond asking people what they *think* they want from web products, to observing them using products in the course of their day to see what they really *do* with them.

Unfortunately, their services are often costly.

So how are you going to research these needs, without breaking the bank?

Your first option for doing qualitative research into people's use of the web is low cost: to do some desk research to see what research you can find.

A great start is to find freely published research in how people use the web that user-research agencies share to promote their more bespoke services. Google any of the following agencies, and you're likely to get some useful free insights: What People Want, Webcredible, User Vision,

---

92 http://webarchive.nationalarchives.gov.uk/20121204113822/
    http://www.culture.gov.uk/images/publications/maria-miller-speech-launch-e-accessibility.pdf

System Concepts, Nomensa, Nielsen Norman, Gartner, Digital Accessibility Centre, cxpartners, Clearleft, Bunnyfoot, and Amberlight.

These will tell you how people are using the web at the moment.

What everyone's general needs are for any website or app:

- their desire to be both satisfied and delighted by the user experience;
- their need to be able to access the product's services across the variety of different devices they use, in many different contexts of use.

The days are gone when you could assume that your users would be sitting at a desk, whether at home or in an office, when using the website. You can no longer assume they will be using a computer with a certain amount of processing power and a large screen. And you can't assume that the environment in which they use your product is static and quiet, or that they will be completely focused on your product when using it.

One of the reasons why accessibility is getting more and more important every year is because we are all 'blind', in relation to the screen, when we are driving a car – we should not take our eyes off the road or we might crash. We are all hard of hearing when we are in a noisy environment and are trying to listen to the audio of a breaking news video. We are all motor impaired when our iPhone is in our pocket because we are jogging. All of these aspects of the context in which people use devices feed more and more into the idea that impairments are not just experienced by disabled people – that we are all impaired in some senses at different times. And because we cannot assume that people have all of their abilities available to them when they are using a website or mobile app, thinking about people who are impaired due to a disability can help you understand how everybody may use your product in those contexts where they are 'temporarily impaired' because they are doing something else at the same time. (see Step 9)

What are your disabled audiences' general needs from the user experience of any website or mobile app?

You can find background information on disabled people's use of the web from the following sources:

- BS 8878's Annex H: 'How disabled and older people experience web products' can provide a good grounding in the needs different groups of disabled people have from web products, and the sorts of accessibility preferences and assistive technologies they use to enable them to access web products.

- The WAI document 'How People with Disabilities Use the Web: Overview'[93] also provides some of the same information, for free.
- If you prefer to consume information via video, case studies of the way people with disabilities use assistive technologies can be found on My Web My Way[94] or AbilityNet's YouTube channel.[95]

To summarize these briefly, the important thing to know about how disabled people will use your product, is that their user experience will be mediated by four technology layers that your product sits on, where accessibility settings and preferences can transform it, if you have coded it correctly to accessibility guidelines, to better meet the needs of the user:

- if your product is a website, accessibility settings in the browser, or browser plugin, may allow users to change your site's font size, colours or display of images;
- below this, users may have installed assistive technologies like screen readers, screen magnifiers or voice-activation software that may allow users to get your site spoken to them, get it magnified on screen, or allow them to interact with it using their voice rather than a mouse or touchpad;
- below this, the operating system of the computer, tablet or smartphone may also include accessibility preferences or in-built assistive technologies;
- and below this, users may have installed specialist hardware to control the computer, tablet or smartphone, such as trackballs or large buttons.

You can find more up-to-date research on disabled people's use of the web from sites like WebAIM,[96] (whose yearly Screenreader Survey[97] is exceptionally useful) or blogs like my own 'Hassell Inclusion' blog[98] where I regularly share my latest user-research insights.

Interview with David Banes, Chief Executive, MADA, Qatar

Jonathan: When we first met each other, the project that we were working on was My Web My Way – a co-production between the BBC, who I worked for, and AbilityNet, who you worked for. We won the Best Accessibility Achievement in 2006 from the British Interactive Media Association. So obviously we did something right...

---

93 http://www.w3.org/WAI/intro/people-use-web/

94 http://www.bbc.co.uk/accessibility/best_practice/case_studies/

95 http://www.youtube.com/user/abilitynet

96 http://webaim.org/

97 http://webaim.org/projects/screenreadersurvey/

98 http://www.hassellinclusion.com/

David: At the time a lot of information about how to customize a computer for disabled peoples' needs was available, but often it had to be mediated at an AT centre by somebody who was a specialist.

I think what we were trying to do with My Web My Way was to say to people with disabilities, 'Actually guys, there's a whole load of things you can do for yourself.' That's what people bought into: 'I can take control.'

It was *My* Web *My* Way. It was really intended at hitting a large community of potential users, mainstreaming information through one of the biggest websites in the world at the time. I think that was why it was so strong. Because people could interact with it, they could look at something, try it out and if it's still not working try something else, without really feeling as if they'd done something stupid.

I think that's why it won the awards: people liked it and it made a difference for them. Lots of people imitated that model afterwards. I suppose we can look back and it's actually quite flattering the number of variations of the concept that began to turn up.

Jonathan: You're now chief exec of MADA, in Doha in Qatar. What first attracted you? You're in Britain, working at AbilityNet, you get a call and someone says, 'Can you help us out in the Middle East?' What made you want to go?

David: I think it was the opportunity to build something on what was a fairly blank canvas – building the complete ecosystem necessary to support disabled people's digital access needs from scratch.

We knew that the services needed to be established, the funding model needed to be established, we knew that even right down to there wasn't that much Arabic assistive technology. So the challenge was to say, 'What can we draw from the experience in the West that we had and how can we apply that to meet a very specific community which in tradition is being under served?'

I really liked the fact that ICT Qatar had set it up, driven forward by the UN Convention on the Rights of Persons with Disabilities. I thought, 'The driver here is the right one, it's a practical response to becoming a signatory.' It was an opportunity to make a difference in the lives of a lot of people, and it's been great to see the impact that has had since in working with other Gulf States, other people within the Arabic world.

Also the support we've been able to get from services in the West – people have shared things, let us localize and sort them into Arabic. Then really the exciting thing for me is that, once we've localized and translated stuff into Arabic from the West, it's actually gone back to the original people that we worked with. Because they've got Arabic-speaking communities in Denmark, Norway, the US...

Watch the complete video interview with David Banes at: http://qrs.ly/s14a6bs

Read MADA's blogs on accessibility in the Middle East at: http://www.mada.org.qa/eAccessibility/EN/blog/

What are your audiences' specific needs from the user experience of your web product? Commissioning or conducting your own qualitative user research

If your desk research gives you valuable insights that you didn't already know about how people use the web, you may decide to go one step further, to look into what free user research won't tell you: what your audiences want from your product.

This second option is for you to commission or conduct user research for your own web product. You could do surveys, or ethnographic research into the context, preferences and specific product needs of your audiences. This is the type of research that all leading organizations do before they start creating a product to make sure they know whether or not their 'great idea' is actually something that will attract any audience; whether it meets a need that actually exists, and how people might want to use the product if it does.

User research aims to provide reliable findings regarding:

- the context in which people may use your product;
- the problem that they wish your product to solve for them;
- their preferences for how you should solve it; and
- how quickly and precisely your product needs to solve their problem, and whether or not there is a trade-off between those two things they would accept.

The aim is to more deeply understand the primary and secondary audiences you've already defined – the audience segmentation – to build up a picture of the different types of person in those audiences. To understand what makes one set of people different from another set of people, and how those differences impact the product you are creating. To understand whether one product could work for all of the different people who might want to use it, or whether you need to work harder to please all the people in your audiences.

To give you an analogy, Ford make motor cars. Cars are designed to get you from A to B, when you are in A and want to get to B. So why do Ford have more than one model in their range of cars? And why for every model of car is there more than one engine size or specification of comfort and functionality extras?

This is all because of coarse and fine audience segmentation. There are many different types of person that might want to get from A to B. They may have different spending possibilities or passenger or baggage requirements. A single man's needs may be very different from a mother's with four kids. A young boy racer and an older person will have different feelings about speed. If I want my car to be a status symbol – if I want to 'pimp my ride' and make it look very flash – my preferences will be different from someone who is not interested or cannot afford that. This is what spoilers were invented for.

Returning to your web product, the question is: how many of the different types, the different segments of users can your product satisfy? Does it make sense for your product to be one product with a number of options trying to do something for everybody? Or does it make more sense, because the needs of everybody are very different, to create more than one product to meet those needs – the way the car industry has always done.

To continue the car analogy, do your different audience segments want a different radio or engine, or do they want a different car?

We'll come back to these ideas of personalization and product variants later in the BS 8878 process at Step 8. At this point it's important for us to do the user research to know how we should make those decisions later in the process.

Personas

And it's equally important to know how to communicate the findings of the user research to people across your product team so they can best design a product that satisfies the needs of all your target users. To do this BS 8878 recommends you create 'Personas', which are commonly used for this purpose in most user centred design processes. As there are better and worse ways of including disabled people's needs in personas, please read the following interview with Judith Fellowes – a leading expert in the field – on how best to do this.

Interview with Judith Fellowes, Freelance User Researcher, UK (has worked with BBC, HSBC, VISA, Tesco, Sky, Vodafone, Sony Ericsson)

Jonathan: You have a particularly good perspective on how to include disabled people in personas. What is a persona and what would you do with it?

Judith: A persona is a representation of who your user might be. The idea behind it is that if you are designing for an individual, it works much better than just trying to design for everybody. I always use the term 'Frankenstein design'.

If you are trying to accommodate the needs of everybody, you end up with something that just doesn't work for anybody. The idea is that if you are focusing on an individual, then you can create something that's a lot more coherent. In reality what you might be doing, is you might be focusing on a couple of personas, a couple of people, who have different needs. For example, you might be saying, 'We've got this audience who are pretty technical and they can understand most things; and we've got this audience, who perhaps need a helping hand.'

Just by having those people, it helps you focus, because it helps you understand. One of the problems with technology is that it's built by really techie people. Personas help the whole team step outside designing for themselves, as they can have this vision of this person.

We don't just make up the personas. They are based on research. A typical process might be, that you do some interviews with your target audience and then you look at other research and literature, and work at amalgamating the two and see what trends come out. I like to workshop these things together.

But, you end up with a focus of people who have these characteristics, so you can understand that when you're designing for 'Eric', he hasn't got a very long attention span, so if you can't get his attention in the first five minutes, he is going to pick up the phone and call the helpdesk.

So you can mix it all in with what do you want the users to do on this page, or with this device. What do they want to do? Then start understanding what personalities you have got out there, and how to design for them.

Jonathan: Personas aren't new. But I still find it disappointing that, even at large user-centred design conferences, there seems to be little understanding that any of these personas might need to include access needs, if you want them to be representative of people in general.

There seems to be two things that happen, stereotypically. People either don't even consider whether anyone has an access need when they create personas.

Or when people understand accessibility, they tend to create a set of personas of disabled people and add them to the pile. These personas over here are all about life style choices and how they'll impact your use of the product. These are about people who may not even want to use the product at all, they just have a disability.

One of the things that I really liked about your way of working is that, you think of access needs as maybe one trait in a persona, and the one aspect of what makes up the person that the persona is based on, as being an individual. Did I get that right?

Judith: Yes, I think, well it is part of so many people. At least 20% of the population have disabilities. Obviously, you're looking at how each persona relates to your product, because that's what you're working towards. But then you also need to understand how the access need might impact on that. You know if somebody has got a disability or an access need, it doesn't necessarily take over their lives. It's not how they define themselves as individuals.

So I think it's just being aware... If you've got a persona who is in their 50s, then statistically they might have a problem with their eyesight. They might be developing something like arthritis in their hands.

Jonathan: Or people's impairments may explain their preferences. So it's very possible that people represented by your 'video junkie' persona may have a strong preference to use the video on your website because they are dyslexic.

Watch the complete video interview with Judith Fellowes at: http://qrs.ly/mr4a6bw

View Judith's 'Inclusive Personas with no extra work' video at: http://www.youtube.com/watch?v=JoFWFPMCD2E

An example of how user research can impact on a site – Hassell Inclusion

My site has a lot of words on it. Which will be fine for the relatively small number of people who are visually impaired, but not so good for the millions of people with literacy difficulties.

As my 'Accessibility myths' blog[99] (a summary of some of my user research findings that are most challenging to accepted ideas about

---

[99] http://www.hassellinclusion.com/2012/01/web-accessibility-myths-2011-part2/#text

accessibility) makes clear: text is not the pinnacle of accessibility, despite most accessibility guidelines giving you that idea.

Ask the four million people in the UK who have dyslexia, literacy or learning difficulties. These guys would love you to remove much of the text from your website, and replace it with carefully selected, informational images and video. They'd love it if, for a while at least, we turned the accessibility orthodoxy on its head, and all text had to have a 'video equivalent' created for it 'for accessibility reasons'.

So, based on this user research, it might be much better to include diagrams or even video of the things I'm talking about in my blogs. The only problem is that I'm not so good or quick at crafting those. So – using my 'get a v1 out there and then improve it' principle – I'm going to do all these blogs in text and simple images, and then consider creating videos or podcasts of them and enriching them with diagrams and animations. And, obviously, if my blogs were only available as video, deaf people would want me to include subtitles. And the game continues. In general, the thing to do is to try to achieve multi-modality for all the important stuff – something I really admire about Brian Kelly, who I interview later in the book about why he videos his presentations to go alongside his slides all the time.

Similarly – my desk research into device usage by the general population (see Step 9 for details) finds that increasing numbers of people may choose to use my website on the move, whether on a tablet or smartphone. So it becomes important for my website to give people browsing on these devices a good user experience too.

Now it's your turn

Check out the size of the potential audience who may be interested in your site with Google Adwords Keyword Planner.[100]

Think further about whether disabled and older people will be equally interested in your web product and note down the size of audience you might be excluding if you don't cater for these subgroups' needs. This 'size of excluded audience' is a great way of putting together a business case for work you may want to consider doing to prevent their exclusion later in the process (check out EDC's exclusion calculator[101] for a handy, visual way of working out these figures). And it's a great addition to the documentation you'll be building up for your site at every step in the BS 8878 process.

---

[100] https://adwords.google.co.uk/KeywordPlanner
[101] http://www.inclusivedesigntoolkit.com/betterdesign2/exclusioncalc/exclusioncalc.html

Take time to familiarize yourself with the basics of how disabled people use the web by watching the video case studies in My Web My Way[102]. Talk to your user experience team to see if they are planning to use personas to guide your product's creation, and how they plan to ensure the personas reflect the reality of disability within your product's target audiences if they are.

And write down the key findings of relevant research to your product, in your web product accessibility policy template.

Step 4: Note any platform and technology preferences and restrictions of the product's target audiences

The standard way of delivering an accessible user experience requires you to create your product to comply with accessibility guidelines such as WCAG, and your users to have the computer, tablet or smartphone they use your product on set up with the assistive technologies and accessibility preferences they need to handle their particular needs. Step 4 is all about checking, during your user research, if there is any reason that they wouldn't be able to live up to their end of the bargain, and what you should do about it, if that's the case.

You'll hopefully recall my example from Chapter 1 of the blind pensioner who wrote to me complaining that we had incorrectly assumed that people like him would have the latest version of the JAWS screen reader needed to get an accessibility experience of our new BBC iPlayer, when in reality it was too expensive for him to buy. This is just one example of a technology restriction that the standard way of doing accessibility doesn't handle well.

If you are going to rely on the user to choose the right browser accessibility settings (for example, a person who is dyslexic choosing a setting which changes your site's colours to a more soothing colour scheme for readability) or install the right assistive technology (for example, a person who has a severe vision impairment using a screen reader to transform your site into spoken text) to iron out the differences between their needs and everybody else's, then does that hold in all circumstances?

Ideally, the user's accessibility settings or assistive technology should provide all of those transformations for you, so all you have to do is to code your product to ensure those transformations happen correctly.

When that's working well, accessibility is a shared responsibility between your users and yourselves. But what happens if some people in your target audiences don't have the spending power to buy, or confidence to

---

[102] http://www.bbc.co.uk/accessibility/best_practice/case_studies/

install, the assistive technologies they need? In that situation, should you go to greater lengths than you usually would and design the product to do those transformations itself?

Step 8 of BS 8878 addresses that issue head on; whether you'll need to provide 'additional accessibility measures' — tools embedded in your product that, in and of themselves, remove the need for the user to install assistive technologies to give them a good user experience.

But you can only make decisions at that step if you've noted down any technology preferences or restrictions you find during your initial user research that indicate you need to consider those additional measures.

These are the types of preferences or restrictions you should look out for and note...

Preference, for browsing on a tablet or smartphone: It's important to be aware that mobile browsers usually have many fewer accessibility settings than desktop browsers, so users who need to change background colours and also wish to browse on smartphones or tablets will need the product that you are creating to provide those facilities itself. Similarly, while the inclusion of accessibility functionality 'as standard' on smartphones and tablets is very encouraging, some OSes make it difficult to install assistive technologies that aren't part of the operating system, so alternative solutions may be needed.

Restriction, due to ignorance of accessibility settings and assistive technologies: It is not always the case that you can assume that disabled people know about the existence of accessibility settings and assistive technologies that have been created to meet their needs. One of the most interesting findings of my user research in 2008 was that many fewer people (both disabled and less impaired) use assistive technologies than would benefit from them. Microsoft research says that 57% of American computer users between 18 and 64 years old are likely, or very likely, to benefit from the use of accessible technology. Yet what we found here in the UK is that only about 6 to 8% of UK web users use some form of assistive technology or accessibility preferences in their operating system or browser. See my interview with David Banes at the end of this Step for more insights on this.

Restriction, due to cost of technology: On top of the issues around the cost of screen readers for older people, mentioned on the previous page, it could be that the user has very strong platform preferences due to concerns about cost. To give an example, user research from the UK Department of Work and Pensions in early 2011 found that people on benefits are more likely to use a smartphone as their preferred means of getting online, if not their only means of getting online. While broadband costs are diminishing, broadband is only available if you have a stable address where you live. As many people on benefits find their stability in their mobile phone, and Android phones are so cheap on pay-as-you-go, they use it to access the web via all-you-can-eat mobile data that comes as part of the top-up of call minutes. As we also know that disabled people are less likely to be working than the rest of the population (see previous Step), it stands to reason that the way a number of disabled people would get online would be via a smartphone. So the people out there that are saying that it's only necessary to make desktop websites accessible, and not necessary for mobile web and mobile apps to be accessible, are completely missing the transformation in access to the web that has already happened. It's entirely possible that if there's only one thing you can do – if there's only one of those platforms that you can make accessible, because you don't have time to do everything – the best place to spend your accessibility time and money is on mobile, not on desktop. This sort of counter-orthodox finding is often something that only user research can reliably tell you.

Restriction, due to complexity: As mentioned previously, screen readers are very complex bits of software that require a lot of training to learn. So young children may not have the cognitive ability, and older people may not have the confidence and motivation, for them to learn how to use a screen reader.

Restriction, due to fear: Older people are often scared to download and install new technologies onto their computers, due to stories of friends getting viruses or people getting access to their personal information. That means that, while it's possible and free for them to add a browser toolbar to give them easier control of the text size in their browser, they are unlikely to do so.

Restriction, due to local IT policy restrictions: People could be stuck with old technology if there are IT policy restrictions in place where they use the web. Often IT support policies prevent users from being able to change any settings, to prevent users from changing settings they shouldn't. But these restrictions often also prevent users in offices, libraries or internet cafes from being able to set accessibility preferences in the browser or operating system, or install assistive technologies they need.

This research around preferences and restrictions will be invaluable in making sure the decisions you make later in the process will enable disabled people to get a good user experience of your product alongside everyone else. Relying on disabled people to have the technology themselves to give them that experience may not be a sensible idea as, while it may save you from legal risk, it may deprive you from gaining their custom.

Now it's your turn

Read Hassell Inclusion's 'Accessibility Myths' articles[103] to challenge your assumptions about how disabled people use web products. Then use the questions in the web product accessibility policy template to guide you in thinking about the platform and technology preferences and restrictions of your product's target audiences.

Interview with David Banes, Chief Executive, Mada, Qatar

Jonathan: Taking us back to My Web My Way, we won those accessibility awards in 2006, and yet about 2009 I started picking up that maybe we'd missed a big piece of the puzzle. That even though we put it on the BBC website which had a huge number of people coming to it, we probably could have flagged it up to people a lot better. Because the only way for all those people arriving at the BBC home page to know there were all these riches in the My Web My Way site was if they understood and clicked on the 'accessibility' link.

And when we did the research we found that a lot of people who would benefit from visiting the site had no idea what that meant. We realized that we missed something. 'It's a great product but we actually didn't do the PR, we didn't do the marketing to the people who might need it.' Something that had so much potential was actually being used more by people like you and I, to train accessibility experts in understanding the range of assistive technologies, rather than being used by the people who would actually benefit, who had the difficulties.

David: I think in all my experience across the years, we've always said that the biggest barrier to accessibility is awareness; enabling people to find the products that are available, the services that are available, the information sources. Naming things is so important... What is it people will search for to find this information? What is it that they think they're looking for and how do we match it to that expectation?

I think the other thing that you did which I thought was really interesting was the bit of work where you said, 'Actually, you know the other problem? It's all text and graphics, and when we look at our target users...a significant group of people – that's not their preferred way of learning and discovering information.'

---

[103] http://www.hassellinclusion.com/2011/12/accessibility-myths-2011/

So that took us down the route of video...how did we use video, with all the issues then of captioning and so on. Video as an accessibility aid to learning, not an accessibility problem as it seemed most people thought of it.

Watch the complete video interview with David Banes at: http://qrs.ly/s14a6bs

Read MADA's blogs on accessibility in the Middle East at: http://www.mada.org.qa/eAccessibility/EN/blog/

Step 5: Define the relationship the product will have with its audiences

One big complication for the creation of successful web products is that your different users may have different needs. This step encourages you to consider whether your product should include the one facility that may enable you make it more accessible to many of your users – the ability to know who is using it.

Step 5 is all about expectation management. It's all about understanding that, in the post-Web 2.0 world, defining the relationship your product has with its audiences is vital to giving them a great user experience.

What do I mean by this? Well I believe that there are two different types of web products out there:

1. Type 1 products assume that their relationship with their audience should be 'one to many'. Their owners will try to make their one product work for as many of their users as possible by trying to ensure there are ways for them all (no matter what their persona) to find out how they can do the thing they came to the product to do. They may provide user journeys optimized for different groups of users (as captured in their personas – see Chapter 3) but never for an individual user. An example of this would be the BBC CBeebies

Playtime app[104] that my little boy loves. The main user journeys in the app are all games for its primary audience – children from around 2 to 6 – to enjoy. But there's also a subtle 'Grown-ups' button in the app that takes parents – the app's secondary audience – into a very different set of user journeys, allows them to learn how the games can help their child's education, and how to maximize their child's learning by playing along with them.

2. Type 2 products consider their audiences to be 'individuals'. You see this in every product that requires or encourages you to create a login. Some sites would be of no use without a login. On Twitter without a login, you would have to follow everyone in the world, and tweet anonymously. It would be a free-for-all of people sharing information with everyone else, with no filter mechanism. Which would ruin its purpose – Twitter wouldn't be Twitter. Other sites are useful without a login, but the login improves the product by providing you with a personalized interface. BBC iPlayer has a 'favourites' functionality that enables you to specify the programmes that you like, so you can find them as easily as the 'editorial choices' the BBC suggests you watch. You allow the product to know who you are, and track your usage, as long as the product will use its knowledge about you to give you a better experience.

Type 2 products encourage or require an individual relationship between the product and the user. And that raises expectations. Because if a product can support my 'wants' (for example, an email app allowing me to choose a coloured theme so its navigation controls reflect my personality) then why shouldn't I expect it to support my 'needs'? – the things that I absolutely need it to personalize so I can use it at all (like changing the colours of emails because I can't read text in the default colours the designer chose).

It is interesting that most current websites that include personalization functionality focus this functionality on 'wants' not 'needs'. Yet, if you think of Maslow's famous hierarchy of needs,[105] 'needs' are much more fundamental to a person's well-being than 'wants'. If I can't use the site comfortably, then it doesn't matter if it responds to my preferences around recommendation. It first needs to respond to my preferences about how comfortable it is for me to use.

In the next part of the RuDDeR – Decision – we're going to look at how websites can use personalization mechanisms to enable people with impairments to get a user experience of the site that meets more of their needs (see Step 8).

For now it's important to note that if your site or app has a login mechanism and encourages the user to expect a personalized one-to-one

---

[104] https://itunes.apple.com/gb/app/bbc-cbeebies-playtime/id684211403?mt=8
[105] http://en.wikipedia.org/wiki/Maslow's_hierarchy_of_needs

experience, users with impairments may be more likely to expect you to give them an experience which is personalized to their accessibility needs as well as their wants. Moreover, having already gained the user's buy-in for personalization, it will be easier for you to convince users that the product can be trusted to give them a more accessible user experience if they disclose their personal access needs.

So that's Step 5: define the relationship your product should have with its audiences. Because from there you know how accessibility personalization may or may not be expected and facilitated in your product.

Now it's your turn

Use the questions in the web product accessibility policy template to guide you in noting whether your site will have an individual relationship with its users. You will then be ready to use this information later in Step 8 on user-personalized approaches to accessibility.

Step 6: Define the user goals and tasks the product needs to provide

If you don't have the time or resource to make every part of your product accessible, what should you do? This step gives you a strategic way of prioritizing accessibility work so you can best handle that circumstance during development.

The final step in the Research part of the RuDDeR is to define the user goals and tasks the web product needs to support. This will undoubtedly be part of any product creation process your organization already has – being clear about the 'user journeys' your target audiences will expect your product to provide is the heart of the requirements gathering that any product manager needs to complete before the product can be built.

This obviously builds on Step 1's purpose of the product. The purpose should be one sentence that summarizes the whole product. This is where you delve deeper; where you consider what goals your audiences are going to come to your product to achieve:

* whether the product should support one user goal (Google search started this way, with only a simple text search) or many goals (now it includes search for images and videos, and searches based on your search history or social media usage);
* whether there is any hierarchy in the goals, where one goal needs to be accomplished before another is possible or makes sense; and

- whether all your target audiences will want to achieve the same goals, or whether some goals are more important to some audiences than others.

Differentiating core and non-core goals to facilitate prioritization

One of the key contributions of BS 8878 to practical accessibility is the recognition that you can't do everything for everyone all the time. There are trade-offs in the process of creating products, and that applies for accessibility as much as any other aspect of the product.

So you need to be sure of what the priorities are for the accessibility work that you do. If there is only a limited time that you can spend on making sure the product is accessible, on which parts of the product should you prioritize your time?

And the important thing for accessibility here – from the perspective of the impact on your audiences, rather than protecting yourself from risk of litigation – is to support *complete* user journeys (as Jennison Asuncion advocates in his interview). It doesn't make sense for you to have made one part of the user journey really accessible if the other parts of the journey exclude people. For success, your users need to be able to get all the way from the first step of the journey to the last. It doesn't matter if 'Step' 5 is the most accessible thing in the world, if 'Step' 4 prevents people from reaching 'Step' 5.

At this point, you need to define what goals are *core* to the product and what goals are *non-core*, based on the research you've done on what your users want from your product.

So, for example, on any video-on-demand service, being able to find and play a programme is core. If you can't do that the whole purpose of the product fails. Being able to then share and rate that programme with your friends, that's non-core. Those goals are useful. Many people want to share their experiences with technology. It may be very useful to the VOD supplier that people help spread the word about their great content so that more people see it. However, if the content itself isn't accessible, how can you tell anybody how good it is? All you could really say is that you couldn't watch it. And that's not the sort of thing VOD service providers want you to share with your friends.

I'll give you another example, from my cloud-based accessibility personalization tool, *restylethis*,[106] whose purpose is: 'to allow website owners to add a tool easily to their sites that enables disabled and elderly people to get a more accessible user experience by allowing them to specify their preferences about how the site should look and function,

---

[106] http://restylethis.com

and getting the tool to alter the site to correspond to those preferences'. Our user research found that many people who could benefit from accessibility personalization tools didn't use them because the tool didn't support their particular needs, or it took so long to show them its benefits that they gave up before finishing the process of specifying their needs. So the core goal of *restylethis* was to quickly and vividly give users an understanding of how the tool could change a site to better suit their needs, by getting them to an initial set of preferences which our research found helped many people with their particular disability. Once this had gained their attention and trust, the non-core goal was to allow them to take time further customizing that starter theme to more precisely suit their needs.

These examples illustrate the difference between core and non-core goals – if you can't make the core goals accessible, it doesn't matter how accessible the non-core goals are, as people will already have been excluded (or will exclude themselves) from getting the real value of the product.

So, if you have a set amount of time to spend to make sure accessibility is considered on the project, prioritize the core goals.

Defining success criteria for the completion of a user goal

The second aspect of Step 6 is how you will define that your product is *successful* at enabling its target audiences to achieve each of its users' goals. What will success look like? This is important because it is what you will assess later on when you test the product during its creation, in Step 14.

Firstly, you'll need to break down the user goal into all the steps that will be needed to take your users on the goal's user journey from start to end. Later, in Step 14, we'll look into the 'exclusion audit' that you can perform on products – those you've created, or those you are creating – to do this.

Then you'll need to consider two aspects of success for the user goal:

1. How *many* of the goal's steps will users need to complete for it to have been a successful experience. Is the goal one where, if you can't reach 100%, it's not worth bothering at all? An example of this would be the 'find and buy' workflow of an online store. If you can't actually complete the purchase of a product you've found in the store, what value was there in being able to find it? Alternatively, is there some value in getting 50% of the way? Is this 'all or nothing',

or can it be 'kind of okay'? This is what the ISO Standards for ISO Human-Centred Design of Interactive Systems[107] calls 'effectiveness'.

2. Does the *efficiency* of completing the goal matter? If checkout is possible but slow (it's inefficient) then you may lose customers to more efficient rival retail sites over time.

To continue the example from *restylethis*, it was all or nothing for the core goal. Success was defined by speed rather than precision – the tool needed to get them quickly and completely to a 'starter theme' set of preferences that mostly met their needs, rather than slowly getting them to a set of preferences that totally met their needs. From that point, success for the customization non-core goal was less cut and dry. If the product could give a user the exact shade of green they needed, that's better than an approximation. But if they were only able to reach that approximation, it was still better than the starter theme for their disability.

How close do you need to be for full success for it to be worth it? You need to define that here in Step 6.

Now it's your turn

Use the web product accessibility policy template to guide you through documenting your product's user goals, and splitting them into core and non-core goals.

Interview with Jennison Asuncion, IT Accessibility Consultant, Royal Bank of Canada; now Senior Staff Technical Program Manager, LinkedIn

Jonathan: With a lot of the things that I've done in the UK, I've found that we need to go past the whole idea of WCAG AA conformance. Especially if an organization is maybe contracting out the entirety of their website creation. They actually want to know whether or not this works for disabled people. As we said earlier, if they make it WCAG AA, it could be accessible, but it may not usable for everybody. If they want that usability, how should they specify that in their contract so both sides are very clear about what their accessibility expectations are?

---

[107] http://www.iso.org/iso/catalogue_detail.htm?csnumber=52075

What I've found is that the way BS 8878 is set up around user journeys and saying, 'Actually, the important things are that everybody, whatever their ability or disability, needs to be able to complete efficiently certain tasks on this website.' That's what we've found we actually write into contracts these days. We don't generally do the WCAG AA stuff anymore. We say that the supplier that's creating the product on behalf of the organization needs to provide proof that users in all of these categories can achieve the goals, the tasks that they would come to the site to use.

Jennison: That's spot on to what we do [at the bank]. Without disclosing state secrets...what I can say is, that we take a very practical and rational approach. So if an application we procured from Vendor X has 100 screens which have accessibility issues, we say, 'Let's have the business that's sponsoring this project identify the most high traffic transaction flows and screens. And, if it's an employee-facing app, any additional screens we know there are people with disabilities will be using.' So that ends up becoming maybe 30 screens out of 100. Let's work on those first and then deal with the rest of them after. Because then it's manageable. Because otherwise you're boiling the ocean. You're sitting there with 100 screens – where do you start? We take that approach because we know the application's already been built. It's not like they can necessarily go in there and change everything right away, because sometimes you're dealing with legacy code, sometimes you're dealing with different code bases or all kinds of different things. So we want to make it manageable.

Jonathan: Absolutely. That's why Step 6 of the BS 8878 process is all about being clear about what the tasks are and prioritizing them into core and non-core goals. I love your phrase there, 'boiling the ocean.' For me, where a framework works is where it enables all of the people working on a project to make pragmatic decisions: 'We maybe can't do everything immediately, so where should we concentrate our time?'

Jennison: Absolutely. I wonder if you get the same kinds of questions: 'Well, you have X number of WCAG things that you want us to satisfy. Can you prioritize which ones can we do first if we need to do it that way?' I don't like to tell a person, 'These are the priority guidelines to do first.' I would rather say, 'These are the priority transactions or screen flows to do first. Fix them completely.' Because if you end up in a situation where they're going to say,

'Okay, we'll work on these guidelines first and then these other guidelines next,' what you end up having is an inconsistently accessible experience. I'd rather have a fully accessible experience on five screens than an inconsistent experience across 30.

Jonathan: What I tend to tell my clients is that accessibility is the art of the possible. It's all about pragmatism. But I would rather they not make a task accessible at all than to make five steps of a task accessible and then...

Jennison: ...miss the final submission step, right? Here's an experience I had a number of years ago. There was an airline in Canada where I was able to build the reservation and all of that stuff. The very last step I submitted my credit card number and I'm like, 'This is perfect. I'm about to go.' But before I could do that, I had to solve a CAPTCHA. Of course at the time they didn't even have an audio CAPTCHA. I'd gone through Steps 1 through 7 before that 8th step – I'd already spent 20 minutes on the other steps, because the site itself wasn't that accessible. So I'd made my way all the way through, and then suddenly there's a barrier came up and bit me in the ankle. I couldn't do anything. I had to bucket out and call a sighted friend who had to do the process for me.

Jonathan: I think you're being generous. I wouldn't want anything to do with that company. If that's the experience they're giving you, why should you be their customer?

Jennison: Because it was a cheap flight (laughter). Money's money.

Watch the complete video interview with Jennison Asuncion at:
http://qrs.ly/rd49k5o

Read about Jennison's Global Accessibility Awareness Day at:
http://www.globalaccessibilityawarenessday.org

Part 2 of the RuDDeR: Decide – making strategic decisions based on that research

With your research done, you now have all you need to make good strategic accessibility Decisions for your product, before diving in to the tactical decisions of implementation later.

These strategic accessibility decisions are broken down into six steps:

7. Consider the degree of user experience the product will aim to provide
8. Consider inclusive design and user-personalized approaches to accessibility
9. Choose the delivery platforms to support
10. Choose the target browsers, operating systems and assistive technologies to support
11. Choose whether to create or procure the product in-house or outsource its creation
12. Choose the web technologies to be used in the product

The important thing to note in this part of the RuDDeR is that, while accessibility should not dictate your decisions around technology use and support for different delivery platforms (mobile, wearable, TV, desktop), you need to take the support for accessibility in each of the platforms and technologies you are considering into consideration when you make your decisions. It's no use deciding that you will aim to make your product usable for everyone, including people with disabilities, only to decide to implement the product in a technology or platform that doesn't support accessibility. It's not sufficient to decide on a platform that supports accessibility through an ecosystem of assistive technologies (ATs) without considering which of those ATs your audience are likely to have, and deciding which to support and test the product with. Similarly, it makes no sense to decide to aim for a product that provides a usable degree of user experience for all users, including those with disabilities, only to neglect to include this as a requirement in your product procurement search, or invitation to tender for digital agencies to build the product.

Step 7: Consider the degree of user experience the product will aim to provide

An online game that is usable but not fun isn't really a game. A page informing you of rubbish collection times needs to be easy to read, but cannot really aim to be 'satisfying'. An online HR system that allows you to book leave, but does it slower than the call-centre it replaced, is probably a bad investment. This step helps you to think about the degree of user experience your product should aim to provide for its target audiences, depending on the purpose of the product. Aiming to deliver the wrong degree will cost you – too high may make your development impossible; too low may make your development pointless.

Step 7 is all about considering the degree of user experience the product will aim to provide. Now you have the research in place to make informed decisions, this is the first big decision that will set the accessibility strategy for your product.

Right back to the original days of WCAG 1.0, with its Priority 1, 2 and 3 levels, accessibility has always included the idea of the different lengths you might choose to go to, to make a product accessible.

There's a lot about that idea that makes sense. After all, we all have different aims, different values that we use to decide how far we're going to go to make something happen. It's helpful to decide what your aims are, even if you can't always live up to them.

Unfortunately WCAG 2.0's A, AA and AAA levels, which replaced the numeric priority levels in WCAG 1.0, are a very crude way of setting your accessibility aims. WCAG 2.0 doesn't help you look at the cost-benefits of choosing which of its different levels of accessibility would suit your web product's accessibility ambition. It doesn't specify the costs of success criteria at different levels – the amount of work you'd have to do to live up to level A for alt-text for images is much smaller than the amount of work you'd have to do to meet level A for video captions. And, while the qualitative benefits to users described in each success criteria are useful, no quantitative figures of how many users would benefit are provided, which would be useful in enabling the relative benefit of different levels to be measured or compared.

Even more importantly, while WCAG strives to ensure all of its success criteria are testable, its levels of accessibility speak to the work you need to put in to make something accessible, not to the impact you wish that work to have on your target audiences. Remember: 'it's not what you do, it's the effect it has'.

To help product managers concentrate on what is important, rather than lots of success criteria detail, BS 8878 places the focus of your product's accessibility aims on the user of the product, rather than the technical details of the product's implementation. It looks specifically at what *degree of user experience* your product will aim to provide for all its users, including those with disabilities. Because, in the end, disabled people shouldn't have to become experts in understanding whether the A, AA, or AAA mark given to a product means it's going to be accessible for them. It's a myth that disabled people want 'accessible products.'[108] They want products that work for them, and they'll work out pretty

---

[108] http://www.hassellinclusion.com/2011/12/accessibility-myths-2011/#usability-vs-accessibility

quickly whether they do. If a product helps them achieve the thing that they came to it to do, then it's a good product. If it doesn't, it's not a good product, no matter what label you've stuck on it.

So in BS 8878 we distinguish between three degrees of user experience that you might wish to try to provide for all your users.

The lowest degree is the *technically accessible* level – where you follow tactical accessibility guidelines to create your product, and where, theoretically, if all users use the right assistive technology and accessibility settings, everything will be fine. That's very much the way most product owners use WCAG at the moment. But this doesn't mean your disabled and older users will actually be able to use your product.

The next degree up from there is, I believe, essential. This degree is the one that is referenced, for example, in the UK's Equality Act, which requires you to take reasonable steps to make sure that disabled people can use your website (or app); not access it but use it. That is very important. Web products need to be *usable*. If they're accessible but not usable for a disabled person, then you are still potentially at risk under legislation like the Equality Act, and disabled people are also very likely not to become your customers or recommend your product to anyone else. We all want to be able to use websites reasonably easily. Anything less is not a good website, and users will only use it if they have no alternative – i.e. there is no other way they can get your products and services, and you have no competitors providing similar services.

The third degree is *satisfying/enjoyable*. The ISO definition of usability[109] has always included three elements: efficiency, effectiveness and satisfaction. Efficiency and effectiveness I think are well placed in usability. But satisfaction is rather difficult to pin down. It's the one element that BS 8878 considers is better abstracted out, as not all websites are designed to be satisfying or enjoyable. To give an example: how satisfying can it be for you to find your bank balance on your online banking service? That makes little sense. What you want is a banking site that is effective (where you can find your balance) and efficient (where you can find it quickly). What you can't really have is a satisfying experience. I have no idea what satisfaction would feel like in that case – unless the amount was higher than you expected… However, satisfying and enjoyable can sometimes be central to the whole purpose of the product. If a game is not enjoyable it's not a game. And the number of online games being created is constantly growing, especially with the current trend towards 'gamification'.[110] So, if a game needs to be fun, it needs to achieve the 'satisfying/enjoyable' level of user experience to have any point.

---

[109] http://en.wikipedia.org/wiki/Usability#Definition
[110] http://en.wikipedia.org/wiki/Gamification

To give an example, let's take a game that's old enough for pretty much everyone to know: Pacman. You guide your Pacman around a maze, eating pills to score points, while being chased by ghosts. When you've eaten all the pills in the maze you get bonus points and advance to the next level. The purpose of the game is fun, and fun comes from pitching the challenge of playing the game at the right level. You need to be able to win, but not so easily for there to have been no challenge at all. If the ghosts are too fast, and there's no way of outrunning them, the game is frustrating. If the ghosts are too slow, and it's very easy to outrun them, the game is boring. Neither of those are fun.

So let's look at our degrees of user experience for playing online Pacman. I'm going to do this from the perspective of someone who has limited ability with their hands. They may not be able to use a mouse or trackpad to control the computer. Let's say their ability to control the computer is restricted to one switch: when they want something to happen they press the switch. They could be Stephen Hawking, or a child with motor impairments and learning difficulties. Either way, they want to play online Pacman through their usual means of controlling the computer.

In this case 'technically accessible' means that they can control Pacman using their switch. How could they use one switch to control Pacman, who normally needs up-down-left-right keys? Well, you could have a focus box on the screen that cycles continually between all of the directions: up, right, down, left, up, right, down, left. And when the focus reaches the direction that they want Pacman to go, they hit the switch and Pacman starts moving in that direction until they choose another direction. That makes it technically accessible for one switch to enable Pacman to go in four different directions, so the user can play the game as long as they can wait long enough for the direction they want to go in to arrive in the cycling.

'Usable', in this case, means that the user must also have a chance of winning. If the ghosts are quicker than the speed of cycling of their switch selector, then they cannot win, because while they're waiting for the focus to cycle so they can go up, a ghost comes and eats their Pacman. So, to make the game usable, the speed of the ghost's movement needs to adapt to their speed of interaction with the direction controls.

For the game to be 'satisfying', the right level of challenge – not too easy or not too hard – needs to be found, and the user needs to be able to see progress in their score over time, against themselves and other people, as they get better at playing the game. They may also want to be able to experience all of the other things that make a game enjoyable. It's important, for example, the way something looks or sounds – that's *why we have visual and audio designers to bring the right aesthetics and production values to the game. These things are all part of the experience.*

While few web products are games, I chose this example because the trends in user experience are to try to add satisfaction to as many products as possible, to make them more compelling to use. This is what the explosion in interest in gamification is all about. Applying game dynamics to dull products to make them more enjoyable can pay huge dividends for everything from e-learning to retail. And these game dynamics are exactly those in the Pacman example – the fun, the challenge, the production values, the ability to play against friends in a league. So if more products are aiming to be enjoyable, you need them to provide a satisfying user experience to *each* user, including those with disabilities, because gamified products that only provide a degree of 'technical accessibility' miss the whole point of the gamification.

Here, as usual, BS 8878 doesn't dictate the degree of user experience you should pick for your product. It lets you know what the options are, and asks you to choose the degree that you feel that you can justify as appropriate for the product you are creating.

The final point here is that pragmatically you may need to aim for different degrees of user experience for the different combinations of user goal and user group that you have. Our example detailed how we could create online Pacman to give people using it with a single switch a satisfying user experience. But maybe a person who is blind or partially sighted may not be able to play the game at all without you radically changing it. While I have created games that can be played purely using 3D audio and the keyboard or gesture,[111] that's too much of a challenge for most online games to reasonably accommodate. So you may need to say for that combination of user group and user goal (people with visual impairments playing the game), you will not attempt this. However, it could be that there are other goals in the product such as being in a high score table with your friends, that you can make more accessible to more user groups.

So it's very important for you to set the accessibility aims for your product, with your eyes open to what is needed, what is possible, and what might not be possible. You'll refine your understanding of how much work it's going to be to achieve the degree of user experience you've decided on as you continue through the process. So you may need to revisit and amend your aims, if it becomes clear that you cannot achieve all of them. This is where your understanding of the different user goals and priorities of the different groups for those goals from Step 6 will help you. Some core goals may need to be satisfying to support

---

[111] https://www.youtube.com/watch?v=2hljkSn477k

your product's purpose. But 'technically accessible' might be enough for other goals because they are lower priority for you and your users.

And, as the web evolves into more varied purposes for sites and apps, there could be even more interesting examples in the future. The challenges of accessibility should not constrain this innovation in web products. But disabled people should also not be locked out from enjoying new directions when it is possible to meet their needs. And, as Chapter 1 highlighted, some of the best innovations can come from the challenge of meeting disabled people's needs.

Now it's your turn

Use the web product accessibility policy template to guide you through specifying a default degree of accessibility that you will aim for, for all user groups and user goals. You could base this on a default degree of user experience that your organization has set for all your web products in your organizational accessibility policy, justifying any divergence from that if you consider it necessary for your product.

Once you've decided this, and documented it in the policy document, then check all user goals and user groups to see if you need to downgrade the default degree for any of them. If you feel this is necessary, write this down in the policy document, along with your justification.

Step 8: Consider inclusive design and user-personalized approaches to accessibility

'I don't want 'design for all', I want 'design for me''

Step 8 is all about the limits of inclusive design, and user-personalized approaches to accessibility. To introduce it, let me tell you a story:

During my time at the BBC, we received a number of accessibility comments on the update of the BBC News website in July 2010.

One comment at 8.05 a.m. on 14 July said:

'terrible contrast between the grey text and dark background'.

However, 19 minutes later we received this comment:

'the background colour is forced to white high contrast – contributes to eyestrain and headaches, perhaps a light grey would help here'.

Both of these users had difficulty with reading text in the colours used on the site. WCAG 2.0 supports the needs of the first person, who wanted greater contrast between the foreground and background colours. However, if the BBC News site had followed WCAG's colour-contrast success criteria even more strongly than it had already done, to help this first user, the site would have become even harder to use for the person who wanted less contrast between the foreground and background colours. Doing user research into this conundrum we found that there were as many people who wanted less contrast because of dyslexia or other literacy difficulties, as people who wanted more contrast between foreground and background colour because of vision impairments. Here the WCAG AA success criteria didn't help us get what we needed, which was to give both sets of users a good user experience.

If you were in that circumstance what would you do?

In this case I wrote back to both users letting them know that there were controls in their browsers that could help them override the colours that we chose for our website and replace them with the colours they wanted. I referenced the award-winning website My Web My Way[112] that I'd commissioned in 2006 to document how users should use the accessibility settings in their operating system and browser to customize their web experience. However, through conversation with them, I quickly found that providing information wasn't enough. Even though they were now aware of the controls in their browsers, they were scared of using them. The solution we had provided did not work for them because they weren't confident enough in their technical abilities to do what was required of them.

At this point the BBC's motivation for caring about accessibility was key. If the BBC had cared about accessibility purely from a risk-mitigation viewpoint then this example would end here, as the BBC could be confident that it would have mitigated its risk by following WCAG 2.0 AA. However, the BBC's motivation for accessibility was based on aiming to ensure that as many BBC licence fee payers can use BBC products as reasonably possible. Therefore, we needed to go beyond the guidelines to find solutions that really worked for our users.

Our resulting user research, both qualitative in labs with real people, and quantitative desk research, found that there were a huge number of people who were experiencing similar difficulties because of the lack of accessibility personalization features on the BBC site[113]. Using this research, I was able to create a business case based on the number of people encountering these difficulties, and the impact of those difficulties on their use of our site, to fund the creation of a prototype tool to investigate how we could help them. The prototype BBC Preferences System, or MyDisplay as it was called, gained quite a few

---

[112] http://www.bbc.co.uk/accessibility/
[113] http://www.slideshare.net/jonathanhassell/2010-mydisplay-accessibility-preferences-arent-for-sissies

users and it won't its own awards.[114] However, the BBC weren't in a position to do the one thing its users really wanted, which was to make it available on all websites. As this would have been outside the BBC's remit as a broadcaster, they decided they weren't able to take it further.

A couple of years later, after I'd left the BBC, I was able to extend the research, with support from the Technology Strategy Board, and develop restylethis – *a cloud-based tool with a completely revised architecture and coding. Nevertheless, the original BBC experience was a very useful proof of concept activity.* restylethis *can now add accessibility personalization to* <u>any</u> *website.[115] The additional research is referenced later in this Step.*

This is an example of the limitations of the non-individualized inclusive design approach to accessibility, which is the one commonly used in the industry at the moment. The aim is to create one website or app that, through the right use of guidelines like WCAG 2.0, is able to be transformed to the user's needs by their assistive technology, or use of browser or operating system accessibility preferences.

This approach – where users provide the assistive technologies to help their needs – works well for product owners, and should always be considered first on web projects.

However, as the research that you will have conducted in Step 3 of the BS 8878 process may have already highlighted, not all users have the assistive technologies they need to make an inclusively designed website work for them.

Dealing with differences

There may also be occasions where different groups of users need different things from a website or its contents, as discussed in Step 3. For example, people with learning difficulties benefit from sites that are as simple as possible, that may even dispense with providing the product's non-core goals to provide an interface that is optimized to access the core goals. Their needs, in this respect, are completely at odds with the needs of the product manager of the website who, like every other product manager, needs more new functionality to show off in new versions of the product. Similarly, different users of a video may want completely different versions: blind and partially sighted people want an audio-described version; people who are hard of hearing will want captions; and people who use sign language will want a sign-interpreted version.

---

[114] http://www.imsglobal.org/pressreleases/pr100524.html
[115] http://www.restylethis.com

Educationalists have established that different people learn in different ways, so e-learning sites always try to give people a number of different ways to learn – through reading, watching, building, or playing – that are based around their different learning styles.

Inspired by this, BS 8878 takes the standard inclusive design approach, and adds two other optional *user-personalized approaches* for providing accessibility, to enrich it:

- to embed the ability for that one web product to be *personalized* to the needs of specific members of its target audience; and/or
- to create a *range* of related web product variants, each of which has the same purpose but is personalized to the needs of specific members of their target audiences.

Tactical accessibility guidelines like WCAG 2.0, which generally take an inclusive design view, do recognize user-personalized approaches and may summarize them under the heading of 'additional accessibility measures'. Quite correctly, WCAG advises that these additional accessibility measures should always complement and never replace inclusive design approaches.

The huge unmet need for personalization

While BS 8878 agrees that inclusive design is always the best start, it also recognizes that, unlike the non-digital product world where personalization of products is difficult and inclusive design is often the only way of creating a product that can be used by the widest audience, software personalization is something that is comparatively easy, and is something that modern web users have become conditioned to expect (as discussed in Step 5).

Some websites and apps include 'style switcher' accessibility preference tools, like *restylethis*, to allow the user to personalize the font size or change text and background colours – as recommended by a WCAG 2.0 AAA success criterion.[116] While these tools should not replace the ability of the website to respond to the user's accessibility preferences set in the operating system or browser, they do provide a simpler interface to this functionality. They are also independent of the accessibility features of the user's operating system or browser. This can be exceptionally useful as mobile browsers commonly have less accessibility features than desktop ones.

---

[116] http://www.w3.org/TR/UNDERSTANDING-WCAG20/visual-audio-contrast-visual-presentation.html

The importance of the unmet need for text personalization facilities (or customization), whether in the product, operating system or browser, is slowly becoming more recognized, after research by Shawn Henry and myself[117].

Interview with Shawn Henry, Accessibility Evangelist, author of *Just Ask*

Jonathan: Can you say something about how the TAdER project started?

Shawn: It was really to fill a void. I was needing text customization to read websites, PDF documents, and other electronic text. In some situations it was easy to make the text work and in others it wasn't – text customization was just not available. There wasn't functionality in the products. And when I spoke with product managers they said, 'Well we don't hear a lot of people saying they need this.' When I managed to convince some, they said, 'So what do we need to do?' And I found that there wasn't a good resource to point them to...So the project started by gathering stories, experiences and information so that we could show the need for text customization.

Jonathan: The verbatim comments on your www.TAdER.com site are great at that. 'It's giving me headaches and nausea.' Is that really the case?

Shawn: Yes. I was so surprised at the range of issues – nausea, dizziness, severe pain, confusion, inability to read – that I had to ask people for permission to publish their actual responses; real user stories, not personas, but real people.

That's why I subtitled my talk today: 'What you don't know can hurt you.'

Because if you provide electronic content in a way that users can't customize, you're causing these reactions. Reading your content is hurting people. And it's hurting you, because you want people to have a good experience.

Jonathan: What sort of impairments do the 400 people who completed your survey have, and how many people do they represent in the population?

---

[117] http://www.slideshare.net/jonathanhassell/2010-mydisplay-accessibility-preferences-arent-for-sissies and http://www.slideshare.net/jonathanhassell/20131108-ucd13jhassellslideshare

Shawn: The statistics are on the site. And some are surprising. We often focus on accessibility for people who are blind, and certainly it's absolutely necessary. But there's over seven times more people with low vision than who are blind. And some estimates say 15–20% of the population have symptoms of dyslexia.

Jonathan: The 'official' figures for all disabled groups are only around 20%, so it sounds like people who are dyslexic aren't included in those figures…

Shawn: Yes, they don't shout about it, and many are undiagnosed.

Jonathan: So there are a massive number of people with these difficulties, but they may not be extreme enough for them to send complaints. They're just dealing with a world that wasn't designed the way they'd prefer to do things.

Shawn: Yes. And there's a lot of people who are ageing, and don't want to admit that they might need accommodations, don't even realize that they are possible. When I showed my father how to increase text size in his browser, he was thrilled. He didn't even know to ask for it.

Jonathan: The second aim of your project was to quantify people's needs…

Shawn: A lot of things we're familiar with: colour, font size, font face. We looked at line width, capitalization, style, whether text is in bold or italic, and the impact of hyphenation. What I found most interesting is the need to be able to increase the text size and not have to scroll horizontally.

Jonathan: I'm sure most people can relate – nobody likes horizontal scrolling. It's like 'Usability 101'. So as soon as you go into screen magnification…

Shawn: You're scrolling all the time, unless the page reflows the words, changing the line breaks so all the text stays within the width of the window. There's also no single solution that works for everyone. In the style sheet study some people preferred serif fonts and others sans-serif fonts.

Jonathan: My research found that when it comes to colours, people with low vision and people who are dyslexic couldn't be further apart.

Shawn: And it's not only that you can't make something that works for everybody, many users' needs conflict with designers' aesthetics.

Jonathan: The draft for public consultation of BS 8878 was one of the first times that people on the autistic spectrum had engaged with setting accessibility standards. You could tell, as their opinions were just so unorthodox.

They had worked out what colour combination would be able to be read best by most people in the world. They averaged out all of these different things and arrived at a light blue background with a brown or 75% grey text on it.

Their first request was that every website should use those colours, so everyone had an equal experience of the site. Their second request was that sites include a tool for people to change those colours if they didn't like them. I remember thinking, 'What they're really saying is they would like every web designer out of a job.'

Shawn: That's not going to fly.

Jonathan: Yes. Their first request was so 'lowest common denominator' that it's not going to help anybody. But their second request made complete sense, so it's in BS 8878. And other standards are slowly supporting personalization.

The American 21st Century Video Accessibility Act requires text customizations for presenting captions in online video players. The weird thing is that organizations that put these 'caption personalization' video players on their sites don't provide that functionality for the text outside the video player...

Shawn: And many people need that functionality – they aren't aware of what customizations are available in browsers, and very few can learn CSS to be able to create their own style sheet to make web text display the way they want.

Jonathan: So this is a massive opportunity for companies – there are large numbers of people who are getting a bad experience of websites, and if you gave them a better one, they would be likely to use sites more. If you're getting nausea from using a site, you're not going to be buying anything on it, are you?

Watch the complete video interview with Shawn Henry at: http://qrs.ly/yb4a6bx

Read all of her TAdER research at: http://www.tader.info

'Alternative content' and product variants

The original idea of 'additional accessibility measures' was a response to a time when assistive technologies like screen readers weren't able to handle plug-in content like Adobe Flash, so WCAG required product owners to provide disabled users with 'HTML alternatives' to that content, assuming that was possible.

The need for these alternatives due to the choice of technology is now less common, with the creation of a WCAG 2.0 techniques document that Flash developers can follow to make their content accessible, and with the introduction and widespread usage of HTML 5. However, alternative versions to meet the different needs of different users can still make sense where a 'one size fits all' approach doesn't work for significant numbers of your target audiences.

For an example of a situation where very different product variants were necessary, here's my interview with my regular collaborator, Martin Wright.

Interview with Professor Martin Wright is Director of Gamelab UK

Jonathan: We first met back in 2005. You won my first BBC jam commission. I was trying to come up with e-learning games to help deaf children with reading and writing. Your proposal showed real understanding of deaf children.

Martin: As soon as we saw that particular invitation to tender, we said, 'This is the one for us.' I had extended one of my products from the 90s called Alphabet Soup to have a deaf capability. I'd worked with deaf students. I'd understood the cultural differences and where deaf people were coming from. Where literacy is taught coherently it is very much phonic based. I also understood that British Sign Language is not just an extension of English, it's a language in its own right. It has its own grammar and semantics and so on.

Jonathan: Your proposal embodied, for me, what I was trying to do at the time – this idea of beyond inclusion; that if you were trying to create a literacy product that worked for everybody, you needed to understand their context. You couldn't just say, 'Let's just add a few BSL videos to our standard product.'

Martin: One of the things that is vital in the whole business of interactive design is understanding the other. That's been very central in everything that we do. If you're going to understand deaf people, first of all you need to meet with deaf people. Going into deaf schools was a key feature for the work we did for you.

Jonathan: I'm interested in how the requirements of the children and young people that you're creating products for almost forces you to be innovative...

Martin: I'm a problem solver by definition. My original background is an engineer, looking for solutions to a problem. You look at a particular situation and you say, 'What is it we're trying to achieve here?' It's always with the end in mind. What technologies out there are sufficiently mature for us to be able to exploit them stably? For your project we picked up a piece of technology that had been used in the Post Office – 3D signing avatars. We had to adapt that into a cartoon context, and immediately applying this very clever technology to a game space was very powerful.

Jonathan: You seem to enjoy the challenge of innovation...

Martin: Everything we've done in media production has always been about pushing boundaries, extending envelopes. That's the raison d'être of Gamelab – to exploit knowledge and research that's never been fully exploited...

In 2006 you presented us with the problem of teaching maths to blind kids. We went to some blind schools and did some research into Braille maths and the technology they're using. Maths was being taught in a very physical tactile way. Whilst that has its place, it's not really getting to the essence of the subject. We started thinking about stereo audio and came across an extremely precise [3D audio] technology that had been used in the Danish defence industry for talk-back within tanks and plane cockpits. We asked the company to provide wrappers for their tech, which we then embedded into our delivery technology.

Jonathan: You've got innovative technology, you've got a wealth of experience in creating games and taking something which can be quite dry and mathematical, and a learning aim that you're trying to get kids to. You've made maths games that you could play using just your ears and a keyboard. Is there a market for the sorts of products that you're creating?

Martin: The markets for those are minute, it's not what a commercial company would do. We're a social enterprise and are all about making a difference.

Jonathan: Since 2005 we've been creating things together for disabled people but in a way that actually has great production values at its heart.

Martin: I've used the phrase 'reverse inclusion' [Making] audio-games so cool that non-blind kids want to play them too. That's the vision. One of the drivers for our Boris games to help students learn better Makaton signing through sign language recognition via the Microsoft Kinect is about getting siblings and peers to join in the game, so they become more conversant in Makaton too.

Jonathan: Do you see potential for the technologies that you've developed for disabled people breaking out to deliver something for a wider audience?

Martin: We'd like to think so, yes. We have this repertoire, like a toolbox of technologies we've used already. And we have examples we're working on of using them beyond just disabled audiences...

Watch the complete video interview with Martin Wright at: http://qrs.ly/jf4a6c9

Read his blogs on innovation and gamification at:
http://www.gamelabuk.com

Now it's your turn

Use the web product accessibility policy template to guide you through considering whether it would make sense to add user-personalized approaches to accessibility to your product. If you think you might need to create product variants, I'd recommend you to read my blogs on 'beyond inclusion and reverse inclusion'[118] for inspiration on: when to do it, how to do it, and the innovation opportunities that can come from it.

Step 9: Choose the delivery platforms to support – mobile accessibility

'In the past five years we have seen more mainstream accessibility features in mobile products than in the entire history of IT before. For the first time major vendors are competing for accessibility, because accessibility features on mobile phones and mobile devices in general are useful to everyone, not only persons with disabilities. So you have scale.

For instance, if you're driving in a country or region where it's not authorized or permitted to use your phone when you're driving, you need to be able to activate your phone by voice, you need to do everything without touching your phone. That is very effective for a person who is paraplegic. You could be trying to read a text message to tell you where to meet someone in a very sunny place, so you just can't see your screen. Well, text to speech becomes a very good tool for you. So how about that for blind persons? When SMS started to expand very quickly, it became the preferred vehicle for deaf persons to communicate between themselves, with their parents and friends.

---

[118] http://www.hassellinclusion.com/2011/10/beyond-inclusion-and-reverse-inclusion/

Mobile technology is always there, in your pocket, in your hand; you can carry it, it's available all the time. GPS can tell your geographic position, and you have near field communication to activate stuff in your home. It's unbelievable. And now look at wearable devices, the glasses, the watches, maybe some implant sometime. So you can think about a number of new services and we do that at the M-Enabling Summit once a year in Washington with all the mobile industry. The number of inventions, innovations, new apps and services that people create with those new tools is mind-boggling.'

Axel Leblois, President and Executive Director at G3ict – The Global Initiative for Inclusive ICTs

Mobile is changing the way we use the web rapidly.

Mary Meeker's million-viewed SlideShare 'Internet Trends 2014'[119] reveals that 25% of total web usage in May 2014 was on mobile, compared with 14% a year earlier. Two times as many people globally own smartphones than desktops or laptops. Tablets are selling faster than PCs ever did, growing 52% in 2013, and with much more growth predicted ahead.

Mobile has also changed accessibility massively.

Axel Leblois' quote (from my interview with him) shows the opportunities mobile presents for disabled people. The Pew Research Center Internet and American Life Project 2012[120] found that:

41% of adults with a disability have broadband at home compared with 69% of those without a disability... [however] groups that have traditionally been on the other side of the digital divide in basic internet access – especially those in lower-income households – are [now] using wireless connections as their main way of getting online.

Similar, unpublished research in the UK has found that disabled people are more likely to access the web via mobile, as 'no frills' smartphones on pay-as-you-go tariffs are now the cheapest way of accessing the web, and many disabled people are not in employment or in permanent housing to make broadband an option for them.

Axel's quote also highlights the way mobile has widened the 'audience for accessibility' because we may all benefit from accessibility features as solutions to the 'temporary situational impairments' that we experience due to the different contexts in which we use mobile sites and apps. I used my Mac's high contrast mode to combat the bleaching effect of the sun on my laptop screen when I wrote some of this book on the beach on holiday. When the environment you're in is noisy, captions will help you understand the YouTube video you're trying to watch, just as turning on the captions on TVs in bars enables customers who want to catch up on news to do so without disturbing other customers who just want a quiet drink with friends. And Apple obviously agree with these ideas on accessibility features helping everyone consume web content safely while driving. IOS 7.1's CarPlay[121] is partly based around Siri's voice detection, so you can interact with your phone without touching it (which was initially designed for people with motor impairments), and VoiceOver text-to-speech, so content can be read to you as well as read on-screen (initially designed for blind people).

Mobile as a model for the impact of new delivery platforms on digital product strategy

While mobile is the current focus for much discussion around accessibility, it's worth noting that the various varieties of mobile operating system are just examples of the wider concept of a 'web delivery platform'. And web products are already being viewed on an increasing plethora of platforms and devices, not just desktop and mobile.

To give an example: TV-on-demand sites, like BBC iPlayer, Netflix or HBO GO, aim to provide a 'Martini' service – making programmes available 'any time, any place, anywhere'. They can already be viewed on everything from traditional desktop computers, laptops, tablets and smartphones, to games consoles, connected 'smart TVs', and TV set-top boxes. And they are likely to have added another whole device category (wearables?) before this book gets to press.

There are always new technologies coming onto the market – whether they're a completely new platform or device category, a new browser or version of a browser, or a new technology to implement web products in. There are always at least two or three 'next big things', some of which will actually turn out to be the future of the web, others of which will fail and become footnotes in the web's history.

In 2010, when we created BS 8878, my committee took a punt that we needed to help organizations think about how to do accessibility on mobile and connected TV. Now, four years later, mobile support is a 'no brainer' – hardly anyone makes a product that isn't responsively designed to work well on mobile; and the question is often whether your mobile app should be Hybrid or Native rather than whether you should develop a mobile app version of your product at all. Conversely, connected TV has not become as important as we thought, which is a shame as accessibility preferences and application program interfaces (APIs) have been planned into the UK YouView IPTV platform[122], to give one example, from day one.

---

[121] https://www.apple.com/uk/ios/carplay/
[122] http://www.youview.com/accessibility/

And, as mobile has become established, we're now looking forwards at wearables such as Google Glass, smartwatches and VR headsets, and uses of mobile devices to control ever more aspects of our environment through 'Internet of things' APIs. As the technologies that we can use to create web products evolve, so the range of purposes of web products also expands.

What we all want from mobile and how organizations handle it

Most people are becoming used to reviewing the devices that they have with them 'right now', and choosing to view the content they wish to consume on the one that makes most sense for the type of content, in the context they're in. I'll check my bank balance on my mobile, research mortgage deals on my tablet, and apply for the best one on my laptop. Our web journeys may start and end on difference devices, but we want the user experience to be consistent, and consistently good, all the way through the journey.

Many organizations, notably IBM[123], have responded to the rise of mobile by adopting 'mobile first' design approaches, where the mobile version of a product is created first, and then designers work up to a larger desktop version. There are pros and cons to this approach.[124] However, one thing is clear: while there are many different platforms and device categories that you *could* support, the number of permutations that you *choose* to support is likely to have a considerable impact on the budget and timescales needed to deliver your web product. It will also tend to dictate some of your technology choices, as some older browser plug-in technologies (like Adobe Flash and Microsoft Silverlight) do not work on all mobile platforms. Similarly, you will need to find efficient ways of handling different mobile operating systems that require their apps to be coded in different languages and using different operating system (OS) APIs, as well as handling the proliferation of screen sizes that are now available (which is why most designers currently design for iOS's few screen sizes, and then go on to the 'wild west' of Android when their iOS app is reaching stability).

While the range of delivery platforms to choose from may change over time, the way of thinking about them strategically remains the same. To decide whether to support a platform, product managers consider:

- the benefits of supporting it: the size of its installed user base, and what the platform will allow the product to do (specific functionality that other platforms do not have, that fits the product proposition well); and

---

[123] https://www.youtube.com/user/IBMMobileEnterprise
[124] http://designshack.net/articles/css/mobilefirst/

- the costs of supporting it: how easy it is to create products on the platform.

In this context, the desire to create products that are inclusive is a complicating factor. Some product managers hope that their mobile sites will be accessible if their desktop sites are, which may not be the case. Others hope that mobile sites don't need to be accessible if their desktop sites are, which, bearing in mind that disabled people may be more likely to access web products on mobile than on desktop, rather misses the point.

The support for accessibility on different delivery platforms varies widely, as does the take-up of different platforms by different groups of disabled people. So, if you do not consider these issues when making your platform support decisions before starting development, you may find yourself completely unable to find ways of implementing your products to be as accessible as you're aiming for.

So how should accessibility impact your platform support decisions, in terms of which platforms you create apps for, and which devices you optimize your website's user experience for? And how much should your product adapt to the challenges and opportunities of each different platform, to give all your users an appropriate user experience, in the context in which they will use your products?

Step 9 of BS 8878 addresses both of these issues.

How accessibility impacts which delivery platforms to support

Are you in control or is the user?

The first question you need to answer in deciding which platforms to support is whether you have any control over the platforms your users will use to access your web product.

For any publicly available web product that people will consume through a browser, the user has the control. This is why browser-based solutions to providing a *consistent quality* of user experience over a diversity of devices are essential, as we'll discuss in the next section. The only control you have is how far to take these approaches.

When it comes to apps, however, you have complete control. You can choose to create an app for a particular platform, and make it available via the platform's app store; or you can choose not to create an app for the platform.

What's popular? – in general, and with disabled audiences

While you are looking at the installed user base for a platform, it's also worth looking into how many people with different disabilities are using it, as research has found that these figures may be very different from the general population, and are almost always linked with how well the platform supports accessibility. If a technology doesn't support the needs of a particular group of disabled people, they won't adopt it.

To give a couple of examples, user research that I commissioned at the BBC found that people with motor impairments may choose not to use touchscreen mobile phones as the small screen size exacerbates their impairment. They often choose to use a mobile network-enabled tablet or laptop instead.

And, while 2013 figures for the global take-up of Android are much higher than iOS,[125] statistics from WebAIM found that 16% of screen reader users use cheaper Android devices, whereas 65% use higher-priced Apple devices.[126] This is despite visually impaired people being less likely to be working than the general population. What's interesting is that this is not because Android doesn't include a screen reader – its TalkBack is not noticeably inferior to Apple's VoiceOver[127]. However, Apple have made it much easier for blind and partially-sighted people to choose to buy their products – all their products include VoiceOver as standard, and have done for years. Whereas Android's more complex value chain obscures their messaging to these audiences – they were late to the party, and while TalkBack should now be on all Android phones, people get confused with the differences between phones from different Android licensees. Even for people who often have less money than the general population, it makes more sense to buy a phone that you *know* will work for you, than a cheaper phone that probably might.

Of course, this essential research will also need to be updated regularly because the rate of change of technologies is such that the things you can assume one year are likely to have changed by the next.

What will the delivery platform enable you to do?

While many people focus on the challenges of making mobile apps accessible, it's worth lingering for a moment on some of the features that make mobile such an *opportunity* for disabled and older people.

Firstly, assistive technologies that you might have to buy, or at least install, on a PC frequently come as standard on mobile devices – the technologies that many disabled people need are ready for them to use 'out of the box'. The huge variety of sensors included in the smartphone

---

[125] http://www.slideshare.net/kleinerperkins/internet-trends-2014-05-28-14-pdf/10
[126] http://webaim.org/projects/screenreadersurvey5/#mobileplatforms
[127] http://takesugar.wordpress.com/2014/07/22/accessibility-head-to-head-android-vs-apple/

or tablet device may also be used in your product to help the user – it knowing where you are via satellite GPS, and what you're near via near-field communication; it knowing how you're holding it, and the ambient light; it even knowing personal things like your heart rate, and what your calendar says you should be doing at the moment. For example, while 'use my location' is a convenient time saver for many people, it could be the difference between a blind person who has difficulty knowing where they are, or a person with severe motor impairments who has difficulty typing their location into a box, being able to use a 'store finder' web product comfortably or not.

Moreover, mobile apps that provide personalized, accessible, universal remote controls to a variety of inaccessible real-world objects are potentially a breakthrough solution to give many disabled people more control over the environment around them. Examples of this include:

- 'smart' control of household objects – for example: televisions[128], central heating controllers[129], and lights[130];
- the use of mobile devices and 'movie reading' apps to give people personal audio-described of movies in movie theatres[131];
- the use of e-Readers to give museum visitors personal, accessible, electronic guides to exhibitions as they walk around the gallery[132].

How well do they enable you to create accessible products?

However, the key accessibility consideration for many, when considering what delivery platforms to support is how easy it will be to make websites and apps accessible on that platform. Challenges here include:

- the impact of differences in screen size – for people with low vision, small screens can be very problematic; whereas for blind people, the size of the screen is completely irrelevant as they don't use it anyway;
- the impact of differences in input device – for people who have motor difficulties, touch screens can be much harder to use than physical buttons or tactile keyboards, and multi-finger gestures can be a complete barrier;
- the impact of mobile browsers and operating systems omitting standard accessibility features, such as the ability for the user to override text and background colours or change the size of text on a website through the browser – to get around this, as discussed in Step 8, you may need to provide these as 'additional accessibility measures' in your product

---

[128] http://recombu.com/digital/news/voice-controls-youview-apps-blind-accessibility_M12481.html
[129] https://nest.com/uk/thermostat/life-with-nest-thermostat/
[130] http://www.lighting.co.uk/hardware/controls-the-age-of-the-app/8638906.article
[131] http://blog.laptopmag.com/smartphone-app-helps-the-blind-go-to-the-movies
[132] http://www.slideshare.net/lmorenolopez/inclusion-of-accessibility-requirements-in-the-design-of-electronic-guides-for-museums

For mobile apps, on top of these challenges, you have the challenge of the massive fragmentation in the programming languages and accessibility APIs you use to make apps accessible on different platforms.

HTML 5 'hybrid' apps offer the promise of the same sort of cross-platform portability of apps that HTML enables for websites across platforms. However many organizations choose to develop 'native' apps for each platform, as they allow apps to make full use of the specific functionality in the device.

If you decide to create native apps, your ability to make the apps accessible will depend on the quality of the accessibility APIs the platform provides. While the APIs of most modern mobile platforms are more extensive than some of the platforms that came before them, this does not hold for all platforms. The situation is also changing over time. So you should check out the accessibility documentation of each platform you are considering supporting,[133] to see if it will allow you to deliver to your accessibility aims. You should also check to see whether each platform's 'app store' has an accessibility rating system, or even requires apps to be accessible to allow them onto the store – while this isn't the case in July 2014, advocates for people who are blind and visually impaired are currently debating how to encourage Apple and Google to change their stores to require app accessibility.[134]

The decision to 'go native' will obviously also impact your choice of guidelines to direct accessible production. The more platforms you support, the more sets of platform-specific guidelines your developers will need to master. And, while all follow the spirit of the WCAG 2.0 guidelines, notably its POUR principles (see the panel in Step 13), the implementation techniques and the way they are structured will be different for each platform. To bring some efficiency to this situation, Step 13 will provide advice on ways to align the accessibility guidelines of the different platforms you support.

---

[133] iOS accessibility guidelines are at:
https://developer.apple.com/technologies/ios/accessibility.html
Android accessibility guidelines are at:
http://developer.android.com/guide/topics/ui/accessibility/index.html Windows Phone
accessibility guidelines are at:
http://msdn.microsoft.com/en-GB/library/windows/apps/hh700407.aspx
Blackberry accessibility guidelines are at:
http://docs.blackberry.com/en/developers/deliverables/11936/
[134] http://in.reuters.com/article/2014/07/09/apple-mobilephone-accessibility-idINKBN0FE12O20140709

How should you design your product to provide an accessible user experience across different platforms?

So now you've decided on the platforms you're going to support, how much should your product adapt to the challenges and opportunities of each different platform, to give all your users an appropriate user experience in the context in which they use your products?

BS 8878 advises that you have three options:

1. You could go the traditional route and create one accessible website for desktop computers and browsers and hope the standards you used to create it help it work well on other platforms.
2. You could create one accessible website but enrich it with a *responsive design* and ensure that you test its accessibility not only on desktop but on other platforms too.
3. Or you could create multiple web product versions (sites and apps) that each include an appropriate user interface for that platform, and a functionality set that is appropriate for the context in which your product is likely to be used, and fully test it with disabled people on each platform.

BS 8878 was considered ahead of its time in including options 2 and 3 when it launched in 2010. Since then, the mass take-up of up smartphones and tablets means that option 1 is not really a sensible option anymore, and options 2 ('responsive design') and 3 ('adaptive design') are common practice even in organizations that have yet to start their accessibility journey.

The benefits of responsive design are already obvious to anyone who has used a responsive site – as 'nobody likes horizontal scrolling' and 'no one wants to read tiny text' are pretty much 'Usability 101'. Who wouldn't want a site to rearrange its layout to fit the size of the device's screen, so no horizontal scrolling or zooming in and out of the screen are necessary?

What's maybe not so well known is that responsive design actually has its roots in accessibility. Early experiences of using mobile devices' small screens as windows onto a larger website were very similar to the experience screen magnifier users have had on computers for years. Responsive design is really an updated name for the 'liquid design' or 'text reflow' solutions to these users' difficulties that accessibility advocates were promoting many years in advance of mobile browsers presenting everyone else with the same difficulties. Check out George Zamfir's brilliant SlideShare *Responsive Web Design & Accessibility*[135] for more details.

---

[135] http://www.slideshare.net/GeorgeZamfir/responsive-web-design-a-tool-for-accessibility

While responsive design is a 'no brainer' these days, adaptive design – stripping away the non-core goals of a website to leave a simpler version that focuses on the core goals users' wish to complete when they're on the move – isn't so universally accepted, even though this is at the heart of designing mobile apps. This is a shame, as there is ample evidence that many disabled people prefer the simplicity of adaptive mobile sites over desktop ones, as this quote from the Atlantic's 'What the Shift to Mobile Means for Blind News Consumers'[136] makes clear:

> 'The shift to mobile – and the stripped down, sparse aesthetic that in many cases comes with it – makes web navigation easier for someone using screen readers and other tools designed to help people with varying levels of sightedness. [Blind user Christopher Danielson] will often log onto a website's mobile iteration as a way to cut through the clutter'.

If you do decide to include adaptive design on your mobile website, the separation between core and non-core goals that you did in Step 6 will guide you in deciding which goals you could leave out of an adaptive version of your site. And it is essential to include the ability for users to be able to choose to view the full or adaptive version of a website on a mobile device, in case users really do want to apply for a mortgage on their smartphone. Similar useful guidelines can be found in the best research-based mobile accessibility guidelines – those from the BBC[137] and Funka Nu[138]

Mobile has forced product designers to be responsive to the different capabilities of *devices* people use to view their products. At the same time, taking that further step to be responsive to the different capabilities of the *people* using them – as inclusion proposes – might not be too much to ask. After all, if designers can change their practices to design for the latest advances in technology, such as retina screens, when few people initially actually have devices that include them, why shouldn't they do the same for the needs of people with impairments, who are far more numerous?

Now it's your turn

Use the web product accessibility policy template to guide you through considering what your approach to delivering accessibility on mobile platforms should be.

---

[136] http://www.theatlantic.com/technology/archive/2014/04/what-the-shift-to-mobile-means-for-blind-news-consumers/361062/

[137] http://www.bbc.co.uk/guidelines/futuremedia/accessibility/mobile/recommendations

[138] http://www.funkanu.com/en/Our-approach/Information-web-and-IT/Rules-and-guidelines/Mobile-accessibility-guidelines/

Step 10: Choose the target browsers, operating systems and assistive technologies to support

This step guides you through the tricky issues of assistive technology (AT) and browser support. You have the choice of hiding behind the guidelines for a legal view of accessibility. But if you really are going to follow 'it's not what you try to do, but the impact you have' you need to engage with the realities of the browsers and ATs people have to have a chance of gaining customers through your accessibility choices.

Once you've chosen the delivery platforms you are going to support, Step 10 is all about choosing the browsers and assistive technologies you will support on those platforms.

In some ways Step 10 is the detailed counterpart to Step 9. Choice of platform is about balancing the benefits of maximizing your audience by enabling them to get a good experience of your products on the devices that they have with the costs of supporting each of those platforms. The same is true for the choice of the browsers and assistive technologies that you will support on those platforms.

There's nothing new, or specific to accessibility, about browser support. Browser support has been a necessary inconvenience for all web projects since the late 1990s. I remember writing my first browser-support standard for the BBC[139] in 2001, and updating that standard every quarter against analytics of the browsers that our audiences used to view our site.

Browser support is a reflection of the reality that web development is not as straightforward as the creators of web standards and web products would wish. As web technologies from CSS, RSS and HTML 1.0 all the way to HTML 5.0 and WAI-ARIA are interpreted and presented to users by browsers, it's important for the technology and browser creators to agree on standard ways for how this is done. Ideally, browser manufacturers would abide by the standards, enabling website creators to create one website which would work and look equally good on all browsers, with no extra effort. Unfortunately, this has rarely ever been the case, and the quirks of different browsers and different versions of browsers are always something that coders have had to test for, and work around.

In this context, support for assistive technologies presents a new level of complication to those creating websites. In the same way that website creators would be best served if browser creators all followed W3C web standards in the same way, website creators would also be best served if assistive technology creators all followed the W3C User Agent Accessibility Guidelines (UAAG) in the same way. But unfortunately, as for browsers, this is not the case. Different assistive technologies, and

---

[139] http://www.bbc.co.uk/guidelines/futuremedia/technical/browser_support.shtml

different versions of the same assistive technology, often provide a different user experience of the same website (see Steve Green's interview at the end of this Step). And this is unfortunately true whether that website is coded in HTML 4 or HTML 5, whether it strictly follows the WCAG guidelines or not, and whether it goes the extra mile of following the WAI-ARIA guidelines or not.

While there are more assistive technologies available than just screen readers, they are normally the cause of most challenges, as there are major variations in the way different screen readers create an interactive experience for visually impaired users from the way that web pages are coded. This means that different screen readers may give a different user experience for the same website, unless you code around the quirks of each screen reader, or version of a screen reader. Worse than this, as assistive technologies interact with the browser to provide the user experience, the same version of an assistive technology can sometimes give different levels of user experience on top of different browsers.

A further complication is that there are a large and growing number of assistive technologies available for disabled people to use. On some delivery platforms a standard assistive technology for a particular disabled audience is available – I'm thinking here of the VoiceOver screen reader that comes as standard on all Apple products. But for most non-Apple platforms there are at least two competing assistive technologies available for each user need. And, unfortunately for web product owners, each often tries to distinguish itself from its competition by doing proprietary things that the competitor doesn't.

The result is that, for inclusive web product development, assistive technology support is a *multiplying factor* on top of a project's browser-support policy. As any QA testing manager will tell you, the cost of testing is directly tied to the number of browsers you need to test a product against. And, as any developer will tell you, it may take a lot of time to create code workarounds for browser (or assistive technology) quirks that testing identifies. Therefore, the addition of each browser and assistive technology to support can be a major factor in the costs for the project.

The fewer assistive technologies your product needs to support, the cheaper its development will be. The question is therefore how to decide which assistive technologies to support.

How to choose which assistive technologies to support

As for platform support in Step 9, the first thing to take into account when making this decision is whether or not you have any ability to control or standardize the assistive technologies your target audiences will use. In the case of an intranet, you may be in control – unless you allow staff to 'bring-your-own-device', you will provide all of the technology your staff use to interact with your intranet, including the assistive technologies that your disabled staff use. To give an example, while there are at least five different screen readers available on the Windows platform, most organizations that provide screen readers for their staff standardize on one screen reader that they provide, and they make sure they have a policy in place for keeping all of their screen reader users up to date with the latest version.

While this may cost in licence upgrades, the cost is far outweighed by the savings available from being able to specify that all of their intranet content and applications need to support just that one screen reader.

Unfortunately, the converse is true for publicly available websites and apps. If you recall the example from Chapter 1, of the letter from a blind pensioner who was 'disgusted' that I had tested BBC iPlayer with the most popular screen reader in the UK – JAWS – as the cost of a licence was three times the cost of his laptop and, as a pensioner, he could not afford it. The screen reader he chose to use was the free NVDA, which at the time could not yet handle the recent technologies used in iPlayer. As mentioned in Chapter 1, this complaint kicked off what I believe was the first comprehensive screen reader usage survey, certainly in the UK, if not in the world. While the BBC 'Screen-Reader Testing Guidelines'[140] that resulted from it are now increasingly out of date, the results of similar annual WebAIM screen reader surveys[141] in the United States are an essential free online resource to help you make justifiable decisions about which screen readers to support strategically in your organizational accessibility standards.

Such organizational screen reader support standards form the starting point for choosing the assistive technologies to support for your web product. But they do not define the choice, as different products from the same organization may have different purposes, audiences and production constraints. As in all BS 8878 steps, it is up to the product manager and their production team to choose which assistive technologies to support for the particular product that they are creating, and justify those choices.

The choice of development technology for the product (in Step 12) and the plan and budget for accessibility testing (in Step 14) will be impacted by the choice of browser and assistive technologies to support. So you may need to revisit this step after doing those steps, as the interaction between new technologies and browser and assistive technology support is key to your ability to deliver the accessibility aims you defined in Step 7.

---

[140] http://www.bbc.co.uk/guidelines/futuremedia/accessibility/screenreader.shtml
[141] http://webaim.org/projects/screenreadersurvey/

**Interview with Steve Green, Managing Director of Test
Partners, a digital product testing company, London, UK**

Jonathan: One complicating factor, when you test anything for
accessibility, is that you have many different assistive
technologies out there that sit on top of different browsers.
Interoperability standards mean that shouldn't be a problem.
As far as WAI are concerned, if the people creating the website
comply with WCAG, and the people creating the assistive
technologies and browsers comply with UAAG, all's fine. But
the reality is different isn't it? A website can give different user
experiences on different assistive technologies and browsers.
How do you handle that for your clients?

Steve: Within accessibility testing, we have got several services.
So WCAG testing is one, expert review with assistive
technologies is another. WCAG testing is fairly straightforward,
because they are very prescriptive, technical checkpoints. For a
lot of the checkpoints in WCAG, it doesn't matter what browser
you are testing, because you are just looking at the code. For
example, if it's semantically structured, that's always the same.
There are only a few checkpoints where we test with different
browsers, because we know from experience that we are going
to get different results. One example is zoom. We know that
some websites, when you zoom them in Firefox, behave
differently than if you zoom them in Internet Explorer. So part
of our standard approach is to test that checkpoint with two or
more browsers. Depending on the content, that might apply to
some other checkpoints – dynamic content, hide/reveal, and
tabbed interfaces might also behave differently in different
browsers.

In our expert review, we will typically test with screen readers,
screen magnifiers, and voice recognition software. Within
screen readers, obviously you have got JAWS, NVDA,
Window-Eyes, and VoiceOver, and all of those will behave
differently from each other. On top of that, each version of
those will behave differently from the other versions, and it can
even depend on what operating system they are sitting on.
There is a colossal number of permutations.

So we have to take a pragmatic approach to which ones to
test, depending on the client's budget. We might have to pick
perhaps the most recent JAWS version and the version two or
three back, the latest NVDA, the latest VoiceOver, and maybe
an older version of each of those.

Invariably we find we get significantly different results on each of them.

Jonathan: So when you are handing back those results to your clients, how do you advise them? Is it possible to code around those kind of quirks?

Steve: It very much depends on what the root cause of the problem is. Sometimes it's just a non-compliance in the code, it's not written to standards. In which case, the first thing to do is to correct that. Sometimes it is down to ambiguities in the standards and specifications. Sometimes it's down to a bug in the assistive technology, or the browser. Then, you have got to consider, is it possible and worthwhile to do a workaround. Once we see what the results are, we can have a discussion with the client, with regards to the impact. Because, although two screen readers might behave differently, they might still actually give an acceptable user experience. It's only if there is an actual negative impact on users that we need to start thinking about remediation.

Jonathan: Your perspective on this is different from a number of accessibility experts working on the accessibility features of HTML 5 or WAI-ARIA…

Steve: This is one of the holy wars that rages on. For those guys, they feel that all they should have to do is code according to standards, and their job is done. If the website doesn't work for some people, that's someone else's problem – the browser vendor's or the assistive technology vendor's. I come from a totally different perspective. I'm all about the user experience. I am not concerned *why* it doesn't work for people. What I'm concerned about is *that* it doesn't work. For me, there are only two important people on a development project: the product owner, and the end user. I am coming from their perspective, that we should do whatever's necessary to give a good user experience.

Jonathan: I completely agree. Telling a user that it's their fault, if they're having a bad experience, seems like the bad old days of browser support. It used to be that, when you googled a site, it often came up with a page description of, 'You are displaying this on the wrong browser. This is optimized for IE7' or whatever. Thankfully, that's not how we do things any more.

Steve: Absolutely. Coding to standards is where you start, but it's not enough. People still expect to do browser compatibility, and they will fix anything that doesn't look or behave right. So I find it disappointing that some people aren't prepared to do the same thing for assistive technologies. I can't think of any rationale for not doing it.

Jonathan: How about cost?

Steve: Clients always ask what it's going to cost. That depends on how much they want to understand what they've built. The more budget they give us, the more assistive technologies and browsers we can test with, and the more they will know. Testing is about risk management. If you have no knowledge, you can't manage your risk. The more you know, the more you can do about it. You can either fix things, or mitigate anything that doesn't work by some other means. Even if you don't do anything about it, at least you've quantified the risk; the percentage of users you are going to lose. If you don't test, you don't know.

Watch the complete video interview with Steve Green at:
http://qrs.ly/wq4a6cd

Read his blogs on testing at:
http://www.testpartners.co.uk/blog.htm

Now it's your turn

Use the web product accessibility policy template to guide you through considering what browsers and assistive technologies to support.

Decide which browsers you will support, across the different delivery platforms (and the operating systems on them) that you have already chosen (e.g. OS X and iOS, as well as Windows and Android). Help for browser support can be found by looking at what the bigger sites are doing – just google 'browser support' to see the standards sites such as Yahoo! publish. If all else fails, deciding to support the latest version of all major browsers, and using tools like Modernizr[142] to make this easier, is usually a good start.

Then decide which assistive technologies you will support, across the different operating systems your product will support, using WebAIM's annual screen reader survey[143] and the advice of any accessibility testing organizations you choose to work with – see my interview with Steve Green from Test Partners.

Step 11: Choose whether to develop or procure the product in-house or outsource its creation

Most web products are not created by the companies that own them – they outsource their production to specialist digital agencies. Most digital agencies do not create web products from scratch either – they build products on top of third-party content management systems, and integrate widgets from different vendors to add functionality. So the delivery of accessibility in your product is as likely to be impacted by clear communication of requirements between client and supplier, both in meetings and in tender or contract documents, as by conformance with tactical accessibility guidelines. If you are procuring or contracting out any aspect of your product and you get that communication wrong, the cost and effort to deliver an accessible product can sky-rocket. This step gives you what you need to prevent that.

By this point in the process you'll have defined most aspects of the product you are creating and how accessibility will be upheld in it.

A quick recap: You've specified what the product's purpose is and who its audiences are. You've done user research into how those audiences use the web, and whether they have any restrictions or preferences for using particular technologies or platforms. You've looked at their expectations from your product and the relationship it will have with them. You've looked at what tasks your users will come to your product to do, the relative importance of the different tasks to your users, and what success will look like in enabling them to complete the tasks. You've made decisions on the degree of accessibility that you're going to aim for, and whether or not you will include user-personalization options to help you get beyond the limitations of inclusive design. And you've made decisions about the delivery platforms, operating systems, browsers and assistive technologies that your product is going to support.

---

[142] http://modernizr.com/docs/
[143] http://webaim.org/projects/screenreadersurvey/

You have defined not only what your product should be, but also the degree of accessibility *quality* that you will aim for, and some of the types of accessibility *features* that you expect your product to provide. You've written down all of this information in your web product's accessibility policy.

But before we go into planning the development of the product, Step 11 arrives like a watershed. Because Step 11 is about how you're going to develop the product: whether you will create it from scratch or procure it; and whether you're going to do that in-house or contract it out to another organization.

This is what makes BS 8878 so different from other accessibility guidelines – it does not assume that organizations will develop their web products themselves, and makes the link between accessible product *development* standards like WCAG 2.0 and accessible product *procurement* standards like America's Section 508[144] and Europe's forthcoming Mandate/376.[145] Moreover, it enhances the checklist mentality of Section 508 with more modern and important concerns like assuring accessibility across multiple delivery platforms and social media channels.

All points in the BS 8878 process up to this one are just as valid for either of these options – create or procure. But from this point onwards the way that you will make decisions will be fundamentally impacted by the choice you make now.

If you decide that you're going to create the product from scratch, in-house, then all of your decisions and all of the work, from this point on, will continue to be up to you. If you really aren't going to procure any aspect of your product – even the use of third-party social media like Twitter, YouTube, Flickr or SoundCloud as additional communication channels to the channel that is your website – you can skip to Step 12 and get on with the hard work of accessible product development.

If, however, you're procuring all or part of the product – either from one supplier and then tweaking it to your needs, or by selecting and integrating tools, software, components or services from more than one supplier – or contracting out its creation, you'll need to ensure that you're clear about the accessibility aims and requirements for the product, and that the supplier or product you select is able to deliver those aims.

In my experience, the most intractable situations for delivering accessibility often happen in client–supplier relationships when the client is not clear about what accessibility they require, or completely forgets

---

[144] http://www.dol.gov/oasam/ocio/ocio-508.htm#.UNeWBnOLKQc
[145] http://www.mandate376.eu/

accessibility, during procurement and only thinks of it after signing a contract with their supplier that doesn't mention accessibility at all.

Put in a nutshell: if you don't ask [for accessibility], you don't get [it].

How to use what you've written in your product's accessibility policy to aid successful procurement, outsourcing and supplier relations

If you're going down the procurement or outsourcing route, you'll be at one step removed from each of BS 8878's Steps 12 to 14, where the product development happens.

If you're *procuring* the product, its technology choices (Step 12), adherence to tactical accessibility guidelines (Step 13) and accessibility quality assurance testing (Step 14) will have already been done (or not done). All you'll be able to do is choose between a number of different products that meet your requirements to a greater or lesser extent, and negotiate any product extension or modification that is necessary to bring it up to your requirements.

If you're *outsourcing* the development of your product to a supplier, you will be able to input more strongly into the decisions they make on each of those three steps by providing requirements for them to follow, but you'll also need to rely on the supplier to deliver those requirements.

Either way, the way to get an accessible product via procurement or outsourcing is to be clear about your requirements. So it's essential to specify clearly what the product needs to do, and the degree of accessibility that it needs to provide.

Thankfully, by this point in the BS 8878 process, this is exactly what you've already written in your web product's accessibility policy.

So you should use the information in that policy to:

- help you clearly specify the product that you wish to procure or commission suppliers to build, in your invitation to tender (ITT) or request for proposals (RFP) documentation;
- help you assess product feature lists or supplier proposals to choose the right product or supplier to win your procurement or contract; and
- help you clearly specify what you expect to be delivered by your chosen supplier in your contract with them.

Embedding accessibility requirements in your procurement documentation and contracts

The prevalence of procurement in the creation of web products is the reason why one of the first things I do in my initial engagement with new clients is to encourage them to include an accessibility section in their standard ITT/RFP templates and procurement contracts. This is a template of the organization's *general* accessibility policy, which is then filled out by the product manager with detailed information from the *specific product's* accessibility policy at this stage of the process. As you'll see in Steps 13 and 14, using WCAG 2.0 as a means for specifying the accessibility you require of a particular product always throws up many questions that are better answered by using the more user- and task-focused approach of BS 8878, specifying the product through:

- the tasks (Step 6) that the product's target audiences (Step 2) need to be able to complete;
- the degree of accessibility aimed for (Step 7);
- the platforms, operating systems, browsers and assistive technologies specified (Steps 9 and 10);
- any accessibility personalization that is necessary to achieve this (Step 8).

This approach to specification is identical to what BS 8878 recommends organizations that develop products themselves do: to specify successful delivery of accessibility via proof that the delivered product enables its target users to achieve what they came to it to achieve (the result), rather than specifying success as proof you've correctly followed a set of rules (the means) that may or may not have delivered that result.

I also encourage my clients to be clear about their expectations for how suppliers should *prove* that they have met this degree of accessibility when delivering the product for sign-off and launch, which draws from the discussion of the cost-benefits of different types of accessibility assurance methodology in Step 14.

This more holistic specification of the accessibility requirements of the product (which often requires some form of user-testing with disabled people as proof of the product's accessibility) is very different from many organizations' current 'best' practice for specifying the accessibility of products they are procuring or outsourcing, which is just to require conformance to a technical standard for accessibility such as WCAG 2.0 AA. That is, if they mention accessibility at all.

However, my experience in outsourcing web products (and I've personally commissioned web products with a combined budget of approaching £10 million, and helped advise product managers handle accessibility in the outsourcing of hundreds more products) is that the more *specific* you can be about exactly what you are expecting from your suppliers, the more likely they are to *deliver* what you are looking for, and the better the *relationship* will be between you and your supplier throughout the project.

BS 8878's focus on what the tool or supplier needs to provide, in terms of the quality of the experience users will find when trying to complete tasks with the product, ensures that the product delivered is fit for purpose for use by all the audiences you have specified. Whereas, specifying accessibility against development guidelines like WCAG allows suppliers to deliver a product that meets the technical standard, but which disabled and older people may not be able to use to complete the tasks they came to the product to complete.

One of the major benefits found by organizations who follow the BS 8878 process is that, by the time they write their ITT and contract documentation, they are able to be very clear about what they expect, both in terms of accessibility, and in other aspects of the project. This clarity of expectations benefits both client and supplier.

How to select a supplier or tool that will deliver the accessibility you need

Being clear in specifying your requirements for how accessibility is to be delivered and assured by a supplier or product is one half of the battle in successfully outsourcing or procuring an accessible web product. The other half is in being able to distinguish a supplier that is likely to be able to deliver to your accessibility requirements (or a product that can do so with the minimum of further modification or extension) from one that is not.

By specifying your accessibility requirements in terms of task completion by specific audiences to a specific degree of accessibility across specified platforms, operating systems, browsers and assistive technologies, you are already marking yourself out as an organization that cares about the *actual* accessibility of the product that you are creating for your target audiences, rather than being content with the risk mitigation of solely meeting technical accessibility standards like WCAG AA.

But I'd also recommend that your standard ITT wording should require suppliers to specify *how* they will meet your product's specific accessibility requirements in their tender or proposal.

For suppliers of products or components, this places the burden on the supplier to prove their product meets your requirements, which pushes them beyond the usual claims of conformance with WCAG 2.0 AA or provision of Section 508 VPATs (voluntary product accessibility templates),[146] which are often provided for a product but seldom independently verified. In doing this, the products that are suitable for upholding your product's accessibility aims rise to the top.

For suppliers of product development services, this places the burden on the supplier to prove to you that they have planned for, and will assure, the level of accessibility you need for the specific product you want them to create. My experience is that this, in itself, tends to separate those suppliers that can actually deliver accessibility from those that know the 'right answer' for accessibility is WCAG 2.0 AA but don't necessarily understand what, in practice, is necessary to deliver a product that meets your accessibility aims.

To give an example of this, when I was commissioning e-learning games for the BBC in the mid-noughties, it was always clear which of our 25 preferred suppliers really understood what we were after, because they did much more than mention WCAG in their proposal's response to our ITT's questions on accessibility. At the time, the only web technology that could deliver the games that we needed was Adobe Flash, and Adobe Flash could not be made accessible using the existing WCAG 1.0 guidelines of the time. Therefore, suppliers that simply quoted their WCAG conformance policy stood out as having missed the point and not engaged with the accessibility approach we needed.

So, if 'we create all our products to conform with WCAG 2.0 AA' isn't proof enough that a supplier can be relied on to deliver what you need, what proof is sufficient?

Here BS 8878's process helps again. Because what you need your suppliers to convince you of is that they have done a first draft version of all the work in Steps 12 to 14 in the preparation of their proposal:

- that any technology choices they've made in their proposal have taken accessibility into account (see Step 12);
- that their development plan, timescales and costs have taken accessibility into account (see Step 13);
- that their testing plan, timescales and costs have taken accessibility into account (see Step 14).

If you see evidence that the supplier has followed these steps in their proposal, you know not only that they have taken your accessibility requirements seriously, but also that the plans they have presented to you can be relied upon to deliver the accessibility you require. If you can't see this evidence, you are likely to get what usually happens, which is that accessibility is forgotten until being tested for late on in development, and then needs to be downgraded because no time has been set aside to rectify the accessibility flaws found in the testing.

---

[146] http://www.state.gov/m/irm/impact/126343.htm

Annex L of BS 8878 also includes more questions you could ask of suppliers of product creation services (such as 'what elements of the product development are going to be most challenging for accessibility?' or 'show evidence of how you've delivered accessibility on similar products that you've created in the past'), and of suppliers of tools (such as 'what was your approach to accessibility when you created this product?'). This helps you to score them for accessibility, amongst all the other factors you use for supplier or product selection.

How to handle the situation where no supplier can meet your accessibility requirements

While procurement requirements in BS 8878 and other accessibility procurement standards lessen the likelihood that you will not be able to find a supplier that can supply a tool or product creation service which delivers the degree of accessibility that you're after, there are still situations where that does occur, as Andrew Arch and I discuss in his interview at the end of this chapter.

In these cases, BS 8878 recognizes that it might be necessary for an organization to procure products that do not deliver the desired degree of accessibility, as long as they are making an informed decision that balances accessibility risk against other business needs.

However, in these circumstances, your contract negotiation should include discussions with the supplier to see if they will put accessibility improvements on their roadmap (using the business cases for accessibility from Chapter 3 as leverage), and discussion of what alternative measures need to be put in place for users who are affected by the product's accessibility deficiencies (at a minimum, declaring the deficiencies in the product's accessibility statement – see Step 15).

How to handle remediation of products where accessibility requirements were not part of your contract with your supplier

The real-world, worst-case scenario for delivering accessible products (as also discussed with Andrew Arch) is where you wish to improve the accessibility of a product or service that you've bought from an external supplier where you didn't mention accessibility at all in the contract.

In these circumstances, you, as the purchaser of the product or service, do not have any legal leverage to require your supplier to improve the accessibility of their product, at least until a break clause in the contract.

However, I have helped many organizations through these circumstances, by commissioning accessibility testing of the product to find its accessibility deficiencies, and leading negotiation exercises to go through the list of deficiencies estimating the benefits to the organization and costs to the supplier that would come from fixing each issue, to come to a prioritized list of which issues could be most usefully fixed in the short-term (see the section on my *Accessibility Issue Prioritization Matrix* in Step 14).

The issue of who should pay for those fixes is a contentious one, and the only leverage the organization usually has is based on what they would require from the supplier to not terminate the contract at the next break clause. But you may gain some more leverage by introducing the supplier to the sales benefits of improving their product's accessibility (see Chapter 3), if they aren't aware of them. Whatever the final result, this sort of exercise provides a useful framework for both client organization and supplier to work through the issues to come to the best conclusion they can agree on for how to proceed, and I have got good results and feedback from both clients and suppliers after conducting it.

Interview with Steve Green, Managing Director of Test Partners, a digital product testing company, London, UK

Jonathan: When [accessibility] test results come back, it's a real opportunity for a developer or a designer, whoever it is who created the problem, to become aware that what they did or didn't do has resulted in this. Do you get the feeling that, as result of your testing, your clients are getting better at delivering accessibility? Over time, working with a client, are there less problems than there previously were?

Steve: That certainly happens with some of our clients. Especially development companies who are working with us, maybe five, ten, twenty times a year. Often it's a particular developer who is getting better at accessibility. In some cases they get so good, they almost don't need us anymore.

However, we also see companies who don't improve at all. That is often, so far as we can tell, due to the use of *code libraries*. I can think of a number of our clients where we can almost write down half of the non-compliances before we have even seen the website, because we know they are going to just pull a particular code library off the shelf, make a bunch of changes that are specific to the site they are building, and, for whatever reason, when we report non-compliances, although they might fix it in that particular instance, they don't fold back the corrections into their code library. So the next time they build something, it's got the same faults that everything has ever had before.

Jonathan: That's really inefficient isn't it? If I were the person in charge of that company, and you were getting the same problems coming up over and over again when you were testing my products, I would want you to tell me that something wasn't right in our processes. That fixes weren't feeding back into a code library. Or, maybe we had a great developer who'd learnt to create more accessible code through your feedback, but now they'd left.

Steve: Yes. Sometimes on a particular website, we can even tell which parts were built by one person, and which parts were built by someone else. I don't think that problem is going to go away, frankly. There is a lot of use of contractors, who move from job to job, rather than staying in the same job the whole time. So, for companies who just bring in people to do one project and let them go, there is a big chance they are not going to improve.

Jonathan: What if those companies cared enough about accessibility to ask contractors, before they sign them up, whether or not they're competent in it?

Steve: I don't think anyone is going to say they are not.

Jonathan: So the problem is how to differentiate the guys who *really* know what they are doing with accessibility, from the guys who just *say* they know what they are doing. If I'm a developer who's bothered to learn this stuff – it's maybe my USP – then it is important for organizations to look for that and say, 'We are going to go with candidate three, rather than candidate two, because candidate three is going to save us money. Because when we send the product to Steve and the team to test, we are going to get back a clean bill of health…' How much money do you think the fixes cost? When you have found problems, do you have an idea for how much of those fixes actually get done, and how much it costs?

Steve: We're not really party to that. But certainly when we look at some of the stuff that we are asked to test, you look at it and think, 'Crikey, how on earth are you ever going to fix this?' For instance, we recently worked on a website, and it was beyond belief. Nowhere near WCAG AA. Terrible user experience with assistive technologies. The only way to fix it was to throw it away and start again, which would just be a six-figure development sum.

Jonathan: So it then becomes even more important that you get this right from the start, I guess?

Steve: Absolutely. It seems that a lot of people who are commissioning work, are just taking it on trust, when development agencies or individuals say that they can code to AA or whatever, then the clients are just assuming that they know what they are doing, and no further testing gets done.

Watch the complete video interview with Steve Green at: http://qrs.ly/wq4a6cd

Read his blogs on testing at:
http://www.testpartners.co.uk/blog.htm

How BS 8878 can help client–supplier relationships by aligning expectations

Once a supplier has been chosen, it is also a good idea to get the client and supplier into a workshop to work together to plan the accessibility in a product's implementation in more detail, using BS 8878 as a framework for discussing the necessary issues. Taking care to align and document the expectations for client and supplier for Steps 12 to 14 at the start of the project may take time, but can pay massive dividends as development proceeds, as both sides know they are aiming for the same thing. This results in accessible products, created through transparent dialogue, not disputes, which can arise when delivered products are found to not meet client's aims far too late in the process for accessibility to be delivered with reasonable cost.

For an example of the benefits of using BS 8878 to manage accessibility on large, multi-supplier projects, see Rob Wemyss' case study of Royal Mail's use of BS 8878 in my CSUN 12 SlideShare.[147]

---

[147] http://www.slideshare.net/jonathanhassell/case-studies-of-implementing-bs-8878-csun-2012-12145101/31

BS 8878 procurement requirements raising the accessibility bar for suppliers

One interesting impact of BS 8878 on the market for accessible products is that, as BS 8878 encourages commissioners of websites and procurers of tools to think more deeply about what they actually expect from the accessibility of a product, this helps suppliers that are competent in delivering accessibility, or are willing to step up to the challenge contractually, to mark themselves out from those that aren't, and win more business.

In essence, if you are a supplier, BS 8878 gives you a better business case for improving your competence at delivering accessibility, and selling it as one of your key competences or unique selling points (USP). As you see evidence in ITTs that companies commissioning your work care about accessibility and value this USP, you will be able to be more transparent about including the actual costs of accessibility in proposals, and not feel that by pitching the slightly higher costs of developing accessible products you will lose business to competitors that pitch lower charges for inaccessible products. And if you are a tool vendor, and you follow BS 8878 in your tool's development, this will give you everything you need to easily convince customers that are also following BS 8878, that your tool meets their accessibility requirements in procurement.

While Section 508 in the United States and Mandate/376 in Europe do a good job of requiring IT product procurement to take accessibility into account in public-sector organizations, BS 8878 raises the bar for private-sector companies too.

Now it's your turn

If you are going to use any procured components in your product, or outsource its creation to an external supplier, note this in your web product's accessibility policy, and download and use the ITT templates in the support materials for this book (see the support materials on page x) as a guide to start specifying what you will require from any components, products or services you purchase.

> **Interview with Andrew Arch, Assistant Director, Web Policy – Accessibility for the Australian Government Information Management Office**
>
> **Jonathan:** Let's talk about the Web Accessibility National Transition Strategy four-year programme you're doing in Australia to get all government sites to WCAG 2.0 AA by the end of 2014. Do you feel like you're going to get there?

Andrew: We're going to make an awful lot of progress. I think probably the informational sites [are] there. But some of the service delivery is just so complex. The life cycle of those projects, those big software projects that do online service delivery are just much longer than four years.

Jonathan: Every site has got a life cycle for versioning and, as you say, software projects can take a long time. Sometimes people don't understand that and think if there's a problem everything can be fixed right now.

Andrew: Yes, when they signed off on this they probably thought we'll just change the colours and we'll change the font, job done. But it's much more complicated than that if you're relying on external suppliers of your systems. You may have an HR system, for instance, that does all your recruitment and HR management, and you've got a five-year contract, and it was delivered with very minor accessibility in mind. People are going through procurement reviews and saying, 'Okay, when is this due for relicensing or renewal?' and saying to the big companies – international companies in many cases – 'We need accessibility built into this.'

In the meantime, they can tweak things. I know our own internal HR system was upgraded recently and we ended up with a pale blue font on a grey background by default. I can't read that. I've got a particularly bad screen and I haven't asked for it to be changed because it actually highlights issues. I was looking at other people's screens and it was sort of okay, but you'd ask around and people would agree, 'It's hard to read'. But they just accepted it. We sent off a message and the developer came back and gave us a look at a trial, 'Is this better?' 'Yes,' and so they rolled it out.

But there are other aspects of particular HR systems, if you're a keyboard-only user, that you'll find incredibly difficult. But we're locked into that – that was a pre-requirements purchase. One of the things we're actually looking forward to is the upgrade of US Section 508 and its harmonization with WCAG 2.0. The US government is such a big purchaser, the biggest purchaser in the world of ICT, so we're hoping it's going to drive things a bit faster than Australia can.

Jonathan: I get you. Because at the moment when you ask suppliers, 'Will it allow us to live up to our accessibility requirements?' they don't know.

Andrew: That's right, yes typically.

Jonathan: It's that international element of what drives accessibility which makes international accessibility events like CSUN so useful. We have multinational organizations, and tool vendors who are trying to sell products all over the world. And yet I got really sick when I was at the BBC of organizations saying, 'That's the first time anyone's ever asked us for accessibility.' It's like: 'Really? Can that actually be the case?'

Andrew: Yes. We've just provided some advice to agencies around procurement. It's not something that you check at the end of the process. You've got to make sure it's written into the requirements before you go to market so that the suppliers know that you're expecting it. Then you've got to check progressively, if they're building something for instance, that they're actually doing it, because by the time it gets to the end you've got to roll it out and you're not going to go back and fix it.

Over here [in the USA], I've heard anecdotes of organizations who have left it until the end, met the business needs but not the accessibility needs. And the accounting and legal people said, 'It's too hard, we're just going to have to wear it.' Our [Australian] Human Rights Commission says, 'If it's not accessible it's not fit for use' and I like that phrase. You haven't purchased something that's actually fit for use if you haven't purchased something that's accessible, and meets the needs of all users. We try and get that message across – so it's not an afterthought…

Watch the complete video interview with Andrew Arch at: http://qrs.ly/bz4a6bo.

Read his great resources on Web Accessibility for Older People at: http://www.w3.org/WAI/older-users/

Step 12: Choose the web technologies to be used in the product

Whether you are creating the web product yourself, procuring it or outsourcing it to other organizations, the web technologies used in the creation of the product are another key element that impacts on how accessible you can make it.

So Step 12 is all about defining the web technologies to be used in the product's creation.

If you're creating the product bespoke, then the choice of web technologies is up to you. If you're outsourcing it, you'll need your supplier to choose the technologies as wisely as you would. And if you're procuring components or content management systems to build it from, you'll need to carefully consider their accessibility capabilities before selecting them.

Choosing the web technology for bespoke products

So how do you ensure the web technologies you choose will allow you to create a product that is accessible?

Thankfully, WCAG is very helpful here. You should search to see if any technology that you consider using supplies *techniques documentation*[148] for WCAG 2.0. If it does, then following those techniques will enable your coders to use best practice for making accessible products with the technology. If techniques documents do not exist for the technology, then you'll need to examine it further, to check whether or not the technology exposes content, structure and functionality to assistive technologies on the platform, and allows web products to live up to WCAG's POUR principles (see the POUR panel in Step 13).

To give an example, support for accessibility in popular desktop web technologies is now pretty good. The advent of HTML 5 enables more of the rich media functionality of modern websites to be coded in a non-proprietary standard that has had accessibility considered from day one (although some of the newer elements of HTML 5 – like Canvas – are still less supported[149]). If HTML 5 does not give you what you need, and mobile isn't important for you, accessibility techniques for Adobe Flash have been available since WCAG 2.0 was created in 2009[150], although Silverlight still has only limited accessibility support (and no accessibility support beyond Microsoft Windows).

---

[148] http://www.w3.org/TR/UNDERSTANDING-WCAG20/understanding-techniques.html
[149] http://www.sitepoint.com/web-foundations/introduction-html5-canvas-element/
[150] http://www.w3.org/TR/WCAG20-TECHS/flash.html

As discussed in Step 9, the key technology challenge these days comes from mobile apps, which are coded in different languages and using different APIs, depending on which mobile operating system you choose. Mobile apps also bypass the browser accessibility preferences/settings layer which has provided accessibility customization for years. Thus, mobile app developers need to look more closely at how the APIs they use for creating mobile apps will interface with accessibility settings and assistive technologies on the smartphone or tablet – both assistive technologies that are part of the standard operating system, and assistive technologies that may be able to be installed onto the device (something Android and Windows Mobile facilitate more than iOS). As different mobile operating systems (OSes) provide different levels of accessibility support, it is entirely possible that – unless you provide 'additional accessibility measures' in the app itself (as discussed in Step 8) – the accessibility you will be able to deliver in the versions of your mobile app for different operating systems will be different. This should be taken into account when reviewing the choices for which mobile OSes to support, and whether your apps should be native or hybrid, that you made in Step 9.

Choosing content management systems and authoring tools

While web technologies are more supportive of accessibility than ever before, fewer and fewer websites are being built from scratch these days. Most websites are now built on top of some underlying content management system (CMS), such as Drupal, WordPress, or SharePoint. Similarly, pre-built components or widgets are often used to add common functionality to websites, however they are built – for example: embeddable media players from YouTube, Vimeo[151] or Brightcove[152]; global comment systems like Disqus[153]; or the ubiquitous social media buttons provided by Facebook, Twitter, LinkedIn or Google+.

These content management systems are empowering more and more website owners to create their own websites without needing to learn how to master web technologies, or contract someone else to do it for them. The web these days is a much easier place in which to create both content and full websites.

However, different CMSs and widgets may have different levels of support for accessibility built in (for an example, see the interview with Graham Armfield on WordPress accessibility).

---

[151] https://vimeo.com
[152] https://www.brightcove.com
[153] https://disqus.com

Interview with Graham Armfield, UK WordPress Accessibility Consultant

Jonathan: Hi Graham. Your day job is to create websites for your clients using WordPress, Graham. Can you tell me what WordPress is and how it helps you create sites?

Graham: WordPress is the most popular content management system in the world at the moment. It's a way of easily building websites where you don't actually get involved in coding up the pages any more. WordPress is based on what are called 'themes', which are a series of templates. In order to create a WordPress website, you either pick a theme off the shelf, or get someone like myself to build one for you. You can customize the functionality with a series of plug-ins, and these are little nuggets of functionality that add functionality to your site; whether it's to do with improving searches or presenting content in a slightly different way. Then once you've got that going, the individual site owner can put whatever content they want into it. Whether it's a blog, a business website, a website for a band or just a hobby website.

Jonathan: What sorts of organizations are using WordPress for their sites?

Graham: It used to be a purely blogging platform, so it was very much very small organizations and individuals. However, a lot of corporates are embracing it now. Not necessarily for their online banking offering or something like that, but for their brochureware or their blogging platforms to relate to their customers more.

It's a secure and sustained product, which is being improved all the time, and which more and more companies are embracing. Hence the figure of it being used by over 20% of the websites in the world.

Jonathan: So how easy is it to make a WordPress website accessible?

Graham: That is a tricky one, Jonathan. There's nothing in WordPress itself to hinder the accessibility of a website – I'm constantly working to make sure that's the case. But, when you start off with a WordPress website, you need a theme of some sort. So your site's accessibility depends on whether or not the person who built that theme actually thought about accessibility. There are thousands of themes out there that are free to use that you can choose from.

Unfortunately, very few of those are accessible. I think the ones that are pretty good from an accessibility perspective, you can count on the fingers of one or maybe two hands. And only a couple of those can create the sorts of sites a company would want. It's currently a choice between accessible or suitable for corporate/SME use. It seems you can't have both.

Jonathan: Which is a shame because, if themes had accessibility 'baked in', then website owners would get accessibility 'for free', without needing to worry about WCAG 2.0 and all those complicating factors.

Graham: The plug-ins would also need accessibility baked in. And it's not a panacea – there's still a responsibility on the content authors to follow simple accessibility guidelines when they're creating content.

Jonathan: So you've already got a set of things that you hand out to people and say, 'These are the things that you need to make sure your website is maintained with accessibility in mind'?

Graham: You're absolutely right. Most of the clients I deal with are not technical at all. They might have seen HTML, but they don't understand how it works, and they're not interested. The beauty of having a WordPress site is that they don't need to get involved in that. The WCAG 2.0 guidelines are very useful for me when I'm building a bespoke site for them and testing its accessibility, because they give you a reference point. But they're quite impenetrable for people who are not technical. I give my clients a crib sheet – an idiot's guide to writing accessible content. It includes things like:

- Put headings in to segment the content, and you'll get better SEO.
- Make sure each link actually describes what it does – no 'click here'.
- Make sure you label images, and maybe include transcripts or captions for video.

This stuff is all easy to do within the WordPress editing area. So why not do it?

Jonathan: So do your clients seek you out because you can create them accessible sites? Or is it something that is just an added extra part of your service to them? Do they value the accessibility that you bring?

Graham: It's a bit of both. I have clients who have been referred by people who have valued the accessibility that I've put into their sites. I have clients that come to me specifically because they heard that this is what I do. But I also have clients who come to me who have never heard of accessibility.

During the requirements process when we're talking about the website that they would like, I always mention it there. Many people have never thought about how people who are blind or motor-impaired, for example, would use their website. But when you explain it to them, they really get it.

Watch the complete video interview with Graham Armfield at: http://qrs.ly/s24a6br

Read his blogs on Accessibility and WordPress at:

http://www.coolfields.co.uk/blog/

So how do you ensure that the CMS or widget you are about to select will allow you to create an accessible product?

What you should look out for is any mention of accessibility, and conformance with WCAG 2.0 or ATAG. ATAG[154] are WAI's lesser known, but equally important, 'Authoring Tool Accessibility Guidelines' – a set of guidelines that authoring tool (CMS) creators can follow to ensure their tools are able to produce accessible web products (see the discussion in Step 16 for how CMSs which conform with ATAG can help uphold accessibility during post-launch site content maintenance). If accessibility isn't mentioned at all in the tool's documentation, your only option is to ask the tool developer directly what level of accessibility their tool supports, and if accessibility improvements are scheduled in their development roadmap.

---

[154] http://www.w3.org/WAI/intro/atag.php

It's worth giving an example of the complexity of the decisions you may need to make when you create a web product based on a content management system. The standard installation of WordPress – the most popular 'website builder' out there, and the one I use on my Hassell Inclusion website[155] – does allow you to create accessible websites. However, most WordPress themes – the mechanism you use for setting how your website will look, and what functionality it will contain over and above the default WordPress functionality – have not been built with accessibility in mind. Similarly, most WordPress plug-ins – the mechanism WordPress uses for further extending its functionality into providing newsletters and aiding SEO optimization, for example – have also not been built with accessibility in mind. This means that, while WordPress can be used to create accessible websites, most professionally produced WordPress themes and plug-ins that allow you to quickly build an impressive, professional, capable website are currently unavailable to organizations who also wish to ensure that their website is accessible. Thankfully, numerous accessibility advocates are trying to change this situation, through the Cities project.[156]

Why create a website at all when you can use a social media platform?

An even more pressing issue, which may be finally getting some attention in the communications industry and accessibility community[157], is how accessibility is impacted by the trend for organizations to dispense with creating a website completely and create a product page on Facebook instead. This is important because, by making this decision, they are making themselves dependent on the accessibility features that Facebook provides[158].

Moreover, almost all organizations now use Facebook, Twitter, YouTube, Flickr, SoundCloud, SlideShare and other social media websites to extend their site's rich media content capabilities, and to act as further channels to communicate with their audiences.

While it makes complete commercial sense to use as many channels to communicate with your audiences as they are already using, this multi-channel approach to audience engagement presents challenges for accessibility. You must take into account the accessibility of the organization's presence on *each* of those channels, most of which is not under your control. So your content strategy should include a pragmatic constraint that all important messages communicated on social media must also be communicated on the most accessible of your channels,

[155] http://www.hassellinclusion.com

[156] http://accessiblejoe.com/cities/

[157] http://www.fcc.gov/events/accessing-social-media

[158] https://www.facebook.com/accessibility

which in many cases will be your website, over whose underlying technology and design you have most control.

A useful separation of labour

The number of available web technologies, content management systems and other authoring tools is likely to continue growing in the future. So the community working on accessibility is likely to become split into two camps:

1. those who are working to create authoring tools that have accessibility baked in; and
2. those who work to select the most suitable authoring tool and components for enabling them to create accessible web products.

The first camp need to be experts in creating tools that get the best out of the accessibility present in underlying web technologies, using guidelines like ATAG, WCAG and WAI-ARIA, and communicating the accessibility properties of their tools in a language that non-technical website owners can understand.

The second camp need to be experts in searching for tools and components that balance all of their requirements, including accessibility. This may often require difficult decisions to be made where popular components are not fully accessible, or where the most suitable components to meet the website owner's wider set of requirements do not meet their accessibility requirements. These are some of the biggest challenges for inclusion in the future (see Chapter 7).

For the creators of authoring tools, themes and plug-ins to take accessibility seriously as a requirement for their work, they need to feel the demand for accessibility from clients of their tools. BS 8878 helps raise the bar here by ensuring that website owners are clear about what their accessibility requirements of web tools are, and why accessibility is important to them, so tool creators will build accessibility in to more and more of their tools.

Now it's your turn

Use the web product accessibility policy template to guide you through choosing and justifying the technologies, content management systems and authoring tools you will use to help you build your product. Also consider how accessibility is supported in all the social media channels you plan to use to communicate with your audiences, and create strategies for getting around any accessibility deficiencies in those channels.

Part 3 of the RuDDeR: <u>D</u>o – developing and launching the product

Finally, we come to '<u>D</u>o' – actually developing your web product, using the decisions made in the previous six steps to guide you.

This part is all about the impact on accessibility of the large numbers of *tactical* decisions your development team will make as they develop the product day by day.

At its heart are two simple recommendations:

1. Develop your product by thinking about accessibility from the start, rather than waiting until the product is almost ready to launch to audit its accessibility, which tends to uncover large numbers of problems, at such a late point in development that it's too expensive to fix them. If you fail to do this, the product is likely to launch with many accessibility deficiencies in it, just waiting for a user to experience them.
2. Use tactical accessibility guidelines to inform *all* the development decisions they have bearing on (Step 13), and test the product at sensible points in its development (Step 14). Do this, and you may find a few problems that you can fix before launch, and possibly some that you decide to leave to fix in the next iteration of the product, which is fine, as long as you inform your disabled users of this decision (Step 15).

Inherent in all of these steps is the concept of consciously *planning* for accessibility through the creation of the product:

- planning to deliver accessibility in each stage of development;
- planning to test for accessibility throughout development; and
- planning to communicate accessibility decisions in the product's launch.

Each of these plans need to be created and harmonized with the others, and integrated with your general plans for the product's development. And progress against them all needs to be actively monitored throughout development.

Of course, you may have decided (in Step 11) to procure the product or to outsource its creation, so each of the two planning and implementation steps (13 and 14) mention what you should do in each of these circumstances.

The final key concept for this part of the RuDDeR is the idea of *priority*. If you find during development and testing that you cannot deliver all of the accessibility aims you have planned for, or fix all the problems that your testing has found, you should use cost-benefits analyses to help make justifiable decisions. These will help you decide which aspects are most important, and should be prioritized, and which aspects are less important, and so could be sacrificed, if that is necessary to deliver your product on time and to budget.

Each step will use a key tool that will help you prioritize – the *Accessibility Issue Prioritization Matrix* that has helped so many of my clients.

Step 13: Use tactical accessibility guidelines to inform development of an accessible product

The greatest number of accessibility decisions you make on a project happen when you're actually developing the product. This is the part 'everybody knows' – using WCAG 2.0 guidelines in your development. But WCAG 2.0 is like the 20 tonne behemoth of accessibility. It's fabulous when it's helping you. But the strictness of its rules may crush you if you haven't found out enough about the reasons for those rules, how to sensibly apply them, and when it is justifiable to opt out of a rule. Thankfully, this is one of the strengths of the BS 8878 process: by the time you arrive at the guidance WCAG gives, you've already established the strategic grounding for making sensible tactical decisions about how you're going to deliver accessibility for your product, based on justifiable reasoning.

Now you're ready to develop your product. You need to plan tactically to ensure accessibility is covered well across all of your product's development, and monitor your team's work so the product you deliver meets the accessibility aims you intended.

When you're developing the product the *number of decisions* made per day goes through the roof... Now we're into tactical rather than strategic decisions, and they need to be made more frequently and quickly. They're also being made iteratively – you're likely to go round the process of making a decision, checking its results, and revisiting the decision to tweak it, quickly.

And the *number of people who make decisions* also expands hugely, as does the number of places in which they are making those decisions. Responsibility for decision-making needs to be devolved from the core team led by the product manager, to staff who could be working all over the globe, and different suppliers who may be developing different parts of the product. And all of these may be making decisions in break-out sessions, email discussions, daily stand-ups, or at their desks, making decisions on their own.

Your ideal set of tactical accessibility guidelines

All these people are unlikely to have the specialist expertise on hand, or time to research, which of the many tactical decisions they make every day will impact the accessibility of the product. They need to know how to make those decisions that do in a way that includes as many people as reasonably possible.

So, on top of the *strategic* research and decisions from the previous 12 steps – all gathered in the web product accessibility policy, for easy reference – your team needs a set of *tactical* guidelines to help them: that have been created by accessibility experts; are based on their understanding of the needs and preferences of people with impairments, and how those needs impact those people when they use the web; and explain how designing or coding pages in a particular way can give them a user experience which suits their needs.

Your team need to be able to rely on the set of guidelines as a complete tactical guide. Each guideline needs to be *necessary*. The whole set needs to be *sufficient* to include all of the tactical things team members need to do to deliver a web product that meets the strategic aims you set in Step 7. And these guidelines need to be appropriate for the type of product you are developing (Step 1), the audiences it is designed for (Step 2), the delivery platforms it supports (Step 9), and the technologies in which you will implement it (Step 12).

Your team also need the guidelines to be able to be used as a stable measure to audit your product against in testing, as we'll discuss in Step 14.

As no set of guidelines could ever predict the future of what web products could be or become, or replace well-researched local, product-specific expertise, where it is available (see Sarah Lewthwaite's interview), you need them to include a sensible *exception process* to handle new situations that their creators hadn't anticipated. Guidelines should never be the end of the discussion; they are its start. They're a gift, not a straitjacket.

To help team members make justifiable decisions, as part of this exception process, they need each guideline to include the sort of cost-benefit information that is needed for all good decisions – in this case, which group of people each guideline helps, by how much, and how many people there are in that group; and how much it is likely to cost to implement the techniques needed to follow the guideline.

To help in deciding on exceptions prompted by lack of resource in the team, you need to know if any of the guidelines are *more important* than others, and so should be prioritized (for example, because they bring greater benefits, or are less costly to implement). Also, you need to know if there are *links and dependencies* between guidelines (for example, if one guideline only solves a user's need if you've already followed another), so if you opt out of one, you might as well opt out of both, as you won't get the value out of following the second guideline without following the first. In many sets of guidelines this information is often provided through the concept of levels of conformance, or segmentation of guidelines into MUSTs, SHOULDs and COULDs.

Finally, your team need a quick way of summarizing the large number of accessibility decisions that they make in their web product accessibility policy.

So guidelines should be *easy to reference*, so your team can quickly state what set of guidelines they've conformed to, and only note down any places where they have diverged from it – what guidelines they didn't follow, and why they considered them to be justifiable exceptions.

Which accessibility guidelines to use to direct your product's creation

So that's what you need – the ideal set of tactical accessibility guidelines for your product. You need to decide which of the sets of tactical accessibility guidelines that are available are the best approximation to that ideal, plan for how to use them most effectively during development, and find ways of enriching them where they aren't ideal (for example: adding a process to confidently deal with any situations where implementing the guidelines doesn't feel reasonable and exceptions may be called for).

The obvious key source for these tactical accessibility guidelines is the Web Content Accessibility Guidelines – WCAG 2.0 – from the W3C, which have now been ratified as international standard ISO/IEC 40500:2012.[159]

While WCAG 2.0 isn't perfect, it's a massive achievement and gift to accessible web development, as it encompasses most of the checkpoints – or *success criteria*, as it calls them – that are important when you are developing a website. It also provides at least one *implementation technique* for achieving each success criterion, enabling:

- interaction designers to understand how the needs of disabled people should impact how they create information architectures and interaction design wireframes;
- visual designers to understand how the needs of disabled people should impact how they create visual designs;

---

[159] http://www.w3.org/2012/07/wcag2pas-pr.html

- client-side coders to understand how to create accessible, semantic HTML, CSS or Adobe Flash that, when viewed through assistive technologies, meets the needs of disabled people; and
- content creators to understand how the needs of disabled people should impact their creation of text, images, audio and video.

WCAG includes a large number of success criteria that people with each of these job roles can use to check their work for particular issues which impact the accessibility of the product. While the value of WCAG 2.0[160] and its achievability have been questioned,[161] much work has been done globally to establish it as the world's one harmonized technical accessibility standard – it's the most-known accessibility standard in most countries, and has been directly included in legislation such as the EU proposed directive on accessibility of public websites,[162] Canada's province of Ontario AODA,[163] and work going into the refresh of US Section 508.[164]

As such, it's the obvious set of guidelines to *start* with.

However, that's not the *end* of the story. WCAG 2.0 is not the only set of tactical accessibility guidelines available, and – depending on the type of web product you are creating – other guidelines can be useful in modifying or enhancing WCAG to better guide accessibility work on your product.

Interview with Sarah Lewthwaite, Research Associate in Education at King's College London

Jonathan: A lot of people in the world of accessibility are all about standards. So your perspective I believe is crucial, which is why I wanted you to share it. You're looking at accessibility from a much more person-centred perspective. It's more varied, it's a lot more culturally and context-specific, and that really struck a chord with me. You've even said that standards like WCAG might actually be getting in the way of accessibility. Can you tell me more about why you think that is?

Sarah: My perspective on the field comes very much from a sociological disability studies background, which is about critiquing things; it's not necessarily criticizing them, but just looking at strengths and weaknesses and trying to draw out things which might be hidden in any particular discussion.

---

[160] http://www.cs.york.ac.uk/hci/publications/001/index.html
[161] http://openconcept.ca/blog/mgifford/wcag-20-aaa-journey-not-destination
[162] http://www.hassellinclusion.com/2012/12/clear-eu-accessibility-law/
[163] http://openconcept.ca/blog/mgifford/aoda-wcag-20-when-it-matters
[164] http://www.dol.gov/oasam/ocio/ocio-508.htm#.UNeWBnOLKQc

So one of my concerns with WCAG is that a standards perspective can be idealized and static. It gives you one view on a particular terrain and in doing so it can obscure other perspectives. With WCAG you're trying to hit a checklist, so there may be other alternative ways forward which are then difficult to see or pick up because you're focusing on this conformance/compliance issue.

Specifically, I think WCAG as a guideline is one thing, but it's increasingly judicially – legally – enforced, and when that happens, attention comes to hitting this kind of compliance issue head-on. In doing so it means other ways forward are harder to pursue. This matters because I think globally WCAG presents what I would say is a very Western view on what disability is and what accessibility requirements are. As it's increasingly applied globally, there's a question of whether the requirements – WCAG requirements – are actually appropriate to every context across the globe.

Jonathan: Can you give us an example of this?

Sarah: Because of the nature of standards-making, there's always going to be a lag in how they're made. For example, the rise of mobile – particularly in the developing world now often referred to as 'phone-first economies' – has blindsided certain major technical companies. They were expecting the PC to remain the be-all-and-end-all of how people access the internet. So standards have focused on web pages, accessed via browsers, on desktops. Meanwhile, a mobile revolution takes place and mobiles now are very popular across the globe. But for Africa, and the Far East, it has been far more important than I would say it has been to the UK or some Western nations. Standards haven't been able to account for that; they have to be reactive to a certain extent.

Jonathan: So, we've got a set of quite inflexible rules that haven't kept up with the realities of how people increasingly, across the world, want to consume the web. So, in codifying one way of doing accessibility, it may be getting in the way of the purpose of web accessibility, which is about people?

Sarah: That's certainly part of it. I think there's a certain hierarchy of expertise, and WCAG holds that position of power to perhaps the detriment of local expertise, regional expertise or national expertise.

There isn't space within that checklist for other voices – maybe a developer voice or a disabled user's voice, which of course is very important. [It doesn't leave room for] that kind of personal usability testing [which] is where we make knowledge about accessibility.

Whereas, one of the strengths of BS 8878 is the way it draws on more local expertise. The person using the standard can apply themselves and their knowledge, and can engage the knowledge of those around them to create maybe more robust, effective outcomes. It offers a framework that allows people making decisions to develop their expertise, rather than hit a checklist.

Watch the complete video interview with Sarah Lewthwaite at: http://qrs.ly/kk4a6c2

Read Sarah's blogs on Social Media, Disability and Higher Education at: http://slewth.co.uk

Here's a guide to deciding which guidelines you will use to inform your product's development, depending on its product-type, delivery platform and target audiences.

How the type of product should influence your guideline choice

The most common example of a product-type that would benefit from the addition of another set of accessibility guidelines to WCAG 2.0 is 'Rich Internet Applications'. A great many web products these days include complex or transactional interaction, whether they are online banking sites, or online 'Software as a Service' replacements for desktop applications like word processors or webmail portals.

For them, you should consider using WAI-ARIA[165] (often abbreviated to ARIA) terminology, so the increasing number of assistive technologies (and browsers) that support ARIA can give an improved accessible user experience to people using them.

Similarly, as mentioned in Step 12, if the web product you are creating includes any authoring elements – if it's a content management system like Drupal or SharePoint, or even a simple commenting system – you should use the 'Authoring Tool Accessibility Guidelines (ATAG)'.[166] These guidelines advise you: how to make your authoring tool functionality accessible, so that people with disabilities can create web content with it; and how to embed features in the tool that will help authors to make that web content accessible.

Finally, as online games are becoming more and more prevalent, and are a big challenge to make accessible, using specialized game accessibility guidelines[167] rather than WCAG can help game developers to cater for the needs of gamers with disabilities and other impairments.

How the product's technology or platform should influence your guideline choice

If your product includes non-W3C implementation technologies, WCAG 2.0 already covers some of these – like Adobe Flash, for example – through its technique documents.[168] However, some technologies have their own separate guidelines. For example, web products that need to include information in the form of electronic documents, for reasons of security or precision of formatting, will need to use PDF/UA[169] – the universal accessibility standard for PDFs, also known as ISO 14289-1 – to define what accessibility means for PDFs, and provide document authors with a clear means of achieving WCAG 2.0 conformance for PDFs. See my interview with Shannon Kelly for more details.

---

[165] http://www.w3.org/TR/wai-aria/

[166] http://www.w3.org/WAI/intro/atag.php

[167] http://gameaccessibilityguidelines.com/

[168] http://www.w3.org/TR/WCAG20-TECHS/flash.html

[169] http://www.pdfa.org/publication/pdfua-in-a-nutshell/

Interview with Shannon Kelly, Accessibility SME for PDF documents

Jonathan: Why are PDFs important? Why not just use HTML?

Shannon: We know PDF is not going to go away – many organizations are regulated to have a PDF format as their official record for archive. And customers often need these official documents.

If you have tax issues or you want reimbursement for expenses, you have to provide that documentation as PDFs. You can review your bank balance through online portals, but if you are going to get a mortgage or make a major purchase, oftentimes you have got to provide some resources that say, 'Yes, I am financially capable of taking on that loan,' which means they want to see your bank statements. So organizations provide PDFs online.

Jonathan: Do they need to be created in a particular way to be accessible?

Shannon: Yes. But back when I started in 2001/2 there were no real standards. I learnt about the tag structure underneath of a PDF, that's not visible to the naked eye, but is visible to screen readers. I worked with several of the local Lighthouse [International] organizations and brought in non-sighted screen reader users to work out how these documents needed to be structured so that an individual could access that information, have it read back to them and navigate through it, using just their keyboard.

Jonathan: But unfortunately the mechanisms organizations use to create these documents often don't include the tagging they need to be accessible...

Shannon: Yes. Depending on the size of the contract we had with the Federal Government I could be running a team of anywhere from 75 to 100 operators, sitting in a large room, in cubicles, doing nothing but manually manipulating the tags on these documents, to make them accessible. Those documents numbered in the millions of pages. An average page could take us as little as ten minutes, or as much as eight to ten hours, depending on how complex that document is.

Jonathan: So you established that process – rather like I created the BS 8878 process – to enable organizations to achieve consistency. And if those PDFs are company reports that come out annually, then the process can cope with it. But if they are individual personalized statements that go out every month, then you are not going to be able to afford to actually service those disabled customers in that way. Hundreds of people manually tagging documents is just not going to work, is it? That's just not scalable.

Shannon: Absolutely. If you are a major bank with a million customers, even if only 1% of them – which is a very conservative number – had a visual disability, doing the math, you are looking at 40,000 pages every 28 days for that billing cycle. So it simply doesn't scale, you are absolutely right.

Jonathan: Now you've found a means of automating that process so it is easier and cheaper to do. How does your solution do that?

Shannon: There are a lot of automation tools that will allow tags to be applied to a PDF, but just not necessarily the right tags in the right order, and that was the real issue. No matter what solution you look at, it requires a human to be involved in the process.

Even though we now have a multitude of compliance standards – PDF UA format, separate standards associated with the US Section 508 under the ADA Rehabilitation Act, and also WCAG 2.0 – when it comes to usability, you have got to apply common sense.

A human has to be involved no matter whether you are doing it manually or you are considering an automated solution. With the solution that is available today, you essentially get a human to build a template for the structured data – how a document should be read, in what order, and how the elements on a page should react with screen readers – and you apply the accessibility rules to that template.

Once you've created that template, the data that flows through that template – individualized, high volume, often private, clearly structured data, like in notices, tax communications, or bank statements – incorporates those accessibility rules.

It doesn't require operators at a desktop to be manually touching things up. You create one template, then all the data that flows through that template can come out perfectly accessible – properly tagged, compliant to WCAG 2.0 Level AA – at the other end.

Watch the complete video interview with Shannon Kelly at: http://qrs.ly/y94a6c0

Read Shannon's blogs on PDF accessibility at: http://pdfaccessibility.com

It is delivery platforms that have the greatest impact on your choice of tactical accessibility guidelines. And the most obvious, and pressing, case where you need to mould the guidelines that you use to the technologies used in the web product you are creating, is products designed to be 'mobile first' (see Step 9).

The POUR principles at the heart of WCAG 2.0 hold no matter what delivery platform you are creating products for.

WCAG 2.0's four POUR principles

The WCAG guidelines and success criteria are organized around the following four principles, which lay the foundation necessary for anyone to access and use web content. Anyone who wants to use the web must have content that is:

1. Perceivable – information and user interface components must be presentable to users in ways they can perceive (they can't be invisible to all of the user's senses).
2. Operable – user interface components and navigation must be operable. The interface cannot require interaction that a user cannot perform.

3. Understandable – users must be able to understand information and the operation of the user interface.
4. Robust – content must be robust enough that it can be interpreted reliably by a wide variety of user agents, including assistive technologies. Users must be able to access the content as technologies advance. If any of these are not true, users with disabilities will not be able to use the web.

However, WCAG's success criteria are based on the presumption of a desktop computer with mouse and keyboard, and support from browser accessibility settings and assistive technologies.

For mobile websites, differences in mobile device capability (screen size, input devices, sensors and the like) and context of use require some of WCAG 2.0's success criteria to be reinterpreted to be appropriate for mobile sites. This can be aided by using WAI's 'Shared Web Experiences: Barriers Common to Mobile Device Users and People with Disabilities' document,[170] as discussed in Step 9.

For mobile apps, the accessibility guidelines of the operating system (OS) you are developing for are equally, if not more, important than WCAG. Unfortunately you will need to get on top of the different accessibility guidelines for each OS, and then work out how they link back with WCAG 2.0's A, AA and AAA, if you wish to harmonize your guidelines across the delivery platforms you support (including desktop browser), and help to minimize legal risk.

Thankfully, the BBC's Mobile Accessibility Guidelines[171] may provide a way out of this complexity. They include a single set of sensible accessibility checkpoints for mobile websites and apps, with implementation techniques for HTML 5, iOS and Android for each checkpoint. While they don't link these checkpoints with WCAG 2.0 success criteria, it is not particularly hard to do this, as I have done for my clients. They come highly recommended, as do Funka Nu's Mobile Accessibility Guidelines,[172] which are a mix of accessibility and usability guidelines for mobile, based on findings from hundreds of hours of user-testing.

---

[170] http://www.w3.org/WAI/mobile/experiences
[171] http://www.bbc.co.uk/guidelines/futuremedia/accessibility/mobile_access.shtml
[172] http://www.funkanu.com/en/Our-approach/Information-web-and-IT/Rules-and-guidelines/Mobile-accessibility-guidelines/

How the product's target audiences should influence your guideline choice

The final thing that you should take into account when choosing accessibility guidelines is the impact of the specific needs and preferences of the *target audiences* for your product, which you looked at in Steps 3 and 4.

This is important as there can be situations where the assumptions underlying WCAG 2.0 do not hold for your audience. To give an example: WCAG's guidance for making websites accessible for blind people assumes those blind people will be using screen readers to access websites. However, this often doesn't hold for blind children.

In my time as Accessibility Editor and Special Educational Needs Commissioner on BBC Jam, my challenge was to ensure that the e-learning games we were creating to help 5 to 16 year-old children in the UK learn different curriculum subjects were accessible. One essential bit of user research, which ensured that we didn't make the wrong strategic choices in our approach to accessibility, was the finding that no blind child below the age of 8 in the UK was using a screen reader. If we had made our maths games accessible following WCAG 1.0, and required 5 to 7 year-old blind children to use screen readers to play them, most of the challenge in the games would have been in how to learn to use a screen reader. Learning maths skills, in comparison, is much easier. Thankfully, our research found this before we started any work, so we created Adobe Flash-based e-learning games, which used simple keyboard skills, audio soundscapes, and simple text-to-speech directly, rather than through a screen reader.

Similar findings are apparent with the ageing population. WAI-AGE conducted research into the similarities and differences of the needs of disabled people and older people, who increasingly experience multiple minor impairments as they age .They found many similarities in need, and that WCAG 2.0 is useful for making sure that older people can get a similarly good user experience of websites. However, they also found that older people are less confident in their use of accessibility settings in browsers, and in purchasing and installing assistive technologies to help their needs. So they may also benefit from websites that do not require them to have the right assistive technologies to get an accessible user experience. Therefore, if older people feature heavily in your target audiences, you should also consider consulting guidelines that specialize in the needs of older people – notably WAI-AGE's own *Web Accessibility for Older Users: A Literature Review*[173] and the National Institute on Aging (NIA) and National Library of Medicine (NIH/NLM) resource *Making your Website Senior Friendly.*[174]

---

[173] http://www.w3.org/WAI/intro/wai-age-literature
[174] http://www.nia.nih.gov/health/publication/making-your-website-senior-friendly

Interview with Andrew Arch, Leader of WAI-AGE work on the link between accessibility, older people and mobile usage

Jonathan: It still feels like a lot of people, when they think about accessibility, are just thinking about disabled people. The research that you did [on WAI-AGE] was actually much broader than that, about people who are older…

Andrew: I was working with *Vision Australia*, the Australian blindness agency who look after people who acquire visual impairments later in life.

The older you get the more likely you are to have vision problems, as well as the normal degradation of sight with contrast acuity and those types of things that go with it. If you haven't needed reading glasses at school or earlier on, you're going to probably need them by the time you're 50. I have to remember to carry mine with me these days because I get in trouble from my wife if she has to read the menu to me in a restaurant.

Jonathan: It's the one aspect of accessibility that I think everyone can relate to, because it's the one aspect that is there in all of our futures.

Andrew: Yes. And your sight isn't the only thing that deteriorates as you get older. Vision Australia was also looking after a whole lot of other needs. The shop sold all those things like the Oxo appliances because people's dexterity was deteriorating, their strength was declining, they needed larger print…

The European Commission is very, very interested in ageing because in a number of the European countries the proportion of people in the over 65 age group is going up dramatically. They were looking at things like smartphones to keep in touch with the community, being able to do shopping online. All that sort of stuff helps somebody to maintain their independence for longer – it's cheaper for governments to keep people independent for as long as they can, rather than putting them into care.

Jonathan: Older people are one demographic that is actually growing online…

Andrew: Yes. We've got the baby boomers moving into retirement, expecting to continue to use computers. As more and more people travel, the older people who are still home want to stay in touch. My own mother-in-law has been using a computer since just before we came to Europe because her granddaughter was living in London at the time. The family was getting emails and she wanted to be part of it. She went out and bought her computer aged 80.

Jonathan: How easy was it for her to get the technology working for her?

Andrew: Often older people will go to a U3A or local library that runs courses, which most of the time are [run by] volunteers who don't know what you can do to make life easier for people who have impairments. I've been told by people that they've actually got their magnifying glass out to read the computer screen, because they didn't know how to make the fonts bigger. One of the things that we did as part of the WAI-AGE project is to document some of those things so hopefully some of those volunteers could disseminate it.

Jonathan: So what about the rest of the WAI-AGE project?

Andrew: It was based on the idea: 'We know all this stuff about helping those we traditionally refer to as people with disabilities. How much of that applies to older people? Can we just say to accommodate our older people we need to do all the same things? Is there something different that we need to do?' Well, a lot of what the W3C and WCAG have documented applies directly.

Two things that I particularly pick on is that contrast acuity goes down as you get older and the lens also yellows in the eye. That means that older people won't necessarily want black text on white, but once you start using combinations of paler colours they just don't work. The other thing is, that if somebody can show them how to make text a little bit bigger because their sight has declined, it also enables them to click on things a bit better.

What we also found was that usability stuff like consistent navigation and consistent presentation, rather than the technical solutions, made a big difference to them. Most aren't interested in learning how to use a screen reader when they turn 80. They just want to use their computer the way the rest of the family uses it , not to have to use some weird bit of technology.

Jonathan: Our research at the BBC found the same sort of thing – that there was less likelihood of older people using assistive technologies, so you may need to take further steps yourself to cater for their needs if you were creating a product to appeal to them. That's what was in our minds when we created the sections in the BS 8878 process about finding out what you can about the product's audience, so that we can use that information to inform us of their needs as we're going through, rather than make incorrect assumptions.

Andrew: Absolutely. You need the technical underpinning of WCAG because it gives you technical solutions for a lot of things that would otherwise just not work at all. And there's more usability in WCAG 2.0 than there was in WCAG 1.0, which was really, really pleasing. But on top of that, you have to take into account usability.

My personal experience is that usability is more important for people with disabilities than it is for somebody like myself.

Watch the complete video interview with Andrew Arch at: http://qrs.ly/bz4a6bo

Read his great resources on Web Accessibility for Older People at: http://www.w3.org/WAI/older-users/

To summarize, my advice is that you should consider WCAG and any specialist tactical accessibility guidelines that are appropriate for your product, platform/technology, and the audiences for whom you are creating your product. You will find many overlaps, and some contradictions. Where contradictions appear, and the right one to overrule the others isn't clear, or you can't find any respected accessibility guidelines specific to the delivery platform, technology or product-type you're creating, this may be a good time to find an accessibility specialist to advise you.

How to make decisions around conformance and exceptions

Once you've decided on the guidelines you'll use, the next issue you need to decide is how you should approach the idea of conformance to the guidelines. And, if the guidelines you are using include the idea of conformance levels, like WCAG 2.0 does, what level of conformance to the guidelines should you decide to adopt?

To give the obvious example, WCAG 2.0 defines three levels of conformance for success criteria: A (the lowest), AA, and AAA (the highest).[175] These originally approximated to the idea that Level A success criteria were the MUSTs, Level AA were the SHOULDs, and Level AAA were the COULDs. However, over the course of time and people's experience of using WCAG 2.0, most accessibility experts and legislators have slightly moved the goalposts. These days the consensus agrees that Level AA – satisfying all the Level A and Level AA success criteria – are the MUSTs for delivering a reasonable level of technical accessibility; and Level AAA success criteria are COULDs, because the additional benefits of trying to achieve Level AAA are not sufficiently proven[176].

The obvious decision here might seem to be to choose the level of WCAG 2.0 conformance which corresponds to the degree of accessibility you chose at Step 8. Unfortunately, however, the link between technical accessibility, usability and satisfaction, and WCAG 2.0's A, AA and AAA levels is not one-to-one. All three WCAG levels are really different sub-levels of BS 8878's 'technical accessibility' degree of accessibility. Many of WCAG's success criteria address usability issues, especially around the usability of forms. However, WCAG 2.0 only includes 'those guidelines that address (usability) problems particular to people with disabilities', and not all the guidelines necessary 'to make content more usable by all people, including those with disabilities'.[177]

So, if you wish to deliver a user experience that is usable or satisfying for everyone, you will need to add other usability and user-experience guidelines to WCAG 2.0.

The strengths and weaknesses of WCAG 2.0

While WCAG 2.0 isn't everything you need, it does provide a good baseline to work from for tactical accessibility, and the conformance levels it defines quickly give you an understanding of each success criterion's relative importance. You can just pick a conformance level to aim for, which summarizes all of the success criteria at that level and the levels below it. This simplifies documentation of your accessibility decisions, and allows you to easily 'badge' your level of conformance,

---

[175] http://www.w3.org/TR/UNDERSTANDING-WCAG20/conformance.html

[176] http://openconcept.ca/blog/mgifford/wcag-20-aaa-journey-not-destination

[177] http://www.w3.org/TR/UNDERSTANDING-WCAG20/intro.html#introduction-fourprincs-head

which can be useful if you need to prove your accessibility level to regulators or legislators. As mentioned earlier, these are two of the requirements of an ideal set of guidelines – and WCAG 2.0's authors have done much of the thinking for you...

Unfortunately WCAG 2.0 has two deficiencies against those requirements for an ideal set of guidelines, which complicate its value to projects:

1. Limited cost-benefits consideration:
   a) While WCAG 2.0 does give some idea of the *groups* of disabled people who might benefit from each success criterion, the assignment of levels to success criteria does not take into account the *number of people* with that disability (which is useful for assessing its cumulative benefit), nor the relative cost of implementing the techniques to achieve it.
   b) So, for example, the number of people who benefit from captions being provided for video content is huge, and the cost is reasonable; whereas the number of people who benefit from audio-description being added to video is very small, and the cost is large, yet both are set at the same Level A in WCAG 2.0;[178] and none of this essential cost-benefits information is mentioned in the success criteria.
   c) This choice — to only include limited information on the benefits of a success criterion, and no information on its costs, in its documentation — undercuts people's confidence in relying on a success criterion's conformance level to estimate the resource costs of using their implementation techniques or prioritize their accessibility work.
2. Conformance as perfection:
   a) This weakness is exacerbated by WCAG 2.0's definition of conformance as *perfection* in achieving all the success criteria at a given level.[179] Quite sensibly, the creators of WCAG didn't want to require you to understand the links and dependencies between individual success criteria, so they made the success criteria at A, AA and AAA all internally consistent – the things that depend on each other, at every level, are included.
   b) However, this emphasis on needing to achieve all of the success criteria at each level completely misunderstands the realities of web product development. In website development, perfection is not something you strive for; you aim for continuous, pragmatic improvement over versions. Unfortunately, if you need to break this consistency and opt out of a particular success criterion – for example, opting out of the need to include audio-description on all of the video on your video-on-demand site – WCAG 2.0's 'statement of partial conformance'[180] exception process is weak

---

[178] http://www.w3.org/TR/WCAG/#media-equiv

[179] http://www.w3.org/TR/UNDERSTANDING-WCAG20/conformance.html

[180] http://www.w3.org/TR/2008/REC-WCAG20-20081211/#conformance-partial

and unsupportive. It is only defined for third-party content, is rarely understood or respected by organizations that use WCAG 2.0 AA as a legislative battering ram, and does not really provide you with enough advice to make these exception decisions through justifiable reasoning.

c) When you are considering opting out of a success criterion you need to know what the implications of that are – an estimate of the number of people who might have benefited and now won't; and whether opting out will deprive some of the other guidelines that you do follow of the effect they are supposed to have. WCAG's process gives you neither.

Organizations' reaction to the combination of these two weaknesses of WCAG 2.0 is what prompts them to complain that accessibility is a 'ruinous obligation', as they don't feel free to make exceptions when they clearly need them.[181] A more useful reaction has been the creation of additional exception processes like Holland's useful 'comply or explain' principle[182] that sit on top of WCAG 2.0.

I don't believe that it is unreasonable to require organizations to conform with WCAG 2.0 in general – for organizations to educate their staff in how to apply the guidelines to their work (as recommended in the 'Embedding competence and confidence' section of Chapter 4), and require them to do that – even if WCAG is not perfect. You don't throw the baby out with the bathwater.

I do believe, however, that it is unreasonable, when staff have taken time to understand a particular success criterion (its benefits to users, the implications to those users of not following it, and its implementation techniques), to require them to conform to it when the implementation techniques are too difficult or costly to implement in practice on their product. People have a 'gut' for this. They know when something is starting to feel wrong. They know it's wrong to be forced to abandon creating some useful functionality for a product because they can't see how to make it accessible. They know that if they are spending 80% of their time on a feature implementing its accessibility, rather than balancing that time with other quality measures like performance or security, that is unreasonable. The tail should not wag the dog.

So my advice on how to work around WCAG's weaknesses in a robust and justifiable way is:

- Use the WCAG 2.0 variant of my Accessibility Issue Prioritization Matrix (included in the support materials on page x of this book) to give you:

---

[181] http://www.hassellinclusion.com/2013/08/web-accessibility-ruinous-obligation/
[182] http://www.hassellinclusion.com/2012/12/clear-eu-accessibility-law/#owners

- o   estimates for the cost-benefits of each WCAG 2.0 success criterion (calculated from the estimated cost of implementing its techniques, the estimated benefit based on the number of people affected, and the severity of the impact of the success criterion on their ability to use a product); and
- o   information on any dependencies or links between success criteria to inform your exception decision-making.
- Don't get hung up on WCAG conformance levels. Pick AA – it's the level that most people agree on, so it's the most sensible baseline. And, for risk-mitigation reasons, it is the most commonly accepted 'safe answer' for WCAG 2.0 conformance, and should keep you out of trouble if people insist on using WCAG 2.0's levels as a blunt instrument against you. Then add success criteria from other sets of guidelines that are needed for your product. And give yourself permission to subtract guidelines during your development where the exception is justifiable. Document this baseline and exceptions, and spend less time defending your sensible, pragmatic exception decisions, and more time concentrating on the more important issue, which is, can all your target audiences actually use your website?

Used in this way, you get the benefit of all the great thought that went into WCAG 2.0, and you are also allowed to think for yourself – informed by my WCAG 2.0 Accessibility Issue Prioritization Matrix, your own local experience, and the research and decisions you've made earlier in BS 8878's process – when your product's needs are at variance with a success criterion.

If you need more support for justifying this sensible course of action, see my popular blog 'The future of WCAG – maximizing its strengths not its weaknesses'[183] for a fuller discussion of these issues.

Using your product's tactical accessibility guidelines for planning accessibility

Now you've established which tactical accessibility guidelines are appropriate for use on your product's development, and have established a baseline of WCAG 2.0 AA conformance, and a sensible attitude to exceptions, you can start to use them.

Accessibility guidelines are regularly used by many of the people on product development teams to guide their work. However, one role that often gets missed out is the project manager, who is responsible for planning the use of resources across the project. The project manager needs to know how to plan accessibility work across the length of the project for the activities of the different people working on a project to come together to deliver a product that achieves its accessibility goals.

---

[183] http://www.hassellinclusion.com/2013/01/wcag-future/

Thankfully, the project manager has as much to gain from using accessibility guidelines as every other member of the team. Used well, they help you to:

- break down your accessibility aims for the product into the decisions you need to make to uphold those aims on a more granular level; and
- estimate the time needed to deliver accessibility on each aspect of the project.

I'm going to assume that your organization – like most of the rest of the web industry – will be using some form of agile or Scrum methodology to project manage your product's development. So I'm going to use the language of 'product backlogs', 'user stories', 'story points', and 'sprints' here. For those who aren't using Scrum yet, the definition of all these terms, along with why agile makes sense for web project management, can be found in Wikipedia's article on 'Scrum (software development)'.[184]

From an agile project planning perspective, accessibility guidelines break down into two distinct groups:

1. A lot of quality guidelines, requiring you to embed accessibility *as a testable quality onto each existing feature's card* in your product backlog, documented in something like JIRA[185] or Trello[186], and providing implementation techniques and success criteria against which you can test that quality (e.g. implementing designs with the right semantics, so headings are enclosed in heading tags, rather than just marked as bold).
2. A few functionality guidelines, requiring you to add *accessibility-specific feature cards* into your product backlog (e.g. including captions or audio-description functionality in a media player, or including a 'style switcher' tool to enable the user to change the colours of your site to their preferred style).

So you should look through the accessibility guidelines you've selected as appropriate for your product and keep them in mind when you are doing your initial project planning.

Make sure that your scheduling of the implementation of each existing feature uses the accessibility guidelines:

- to help you define what *accessibility* success for the feature means (necessary for your unit testing); and
- to help your team members estimate *how long it will take* them to deliver the feature with the level of accessibility quality required by

---

[184] http://en.wikipedia.org/wiki/Scrum_(software_development)

[185] https://www.atlassian.com/software/jira

[186] https://trello.com

the guideline (alongside other code qualities like performance, robustness or security, or design qualities like simplicity, usability or aesthetics).

And make sure that you schedule the implementation of any accessibility-specific features you need to include to meet the requirements of the guidelines.

Doing this ensures the 'development overhead' for implementing accessibility is embedded throughout your product backlog, rather than 'tacked on' at the end of your development project as an 'after the fact' remediation exercise in fixing accessibility defects you could have avoided creating in the first place. This ensures accessibility isn't forgotten, and is an efficient way of including accessibility across the development, testing and fixing parts of your project.

Using your product's tactical accessibility guidelines for implementing accessibility

Applying the guidelines in your development of product features is relatively straightforward if you have broken down WCAG 2.0's success criteria (and any other guidelines you've added to them) by job role, as I suggested in Chapter 4's section on 'competence and confidence'. With this done, each team member should have a short list of success criteria to watch out for. They should apply a criterion's implementation technique whenever they create a new element of design, content or code that it applies to, or check that the technique is already implemented in elements they are selecting, modifying and incorporating from code libraries or style guides.

If it's easy to implement the implementation technique as specified, then your team should do so. If it isn't as easy as they estimated in the planning process, and continuing to work to apply the implementation technique successfully will cause delays in delivery of features or increase in resource costs, they should do the necessary cost-benefits analysis required to make an informed exception request (see previous section). The project manager and product manager should review the exception request and decide if the project sprint planning can flex to accommodate the extra resource or time needed, or whether to accept the exception and downgrade the accessibility of the element (see next section).

While the quality assurance team may test the accessibility of the elements impacted by each team member's accessibility decisions at a later stage (see next step), it should be each team member's responsibility to *check their own work* on a product, to ensure it conforms with each success criterion for their job role, before passing it on to other members of the team to progress through development:

- Interaction designers should check the accessibility of the information structure in their wireframes, before passing them on to visual designers.
- Visual designers should check the accessibility of their use of colour, typography and images when adding the 'style and look' to the wireframe, before they pass their design comps to client-side coders.
- Coders should check the accessibility of their code – that they've coded the semantics of the design as well as the look of it, provided flexibility for text resizing etc. – before passing it on to content authors.
- Content authors should fill the code templates with accessible content written in simple language, including alt-text etc.

Monitoring and documenting accessibility delivery during the project

Once you've set your plan to deliver the degree of accessibility you are aiming for, you need to monitor your team's progress against that delivery as the project's development progresses. For this purpose the documentation of each development decision is critical for exposing the costs and risks in making justifiable exception decisions.

Often, due to conflicting product requirements, in terms of time, resources or prioritization, a team can't do everything. Sometimes, the work you do to make something accessible doesn't deliver the accessibility you aimed for when you test it (see the next step for how you do that testing), and there's not enough time in the schedule to fix it. Other times, the project may get behind in its implementation, creating pressure to make decisions to downgrade the accessibility aims of some product features to catch up. Where exception requests claim this is needed, the understanding of which of the product's user goals are core and which are non-core can aid your prioritization – do what you can to protect the delivery of accessible core user goals, and take resource from delivering the accessibility of non-core user goals if you need it.

Whatever the reasoning behind exception requests, it is essential for your accessibility decision documentation at this step in the process to give two groups of people the information they need to make informed decisions:

1. The *product and project managers* need to be able to quickly review the cumulative impact of each development decision made, on the benefits, cost and risk profile of the product.
   o They also need to be able to see any relationships between decisions – how one decision has prompted others, or where a request is being made that undercuts previous decisions (for example, where a project has already created or procured a

media player that can play captioned video, but then a decision is made to not caption any of the video being delivered by the project).
o This will enable them to make informed decisions, in the context of the impact of previous decisions, as well as the fit with the accessibility goals of the product. There is a trade-off between denying or accepting the exception request, and therefore either:
  – accepting the resource cost of requiring the implementation of an accessibility implementation technique, or
  – saving the resource cost and incurring the accessibility risk that comes from not implementing the implementation technique,.
o They need some form of dashboard to be able to quickly review how each decision impacts the whole project's level of cost, benefits and accessibility risk, as this is the key way of assessing the justification of each decision, and tracking the accessibility profile of the product as it develops.
2. Other *team members* need to be able to access the detail of strategic research and decisions made in previous steps to provide firm grounding for their exception requests.

Your ideal accessibility documentation management system should support both of these needs, with some form of dashboard showing:

- current levels of accessibility benefit, cost and risk;
- high-level summaries of how many exception decisions are being made, where they're being made, and what sort of decisions they are;
- notifications of key decisions that have most impacted the accessibility profile of the product; and
- a mechanism for allowing the whole team to drill down into detail where they wish to take a better look.

The system needs to be available wherever decisions are made. And it needs to be lightweight so it doesn't take long to document exception decisions once they are made to minimize this overhead on the project's progress.

Ideally, your documentation for accessibility decisions at Steps 13 to 15 should be integrated into the documentation system for other decisions in the rest of the project. This will allow accessibility decisions for one particular aspect of the product to be taken in the context of all the other decisions, priorities and pressures on that aspect of the product and the rest of the project.

The higher-level web product accessibility policy document could be part of the same system, or be a separate living document that links to the project documentation system for decisions in Step 13. Either way, the decisions summarized in the document – especially the documentation of exceptions that will result in *accessibility deficiencies* in the final product you deliver – will be a key resource to be used in Step 15. You'll use it for assessing how much accessibility risk you will incur when you launch the product, for creating an accessibility policy to communicate those deficiencies to your users, and for planning for fixing those deficiencies post-launch.

Now it's your turn

To get your development started on the right foot, download the web accessibility development planning template in the book's support materials – details are in the support materials section on page x at the beginning of the book. Use this to guide you in holding a workshop to plan accessibility as a quality of all features, and the addition of any necessary accessibility-specific features. Put this into your project backlog.

Tools to integrate BS 8878-style accessibility decisions into popular agile project management systems like JIRA are currently being investigated. So I'd suggest you sign up for BS 8878 tool updates when downloading the support materials for this book, to keep up to date on tools as they become available.

Interview with Sarah Lewthwaite, Research Associate in Education at King's College London

Sarah: Being able to handle ambiguity is an essential part of being an accessibility expert.

This is where standards can run into difficulty, because there's always going to be ambiguity at the cutting edge of knowledge-making. When you get to the very highest level in any research, it's about how you handle ambiguity at the edge of knowledge. How you're comfortable with that and confident with it and deal with it, still making decisions about which way to go, what to do, whilst knowing that maybe this isn't going to work for everybody.

Maybe it will work for some, maybe it will work for everybody, maybe it will just work for me, but always keeping that 'maybe' in mind.

I think that's an essential part of accessibility practice: recognizing uncertainty and ambiguity and actually embracing it. Which is difficult because it is difficult.

People want things that are easy and scalable, and a court of law where you might say, 'Did this hit the mark or didn't it?' One of the constrictions of WCAG is also its strength in the sense that it gives people a very black and white view of what's achievable: what hits the mark, what doesn't hit the mark.

It's a weakness but it's also a strength, and that's why I think it is being picked up internationally; it meets legal frameworks in a very straightforward and matter-of-fact way.

But unless you embrace ambiguity, and work out how to use the guidelines to guide you, not constrain you, you can't guarantee robust, safe, accessibility practices. The further you get into the discipline, the more you understand that you need to create knowledge of the specifics of the audience for accessibility – WCAG can only take you so far. The standards should remind people what they need to do. But they also need to be flexible.

If WCAG is our only route to accessibility, there is a risk it becomes discredited, and that would be far more potentially counterproductive than if we can acknowledge that there might be several routes to an accessible future.

While ambiguity and complexity might seem like things you'd wish to remove from a project, what I've found is, that one of the joys of working in accessibility for a lot of developers is they find it challenging. It forces them to be creative. That's one of the big kicks of working in the area, and is part of what being an expert in any discipline is.

People like challenges. Good things don't have to be simple, as long as you've got a map to guide you. I think that's one of the very interesting and useful parts of what BS 8878 does. It gives people a framework that allows them to negotiate ambiguity – ambiguous, difficult situations. It scaffolds you in to a particular area and gives you a way to work through it. It's structured without being reductionist, without reducing everything to a set of checkpoints.

In my view accessibility should be about visionary people wanting to celebrate the diversity of their audiences in their products, not wanting to reduce that diversity to make product creation easier. I'm interested in what happens when we create products where the differences between the people using the product are considered to be a strength rather than a weakness.

Watch the complete video interview with Sarah Lewthwaite at:
http://qrs.ly/kk4a6c2

Read Sarah's blogs on Social Media, Disability and Higher
Education at: http://slewth.co.uk

Step 14: Assure the product's accessibility through production (testing)

This step is the first thing organizations think of when they wake up to the need to make their products accessible – testing them. More money is spent on accessibility testing than any other aspect of accessibility work. And, unfortunately, because organizations don't often plan their accessibility testing strategically, much of that money is wasted. This step will show you how to minimize your testing spend, and maximize its value to your product.

So now you know the specification of the accessibility that you want the product to support. And you've chosen the tactical accessibility guidelines you'll use to ensure each member of your development team knows what they need to do to ensure each individual aspect of the product they touch is created in a way that minimizes excluding disabled people.

To use an analogy from the motor industry: this is like the specification sheet of a car.

But how do you know if the combined effect of their good intentions will actually result in a product that upholds your accessibility aims – to give your users a technically accessible, usable or satisfying user experience (as you specified in Step 7); one that enables them to successfully complete the tasks that they will come to your product to achieve (as you specified in Step 6).

To continue the analogy, no one buys a car based on reading its specification sheet – you buy it based on a test drive.

So this is where testing comes in.

Putting accessibility into the project's test plan

There's nothing new about this desire to test the product as you are creating it. After all, you're already likely to be doing unit testing, integration testing, QA testing, some form of usability or customer experience testing with users pre-launch; and combinations of all of these with regression testing post-launch. Moreover, you'll have put together a plan specifying which types of testing should be used at which stages of development, to strategically tell you whether the product is developing in the right direction and upholding your quality goals.

The reason you do this multi-stage, multi-methodology testing is because everyone knows that it's essential to find problems with the quality of the product's implementation *as early as possible* in development, to minimize the cost of fixing these problems.

So why, then, do most organizations leave accessibility testing *to the very end* of the project, when it will be most expensive to fix problems, most of which could have been found much earlier? And why do they only use *one accessibility testing methodology* – 'WCAG testing' – when many others are available that are more reliable for evaluating whether or not the product is accessible and usable for disabled users?

To avoid wasting time and money in this way, you should incorporate testing for accessibility into *each* stage of the product's test plan. At each step, you should use the accessibility testing methodology that is most appropriate for the type of product you are creating, at the stage of development you have reached, to maximize testing benefits and minimize costs.

If this extra testing sounds expensive, the good news is that integrating accessibility testing into any test plans you already have, rather than doing it on its own, may make it cheaper than you think. Here's an example of how integrating accessibility and usability testing can pay major dividends:

Interview with Andrew Arch, Assistant Director, Web Policy – Accessibility for the Australian Government Information Management Office

Andrew: The general usability that people talk about is equally important for people with disabilities. 20% of the population has a disability. Have you got 20% of the users that you're doing usability studies with for your new product with a disability? In Japan, by the end of this decade, 35% of the people will be over 65. That means that one-third of your users in Japan included in usability studies should potentially be older people. If your target audience is everybody, which it is for most government information or for banking, when you're building personas to act as truth checkers internally as you go through, people with disabilities and older people need to be part of that mix. And the great thing is, the usability companies that do include people with disabilities find just as many, if not more, usability issues because it's more important for people with disabilities.

Jonathan: Absolutely. That was the lesson I learnt when I took on the job of Head of Usability & Accessibility at the BBC. The great boss who head-hunted me for that position, he and I had exactly the same frame of mind which is that these two things needed to be together.

We had a great user-centred design process that people in the usability, in the user research, in the user-experience field were very, very aware of. Then you had accessibility over here as a very technical thing that was really done by developers. The only place it touched the user-experience people was in things like colour contrast.

I remember the first week in my job being impressed that my team were already advanced enough in their thinking about accessibility that they knew we needed to do user-testing with people with disabilities. On one day I saw user-testing of the new BBC homepage with people who had disabilities, and the next day, saw the same page being tested with people who didn't have disabilities. It was impressive.

But I was also able to look at it critically and say, 'I've worked with dyslexic people a lot, and it seemed that one of the people in the 'non-disabled' testing was dyslexic, even though they hadn't declared that on their recruitment screener – I guess because we didn't ask. And the person with a motor impairment that we'd recruited so we could see how they found using the page using Dragon speech-to-text or using the keyboard only, actually didn't have an impairment that affected them using the mouse at all.' The line between the two testing sessions was pretty arbitrary.

Much of the script for each session was identical, even though different research specialists – in this case one internal and one external supplier – had created each script. We'd booked two labs. Even worse, we'd booked two different presentations of the research findings with the product manager so we wasted his time and didn't allow him to compare results. It was obvious, if we'd joined up the two tests it probably would have cost 60% of the combined costs, and we'd get more benefits too.

Andrew: Two-thirds of the cost and you'd have got the same answers.

Jonathan: Is that thinking part of what you're doing in Australia?

Andrew: We're trying to encourage it.

Jonathan: For me, the cost, the efficiencies just make sense. But there's maybe some reticence from the usability community to take on the accessibility stuff.

Andrew: What's happened that I've noticed, particularly in the three years that I was away, and it's really noticeable now, is that the better usability companies are saying, 'Accessibility is part of our responsibility as well.' They've got pure UX experts and some accessibility experts. But it's where they're working together in teams where we're getting the best results.

Jonathan: I agree. Maturity in a usability company is where they've blended accessibility and usability disciplines. Certainly that was what I experienced at the BBC with our preferred suppliers. We wanted all of our suppliers to be able to do that blend of both.

The first time we did that procurement exercise, we found that there were some usability suppliers who people really liked – the way they conveyed the results of the testing were very compelling, there was a real narrative to it, you could really understand what the issues were – who seemed reticent to take on accessibility, possibly because of the technology...Could I use a screen reader? Would I know how to relate to that person? But the second time we refreshed our roster, all the suppliers were up for it.

Watch the complete video interview with Andrew Arch at: http://qrs.ly/bz4a6bo

Read his great resources on Web Accessibility for Older People at: http://www.w3.org/WAI/older-users/

It shouldn't come as too much of a surprise to hear that it is useful to harmonize accessibility testing with usability testing. For, in BS 8878 terms at least, what you are trying to achieve through your accessibility strategy is to create a product that is *usable to all* of its different audiences. Disabled people are just one audience for usability alongside people who, as some disabled people say with a hint of irony, 'haven't become disabled yet'.

Of course, user-testing is only one testing methodology, and not all of the benefits mentioned in the interview would necessarily have been available if the testing had been done earlier in the development process. However, these sorts of cost savings should at least indicate that it's worth looking closely at different accessibility testing methodologies, and whether they can be incorporated into other 'mainstream' testing methodologies.

A summary of accessibility testing methodologies

There are many ways of testing the accessibility of a web product. And, to continue the analogy from earlier, some are about testing 'the specification sheet' (whether the product has been built in the right way), and others are about 'going for a test drive' (whether the product provides an experience users would want to repeat).

To summarize methodologies in each of these categories:

- 'Specification sheet' tests:
  - o You could test against conformance to the accessibility guidelines you'll have chosen in Step 13, either manually or via software automation.
- 'Going for a test drive' tests:
  - o You could put the product in front of its target users, either face to face in a lab, in the setting in which the product will be most used, or remotely using remote user-testing software, and seeing whether they can complete the user tasks that you specified in Step 6, without any prompting or help.
  - o To save money, you could get accessibility experts to do 'cognitive walkthroughs' of those user tasks acting 'as if' they had the different impairment of your target users, to see if they could uncover any barriers to achieving the definition of success you defined for each user task.
  - o And you could check that the user experience and behaviour of your product is consistent against the set of different browsers and assistive technologies your target audiences may use (as you specified in Step 10).

Each of these methodologies may have different costs, and different strengths and weaknesses for producing reliable, actionable findings. Each may also have a particular point in the development process where they are best used. So let's examine each of the accessibility testing methodologies, and where you should consider including them in your testing plan.

'Specification sheet' tests – manual and automated 'heuristic testing' against tactical accessibility guidelines

'WCAG testing' is the most common current form of accessibility testing. However, you could also test your product to check that it has correctly followed any other guidelines that you have chosen. And, with the right training and tools, members of your team should be performing these tests on their own work, as well as your QA team auditing everyone's work.

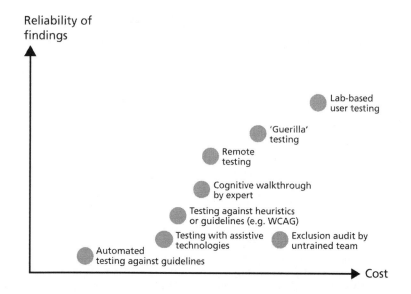

Figure 2 – Estimated cost vs reliability of findings

Here's a guide to where this *heuristic testing* – testing for the presence of issues that are likely to cause barriers for different disabled people to use the page – should be used during your development. At each point, I'll identify:

- what your team members or QA team need to do this testing well;
- what tools are available to help them complete the testing quickly and easily;
- which of the guidelines these tools will help them test;
- where automated tests can produce reliable findings; and
- where extra manual testing is needed.

Accessibility testing of initial wireframes and visual designs

Firstly you should test initial wireframes and visuals against the accessibility guidelines for interaction designers and visual designers in the tactical accessibility guidelines you chose in Step 13. No automated tools exist that can do this for designs. So you should do this manually. And any accessibility defects should be fixed before being implemented in code.

Tools can be useful in making this testing more efficient, for example:

- for checking colour combinations used in visual design, many free colour contrast tools are available, for example, from snook.ca[187] or webaim[188].

Once initial designs are implemented in code, other tools can be used to double-check their accessibility. For example:

- for checking that the order of content is logical on a web page, you could use the free aDesigner tool[189] to visualize the length of time it takes to get to portions of the page when listening via a screen reader;
- for checking that the visual structure of the page does not break when text is resized to 200%, you could use the text-resizing functionality of your browser (see My Web My Way for details of how to access this functionality on different browsers[190]).

Unit and integration testing of code accessibility

During development, iterative unit and integration testing of the code in the product's page templates and components should incorporate testing against the accessibility guidance for client-side developers in your tactical accessibility guidelines. And any accessibility defects should be fixed before content is added to those templates.

Tools can be useful in making this testing more efficient, for example:

- for checking the presence of alt-text, labelling of form controls, accessibility properties set on objects and elements on a web page, you could use the free WAVE toolbar,[191] or automated tools from numerous software vendors[192];
- for checking that a page's mark-up is structured correctly, you could simply use the tab and enter keys to navigate the page as a keyboard user.

You could also test the accessibility of a page template by trying to use it with different assistive technologies. However, to avoid false-positives and true-negatives due to inexperience, I recommend that you do not test with any assistive technologies (especially screen readers, like JAWS), unless you are well experienced in how disabled people who rely on them for access use them. If you are not a screen reader user, but you do

---

[187] http://snook.ca/technical/colour_contrast/colour.html

[188] http://webaim.org/resources/contrastchecker/

[189] http://www.eclipse.org/actf/downloads/tools/aDesigner/

[190] http://www.bbc.co.uk/accessibility/guides/text_larger/browser/

[191] http://wave.webaim.org/toolbar/

[192] Some examples, in no particular order, and with no implied endorsement: http://www.deque.com/products/worldspace/, https://www.ssbbartgroup.com/amp/index.php, http://www.hisoftware.com/products/hisoftware-compliance-sheriff-overview/hisoftware-compliance-sheriff/accessibility-compliance.aspx

need to test a page with one, I recommend using the free NVDA screen reader and Firefox, and following the guidance in Marcho Zehe's useful blog 'How to use NVDA and Firefox to test your web pages for accessibility'[193].

Testing of content accessibility

The content of the product should be tested manually against the accessibility checkpoints for content authors in your tactical accessibility guidelines, and any accessibility defects should be fixed.

Automated tools can be helpful in testing large numbers of pages for some simple content accessibility defects like the absence of alt-text for an image, or a title for a page. However, they cannot check all guidelines – for example, the only way of checking whether the alt-text for an image, or title for a page, is meaningful is to review it manually.

Pre-launch accessibility QA audits

To reduce the legal risk from launching a product without knowledge of how it conforms with the level of accessibility that is most likely to be referenced in any legal case, you should audit the product for conformance to WCAG 2.0 AA before launch.

To gain the greatest legal protection, this testing should be done by an independent (ideally external) expert, who understands WCAG 2.0 AA, and who ideally has not worked on the product up to this point.

The cost of such testing obviously depends on how many pages in the product the expert reviews. To help you make this decision, use the recent WCAG-EM Website Accessibility Conformance Evaluation Methodology[194] to advise you on a justifiable approach for determining how well your website conforms to WCAG.

You should consider fixing any aspects of the product that fail to meet success criteria, or provide justification for why the required fixes are not reasonable to achieve – at all, or before launch – due to other project constraints. Audit reports that include cost-benefits analyses – for example, in the form of an Accessibility Issue Prioritization Matrix (see later in this Step for more details) – will help you to do this in a justifiable way.

WCAG audits will give you a relatively cheap idea of how accessible your product may be to your target audiences, in comparison to user-testing,

---

[193] http://www.marcozehe.de/articles/how-to-use-nvda-and-firefox-to-test-your-web-pages-for-accessibility/
[194] http://www.w3.org/WAI/eval/conformance.html

but are not as reliable. Audits can tell you how well you've followed the specification, but can't tell you how accessible real users will find your product as a 'test drive' will.

'Test drive' tests – testing user journeys with users and experts

Unlike the previous methodologies that test pages against heuristics, 'test drive' tests are based on user tasks.

Task-based testing checks that the product's target users can complete all the tasks that they have come to the product to achieve, using their assistive technology or browser/operating system accessibility settings (if they use them), with reasonable efficiency, and without any external prompting or help.

As this models the actual interactions that people will come to your web product to experience, task-based testing is a more reliable methodology for proving that disabled people can use your product than heuristic testing. To use a road-trip analogy, if heuristic testing checks to make sure you have made all the right turns according to the map to get where you wished to go, user-testing encourages you to look out of the car window to see if you've ended up where you wished to be. While it may be more costly than 'checking the map', it is more reliable because it doesn't rely on the quality of the route in predicting where you should have ended up. It looks directly to see if you actually arrived.

Pre-launch task-based user-testing – user-testing with disabled users, and integrating disabled users into general user-testing

The ideal type of task-based testing is testing with real users.

When you user-test a product with real people with disabilities, there is no simulation, no 'putting yourself in someone else's shoes'. You are working directly with the people who care most about the accessibility of your product, and they will tell you exactly whether they can achieve what they wished to achieve. If not, where the blocks were.

If you are testing solely with disabled users, if may be unclear whether these blocks are to do with 'accessibility' or 'usability'. So that's another reason (to add to those noted in the case study interview earlier in this step) why it's useful to include disabled and older people alongside users with no disabilities in your participants list for task-based user-testing.

Which user groups should you include?

You should consider including representatives of the following groups of disabled and older users in your testing:

- assistive technology users:
    - a blind screen reader user; a vision-impaired screen magnifier user; a low-vision user who uses resized text;
    - a motor-impaired voice-activation user; a motor-impaired switch user.
- non-assistive technology users:
    - a user who is hard of hearing, deafened, or Deaf;
    - a dyslexic user; a user with attention deficit hyperactivity disorder (ADHD) or Asperger's syndrome, a user with a moderate or severe learning difficulty;
    - an older (75+) user.

Of course, this is a default list, which should be modified based on your research in Steps 2 and 3 on which disabled user groups are more or less likely to be in the target audiences for your web product.

For efficiency, much of the difference in user experience that disabled people might experience using different types of assistive technologies *on one particular platform or operating system* is best tested for separately via pre-launch assistive technology difference testing.

However, as there are significant differences in the way assistive technologies function on different platforms and operating systems, you should ensure that you user-test the versions of the product you've created for each of the platforms you chose to support, with the assistive technologies you support on that platform.

BS 8878's *Annex O: A guide to user-testing with disabled and older people* gives more details on how to commission user-testing with people with impairments, or even carry it out yourself.

At what points in the creation of the site or app can you include disabled and older people in user-testing?

It is unlikely that you will be able to include assistive technology users in task-based user-testing of websites or mobile apps in their early stages of development (see my interview with Judith Fellows below), and the costs of including all groups in all rounds of user-testing may be unreasonable.

So I recommend you concentrate on non-assistive technology users at earlier stages of development, and plan to include assistive technology users at later stages, when the product is mature enough for them to meaningfully test.

Interview with Judith Fellowes, Freelance User Researcher, UK (has worked with BBC, HSBC, VISA, Tesco, Sky, Vodafone, Sony Ericsson)

Jonathan: Can you integrate people with access needs in rounds of testing at all points in a project? Or is it more complicated than that?

Judith: There are lots of access needs that you can easily incorporate into all rounds of testing. Where you sometimes might have more difficulty, in testing the early stages of development (where you often test through paper prototyping, or where you've just got a couple of clickable images), is if you have got somebody who is using an access technology which is dependent on having a properly coded interface.

But you can certainly accommodate these users, with a bit of effort. So, for example, most user-tests you might start off with a context interview, and get background on people, and how they like to engage and what they like to do. If you're including screen reader users, or magnification users, you may not be able to get them to have a look at your prototype, but you could start understanding more about how they might want to operate, or how they do operate.

What also works well is getting people to look at others' sites, competitor sites so you can learn from access technology users' opinion of them.

Or you could use the following 'Wizard of Oz' style of testing before you've coded everything up: 'Okay, this is what it looks like, what do you expect to happen?' Then you can build up a pattern of how people would like to work.

There are a lot of different access needs that you could cover, and you're not obviously going to be able to cover them in all rounds of testing. So you might want to make sure that you include people who use access technologies at later stages.

Jonathan: If you actively want to recruit a particular group of people with access needs for some user research you're doing, how should you find them?

Judith: That can be a challenge. The Market Research Society have got a list of recommended recruiters. You can search on their database for recruiters who deal with 'medical' (they don't say disability or access needs, just medical). Some of them actually weren't that helpful. But I did find some recruiters who were quite good.

Jonathan: Or you can try and recruit people with access needs yourself?

Judith: Yes. You can try via social networking direct to individuals. I've found the Deaf UK Jobs website is where all deaf people seem to go for advertising jobs. Just post it on there and you will get people.

I think charities can be helpful to a degree, especially when you can't directly approach people with learning difficulties because they may need someone to support them.

Looking for local groups of disabled people that you can build a relationship with can be more useful than contacting national groups.

You may also get people with access needs in your recruitment when you don't specifically ask for them.

I agree with Leonie Watson who recommends to clients that they should just ask people if they've got an access need in their recruitment, or when they attend research, because I think that can be really valuable.

Watch the complete video interview with Judith Fellowes at: http://qrs.ly/mr4a6bw

Read Judith's blogs on usability and accessibility at: http://mindfulresearch.co.uk/category/blog/

Remote user-testing, cognitive walkthroughs and 'exclusion audits'

If you do not have the time or budget to do full testing of the customer experience with disabled people, you have a couple of less effective, but cheaper, alternatives:

- you could do various forms of *remote user-testing* – testing conducted over the phone or computer, which gets you direct feedback from users in a 'quick and dirty' guerrilla-style;[195]
- you could engage the services of an expert who understands how disabled people use websites and mobile apps to conduct a *cognitive walkthrough*[196] – to go through your product's core user journeys, one step at a time, acting 'as if' they were a person from each of the disabled and older user groups referenced above, noting down any issues or barriers that they consider would hinder that person's progress through the task.

One interesting example of a cognitive walkthrough is the 'exclusion audit' methodology, promoted in the Inclusive Design Toolkit,[197] which is often used to assess the inclusiveness of non-digital products. While it's not perfect, I've had some success using it with product teams with little experience of accessibility. I introduce team members to a set of personas of disabled people; ask each team member to put themselves 'in the shoes' of one of the personas; work with them to break down the core user goals of the product into steps; and assess what barriers they'd find (as that disabled person) at each of those steps. In a couple of hours, this thought experiment gives team members a virtual experience of using the product 'as if' they were one of their disabled users. While the accuracy of the results of this exercise aren't sufficient to prove the accessibility of a product, exclusion audits can be a low cost, highly engaging way of getting team members bought in to considering the accessibility of their product throughout its creation.

When doing exclusion audits for web products, make sure you support the team to understand the added complexity of the technologies that lie between the product you're creating and the user experience your disabled users have. With a non-digital design, in most cases, what you see is what you get – there is no mediating technology between what you create, and the experience the user has of the product. Whereas, for digital technology, there are a huge number of layers between what you create and the experience your audience has – settings in the operating system, settings in the browser, any assistive technology that completely mediates that experience. Moreover, real disabled people have varying levels of awareness that such technologies are there to help them, and varying levels of the ability to purchase them, install them, and learn

---

[195] http://alistapart.com/article/quick-and-dirty-remote-user-testing
[196] http://en.wikipedia.org/wiki/Cognitive_walkthrough
[197] http://www.inclusivedesigntoolkit.com

how to use them with any level of proficiency. This complexity of mediating technologies in the digital space makes it harder for team members to feel confident that they are correctly identifying barriers to disabled people's use of the product with any degree of accuracy, unless they go deeper into understanding the technologies as well as the user's needs before starting.

This is one of the reasons why I recommend that 'exclusion audit'-style cognitive walkthrough testing is used for *educating* team members, but the results of this sort of testing are only *relied* on if the cognitive walkthrough was done by a person who really understands disabled users' needs, and the technologies they use to support those needs.

Interview with Cam Nicholl and Gavin Evans, Digital Accessibility Centre, UK

Jonathan: In 2006, while I was part of the team that created PAS 78, one of the things we were quite aware of at that time was that a lot of expert testing was happening out there, but as people really weren't valuing user-testing with people with disabilities, it wasn't happening quite so much.

We almost wanted to fly the flag for the importance of that at the time, and what we were hoping was that we would set up, not a cottage industry but a proper industry of people who had disabilities who said, 'I may have an impairment that makes using the web difficult for me, I may use assistive technologies and coping strategies to get past that. But actually maybe that can be what I've got to bring. Maybe there are people out there who need that skill that I've got. I am an authentic disabled person saying, 'I can use this or I can't'.

We were hoping that groups of disabled people would band together to say, 'This can be our career, we can be testers.' I don't believe there are very many groups in the world that actually did that, but I'm sitting in one of them now. You have 18 disabled people on your team, and they blitz a product in a day, everyone testing from the particular point of view of the disability they have. You're the guys who set up that service... Why did you do it?

Cam: What drove us to do it is because there were people popping up all over the place saying, 'I'm an expert reviewer and this is right because I say it's right.' There was nobody challenging that, and now our team do challenge that. Yes, we work within the WCAG guidelines. But occasionally we step outside as you heard for yourself this morning. You saw a piece of text that passes WCAG 2.0 that still caused an issue for somebody with diabetic retinopathy. You now are equipped with that knowledge. What you do with it is up to you. You can either say, 'WCAG 2.0 here we come.' Or, 'I'll just tweak it that little extra bit because Gary and other people with the same condition as Gary will benefit.' That's why we did it – to bring a bit of realism to the table.

Gavin: WCAG 2.0 is a good technical standard when you're developing or designing a website, and that's a good starting point. But how does that comes across in the real world for a disabled user or somebody with an access issue…? At the end of the day, why would you use a person that doesn't have that difficulty in testing a website when really a true representation is to have somebody that may be blind or mobility impaired to say, 'Yes that works for me,' or, 'That doesn't.'? Not every single person has the same unique experience, that's true. That's where the guidelines come in, so there is a baseline to say 'that is acceptable' for the majority of users with an impairment. But I think it doesn't cover everyone. We try and provide as much feedback and guidance to clients or organizations as possible to make them aware. To say if they meet the baseline, and also how does it impact on the real person with that disability?

Watch the complete video interview with Cam and Gavin at: http://qrs.ly/8r4a6bu

Read DAC's blogs on accessibility at: http://www.digitalaccessibilitycentre.org/index.php/news

Pre-launch browser and assistive technology difference testing

One final accessibility testing methodology that should be included in your pre-launch plan is testing of the product against the different browsers and assistive technologies you defined in Step 10, by an expert in any differences users would experience in viewing your products across those browsers and assistive technologies.

While different brands exist for speech recognition, screen readers are the main assistive technology that may deliver (sometimes massive) differences in the quality of customer experience of a website or app across different brands and versions.

So it makes sense to test your product with all the screen readers you chose to support, to check that the user-testing results that you achieved with blind people using one screen reader, can be reliably extrapolated to be the case for blind people using other types of screen reader.

This is similar in many ways to browser testing – ensuring that a good user experience is available to all your audiences no matter which of the combinations of browsers and assistive technologies you specified in Step 10 they are using. This is particularly necessary if your web product involves any new or cutting-edge technologies (for example, dynamic/rich internet experiences made accessible through ARIA) that may be supported by different browsers and assistive technologies in different ways.

For more on the impact of different browsers and assistive technologies on the accessibility your users may experience, read the interview with Steve Green in Step 10.

Planning how to choose the right methodologies for your product, budget and deadlines

The project manager, in conjunction with the rest of the team, should discuss and agree where accessibility should be tested in the project's test plan, and which of the methodologies outlined above to use.

Your plan needs to assure you that you are directing the design and development of the product towards the degree of user experience that you are aiming for. Different project budgets will allow teams to do more or fewer rounds of testing, and choose more or less reliable indicators that the product will really deliver what you are aiming for.

Ideally, you should do a number of rounds of testing with users during development – from early 'click-through' testing to gauge customers understanding of the wireframes for progressing through tasks, to testing of the visuals and full interaction as they are added.

Include time for fixes in your project planning

Your development schedule should also include time to *fix* the accessibility problems found in your testing. This seems an obvious point to make, but my experience has found that where accessibility is not a priority for an organization or project team, testing may have been scheduled, but no time is also scheduled to deal with fixing the accessibility problems that the testing uncovers.

Ensuring test schedules can flex alongside changes in the delivery dates of test materials

If planning for how you will assure the product's accessibility alongside its usability, security, resilience and browser/platform independence is essential right from the start, then sticking to the plan during production is equally as important.

One key thing here is the cost of postponing different kinds of testing if the product isn't ready on time. My experience, from managing the BBC's resource of user-testing specialists, is that the ability to accurately estimate the time it will take to develop a product is a rare quality in project teams. Invariably products do not deliver on time, so a user-testing specialist must strive to be flexible about the nature of testing they have scheduled. As it can be expensive to postpone test participants and test lab bookings, development and user-testing teams need to keep in good communication during development. This is to ensure that the value the team wish to get from user-testing is realized, even if they deliver the prototype an hour before testing is scheduled to begin.

How to report test results to aid prioritization of accessibility defect fixes – the Accessibility Issue Prioritization Matrix

Whatever testing methodology you use, it is essential to enable the product team to quickly assess any accessibility defects the testing finds and prioritize fixes on a cost-benefits basis.

Therefore, test results should be reported in two standard ways that enable:

- project management staff to quickly get a *strategic* overview of the number of defects, and their relative importance, based on: an analysis of the benefits of fixing each issue, to the different disabled audiences it affects, and an estimate of the cost of implementing its proposed fix; and
- implementation staff to understand each defect and its impact in more *detail*, and apply the fix suggested.

My experience of reading countless accessibility test reports is that the second of these – the tactical information to help the people who'll actually fix the problem – is usually well covered. However, the essential overview information to enable the results of testing to be quickly and strategically understood, and resources prioritized for fixing, is often poorly done or completely missing, requiring time-poor project management staff to read through hundreds of pages of detail to work out what the test results mean for their project planning.

To rectify this, I created the Accessibility Issue Prioritization Matrix (AIPM) that you already encountered in Step 13. This provides a standard way for testers to communicate the cost-benefits of fixing each issue to product and project managers, to facilitate their discussion of prioritization of fixes with all stakeholders.

The AIPM is a spreadsheet that provides an overview of all issues found in testing, with each line describing the issue found, a unique reference number so it can be easily and precisely referred to in discussions, the solution suggested for fixing it, and values for each of the four key factors that are most useful in prioritizing fixes for accessibility issues that have been found.

The four key factors are:

1. the *extent/frequency of occurrence* of the issue, and the importance of the parts of the product in which the issue occurs:
    * whether the issue occurs in an element which appears: on every page across the whole site or app; on a section navigation page; or on a leaf page;
    * whether the page(s) the element occurs on are part of the product's core user journeys or not;
    * how frequently the issue occurs,
2. the *size of the audiences* that would experience difficulty in using the product because of the issue.
3. the *impact* of the issue on their use of the product:
    * high = a total block to them completing a user journey;
    * medium = they can complete the user journey, but it will be a struggle for them;
    * low = their efficiency or enjoyment of completing the user journey could be improved,
4. the estimated *cost* of fixing the issue.

The AIPM also includes three different cost-benefits measures for fixing the issue, calculated from those four key factors using business intelligence embedded in the spreadsheet:

1. *Value for money* – the number of people affected by the issue multiplied by the impact of how much it affects them (benefits) vs the estimated costs of fixing it.

2. *Political risk aversion* – the political weight (in terms of adverse PR and litigiousness) of the disabled groups affected by the issue multiplied by the impact of how much it affects them (benefits) vs the estimated costs of fixing it.
3. *A blend* of these two measures.

You should choose one of these cost-benefits measures to use based on the motivation for accessibility that you established for your organization back in Chapter 4 (value for money, risk aversion, or both).

You can then use the spreadsheet's reordering function to place the issues in the prioritization order that corresponds to your organization's values, and work through them from the most important to the least important, deciding which fixes you can budget for, and which you cannot.

My AIPM has been so universally useful for all my clients that I have included a version of it for free in the support materials for this book on page x. I would recommend that you review it, together with its documentation and case study, to see whether it would be useful for enabling you to quickly understand and action the prioritization of issues in your project processes. If it's a good fit for you, I'd encourage you to require anyone who does your accessibility testing – whether internal teams or external suppliers – to summarize the issues they find in an AIPM, as well as providing a detailed report.

How to reduce the costs of fixes, where you cannot easily change the code or design

The results of your testing may indicate that there are code problems with your product that will be difficult or expensive to fix. If the product or component is one you procured, so you don't have the ability or competence to make code fixes, then the recent introduction of accessibility remediation tools, such as Deque's Amaze,[198] which create server-side overlays that replace your site's accessibility bugs with stored layers of accessible code, could be the cheapest or only option you have for fixing the problems.

What to do when you can't fix things to please everyone

If the results of your testing indicate that the design, code or content of your evolving product is working for most users but not working for some disabled users, then ideally you should be able to find cost-effective ways of fixing your product to work for those disabled users without negatively impacting the user experience of your non-disabled users.

---

[198] http://www.deque.com/products/amaze/

However, sometimes this isn't possible. A fix that improves the user experience of one disabled user group may damage the user experience of another disabled user group, or the larger number of people with no discernible disability or impairment. In this case – where your testing finds that the ideal of inclusive design isn't possible for your product – the user-personalized approaches discussed in Step 8 are a possible way of getting around these difficulties, if you have the time and money to include them.

Should you launch a product with accessibility deficiencies?

When fixing all the problems, or getting around them using user-personalized approaches, isn't possible, then what should you do? That's the purpose of the next step – working out which accessibility deficiencies you can launch with, and which you can't.

Now it's your turn

Use the web accessibility development planning template to guide you in holding a workshop to plan accessibility testing across the length of your product's development.

Specimen testing plan for BBC Homepage (circa 2008)

Here's a summary of the accessibility testing plan for the redesign of the BBC Homepage in 2007/8. In the case of this key page we conducted:

- initial testing of prototype wireframes of the page with non-disabled people to check their reaction to the idea of being able to rearrange the sections of the page;
- WCAG checkpoint testing for each element of the functionality of the homepage, as it was developed;
- iterative user-testing with disabled and non-disabled people of the complete homepage at the end of every sprint; and
- once that user-testing proved we had delivered a great user experience we did follow-up testing of the page against various different types of screen reader to check that the user-testing results that we achieved with blind people using one screen reader could be extrapolated reliably to be the case for blind people using the other types of screen reader that we supported.

Step 15: Communicate the product's accessibility decisions at launch

By this point in the process you'll have been developing your product for quite some while, and hopefully your iterative testing is finding that most people are not only interested in using your product but they also find it a usable experience. Often the problem is that the product doesn't yet deliver that usable experience to everyone. So the issue is: is it ready to launch?

That's the key decision behind Step 15 of the BS 8878 process: does your product's accessibility need to be perfect for it to be launchable? And if you do decide to launch without perfect accessibility, what are the implications of that?

How good does the accessibility in a 'version 1' product have to be?

The important thing to bear in mind here is that no product is launched which is bug-free. Launch planning is not about perfect products at some vague point in the future, but about having a product that is *good enough* for launch now.

The trick here may be to act like Apple, Facebook, Twitter and many other successful software vendors you can think of: ship early, and then improve your site over time. Check out the version 1 of these and many other successful websites at: 'What the World's Biggest Websites Looked Like at Launch'.[199] I guarantee that you'll be amazed at what is missing from the sites. The thing that makes those giants household names, rather than the hundreds of competitors who failed to win that success, is that question of *when* you should ship. How good does your web product have to be?

That comes down to what's important – what you reckon is the minimum level of quality and functionality for your site to be useful to users and make the right sort of mark against your competitors (assuming you have some). In business talk, if your product demonstrates enough of its unique selling points (USPs) and no more than that, you've achieved your *minimal viable product*, and you should get it out there right now.

If you're too early, your audience may consider it a false start and not bother coming back in the future. Too late, and your audience may have found what they were looking for somewhere else already, so you're now going to have to spend half your time working out how to get them to switch to you.

---

[199] http://mashable.com/2011/12/11/old-web-design/

The important thing here is that while it's you making the judgement of whether you're ready to go, it's your target audience that will decide whether you got it right. They are the people who will make your site successful or not.

So, you will need to consider how good the accessibility of your product needs to be in the definition of your minimal viable product, which depends on how important the disabled groups in your target audiences will be to its success.

For most web products that I have been involved with, the minimal viable product has allowed for launch with some accessibility quality deficiencies, or missing accessibility features, as long as the level of accessibility risk in making this decision is deemed acceptable by the organization's lawyers. You need to make a call on which compromises you're willing to launch with, and which you are not. The only exceptions to this, that I've experienced, are:

- where the product's target audience is primarily made up of disabled people; or
- where it will not be possible to sell the product in key territories unless the product meets a defined accessibility threshold – Section 508 VPATs and selling products into Australia since the 2013 DDA came into force, being the most recent examples of this; and, in the future, Apple and Google may require apps to be accessible for them to include the app in their app stores, if advocates for blind people have their way.[200]

If you do decide to launch without full accessibility, as I believe is inevitable on all but the simplest web product development:

- the decision to launch version 1 with accessibility deficiencies needs to be justifiable;
- the delivery of lacking features or accessibility quality needs to be planned for in subsequent versions; and
- you need to communicate the deficiencies and accessibility fixing roadmap to disabled users via an *accessibility statement* to allow you to manage audience expectations while evolving your product through that roadmap.

This is the reality of modern web product development: most products these days evolve quickly through numerous minor and fewer major versions, whether explicitly via updates through an app store or, less transparently, as tweaks to the website. All features on a product's roadmap and in its backlog are constantly being assigned and reassigned

[200] http://in.reuters.com/article/2014/07/09/apple-mobilephone-accessibility-idINKBN0FE12O20140709

to different product versions. So most product managers wouldn't consider it unreasonable to expect accessibility functionality to follow suit.

Similarly, the usability of websites gets iterated quickly these days through post-launch optimization routines that are designed to test (via ongoing A–B testing, which is now available via Google analytics for free) how small incremental changes to components of a product's user interface impact how many people use your product in the way you would wish. For example, in retail websites, A–B testing focuses on which interface options maximize conversion through the sales funnel. If this is the case for usability, why not accessibility too?

At a more granular level, the accessibility of each item of new content on your website may also be subject to the same decisions about whether to post now or wait for full accessibility quality.

To give an example: if you have live streaming audio of an important news event on your website but do not have the ability to provide captions or a transcript in real time, should you delay publishing that stream until you have the transcript? Or should you publish the stream and place a note next to it saying that captions and transcripts will be available in one day, and if users have any difficulties with that delay they should contact you on your organization's accessibility email address?

Obviously, it would be better to have the full accessible solution available at the time of the news event, so there is full equality of access. But where that is not possible, how many people would actually be helped by holding back the stream until captions and a transcript were available?

This is even more important for news organizations, as one of the main purposes of their websites and mobile apps is likely to be 'to report news items as soon as possible'; this purpose may even be a unique selling point of the organization against their competitors (to always be first with the story, rather than best at telling the story). Where this is the case, the cost to the organization of holding back news coverage for accessibility or any other reason may be too much to accept. This may be the basis for their justification of publishing all news immediately and then enriching it with accessibility cues later in the day (see my editorial blog: 'GLAD vs CNN closed-captions lawsuit: finding a win-win for broadcasters and deaf people'.)[201]

---

[201] http://www.hassellinclusion.com/2012/02/glad-cnn-closed-captions-lawsuit/

Handling trade-offs between accessibility and other values of the product

These trade-offs between accessibility and the product's other values (such as being first to break a story) are things that cannot be found in any tactical accessibility guidelines. They are designed to cover general situations, and be applied to any website. But that doesn't make careful consideration of these trade-offs any less valid and important. This is the reason why I believe that conformance with accessibility guidelines should always be balanced with safeguarding imperatives arising from the purpose of the product and its target audiences – no organization can afford guidelines to dictate conformance if that conformance undermines their product's delivery on its purpose.

Handling these real-world trade-offs is the job of the product manager and the staff maintaining the product. BS 8878 allows them the flexibility to include these imperatives when they are making decisions about accessibility, just as long as they communicate their decisions to the users that will be adversely affected.

So how should you make decisions about any accessibility compromises you are considering for a particular product launch or product version launch?

In essence, the decision is quite simple: do the benefits of being able to launch your product or product version right now outweigh the potential risks of releasing a product with accessibility deficiencies? Is there a way of mitigating those risks by communicating clearly and transparently with the audiences that the accessibility deficiencies may impact?

BS 8878 advises that the best way of mitigating these risks is to provide an accessibility statement, that details the justifiable decisions you've made clearly on your website, or in the documentation of your app in the app store.

What your accessibility statement should include

Accessibility statements have been around for a while. However, most organizations use them in misguided PR attempts to let disabled people know how much work they've done to make their sites accessible. Reading most accessibility statements, you would be forgiven for thinking that the websites on which you find them are paragons of virtue and best practice when it comes to accessibility. However, this is rarely the case. Most accessibility statements generally come over as 'protesting too much', especially where disabled users' experience of the website quickly tells them that the organization does not care about accessibility in the way that their statement portrays.

Thought about more clearly, accessibility statements are tools of *expectation management*. And disabled people's expectations of a web product's accessibility may be different for websites and mobile apps.

As websites, and legislation requiring their accessibility, have existed for a long time, disabled people expect websites to be accessible. So it is likely that the only reason people will visit a website's accessibility statement is because something on the website is not working for them, and they're looking for an explanation. In this situation, the purpose of the statement should be to defuse their frustration. Therefore, basing your accessibility statement around explanations for any *deficiencies* of your product, rather than providing bland statements of conformance with guidelines, makes them much more likely to be useful for disabled users and for upholding your brand reputation. To be effective, the statement needs to be easily found from any page the user visits (for example, through a navigational link that's available on every page).

Mobile apps, however, are still relatively young as a product category, and the link between their accessibility and existing legislation is still being clarified in most countries. So disabled people are used to trying to find out which apps have been designed to be accessible, and which have not. So providing information on the accessibility that you *have* been able to provide in your app in your accessibility statement, and putting it in the app's app store documentation, may be exactly what disabled users are looking for.

How to write an effective accessibility statement

With these insights in mind, BS 8878 recommends that accessibility statements:

- use clear, simple language that the greatest majority of disabled users (including those with learning difficulties) can understand (even if they cannot so easily understand the rest of the site);
- include information on how users can customize their experience of the web product if they are having difficulties using it – either through installing assistive technologies, using browser or operating system accessibility preferences, or accessibility tools on the site itself;
- include information on any accessibility deficiencies the product has, and plans to fix those deficiencies;
- include a contact mechanism for disabled people to use to get help if they still can't find a solution to their difficulties, and suggest that people read WAI's 'Contacting Organizations about Inaccessible Websites'[202] document to make sure their feedback adequately explains the problem they are having, so you can more easily understand and reproduce it.

---

[202] http://www.w3.org/WAI/users/inaccessible

After this information, the statement may include information on how the owners of the website have catered for accessibility in its production, but this should avoid technical terms and jargon.

Finally, the accessibility statement should include the date it was last updated, so that readers can see it is a live document, whose accuracy is reviewed and updated every time a new version of the site is launched.

What is the value of accessibility conformance badges?

Many accessibility testing suppliers offer accessibility conformance badges for products they have audited, to allow organizations to feel more secure about accessibility at launch. However, while the costs of badges are clear, the benefits are harder to assess.

If you are considering paying for a badge, to add to your accessibility statement, consider:

- its value to *you*, the product owners, in providing some sort of external, independent proof and public recognition that your product has achieved a particular level of accessibility – badges from different organizations use different metrics, so, when you're choosing an organization to audit and accredit your site, ask for details on how their audit and badge is going to give you the level of accessibility assurance that you desire (and are willing to pay for);
- its value to *users*, in giving them information on whether the site will support their particular needs – many badges do not do this well, so, when you're choosing an organization to audit and accredit your site, ask what mechanisms they will provide to ensure disabled users understand what the badge means, and how it will allow them to predict whether a site will work for their particular needs.

You can get further information on accessibility conformance badges from my popular blog: '5 things you should know before buying accessibility audit and accreditation services'.[203]

Good examples of accessibility statements

To help you write a best-practice statement, BS 8878 includes a sample accessibility statement in its annexes, and my own accessibility statement[204] on hassellinclusion.com is another good example.

---

[203] http://www.hassellinclusion.com/2013/01/accessibility-accreditation-value/
[204] http://www.hassellinclusion.com/accessibility/

What can happen if you get your communication wrong

It's worth noting that the costs to your organization of neglecting to communicate issues that will affect your disabled users' user experience of your product, or doing your communication poorly, can be more significant than you might initially expect. Here are a few examples from my experience:

- Providing an insufficiently clear explanation of our justifiable reasoning for not providing a completely accessible version of every iPlayer feature resulted in me having to spend a lot of costly time defending the product's accessibility on BBC Radio and TV (see my story in Chapter 2), despite it winning us multiple 'Best Accessibility' awards[205] and being widely recognized as the most accessible video-on-demand service in the UK.
- Depriving your disabled users from having a simple way of feeding back to you their concerns regarding your site's accessibility is likely to raise their existing frustration with your site, and might potentially be a factor in them contacting you through a legal proxy rather than directly.
- Omitting to include instructions to guide disabled users in making that feedback effective is likely to result in costly chains of phone or email correspondence between the user and your customer service team, as they try to get enough information from the user to have a hope of reproducing their difficulty.

Now it's your turn

Create an accessibility statement for your product, based on the advice in this chapter, my popular blog: 'How to write an effective Accessibility Statement',[206] and any deficiencies in the version of your product that you are readying for launch.

> **Interview with Jennison Asuncion, IT Accessibility Consultant, Royal Bank of Canada; now Senior Staff Technical Program Manager, LinkedIn**
>
> **Jennison:** Many companies now have information on accessible features that they have for their business, whether it's a restaurant or whatnot in Ontario.

---

[205] http://www.bbc.co.uk/blogs/legacy/bbc/2009/10/bbc_iplayer_gets_more_audio_de.html
[206] http://www.hassellinclusion.com/2012/05/write-accessibility-statement/

I'm not going to claim to be an expert about the Accessibility for Ontarians with Disabilities Act. But what I will say is that part of what that Act obligates businesses to do is to have plans and information on how their services are accessible.To provide that and make that 'accessible'.

So what I've seen is people will put that stuff up on their website and they'll say, 'Here's information on our accessibility plan.'

Well, I Jennison, who's blind, will download what I think is going to be a useful file. I open it up and it's an inaccessible, untagged PDF. So I shake my head and go, 'What's the point?'

Jonathan: Half-baked implementation is a real own-goal.

Jennison: Continuing the example I mentioned before – of the Canadian travel site with the inaccessible final transition step – through LinkedIn, I found the name of the person who directs the web platform. I remember sending an email to them and also sending a note to their customer service team. A polite note, because as a person with a disability, if I'm going to express or file an issue around accessibility, like anything else, if you want a positive response back...

I just take the perspective of being respectful and factual. There's no point in going to them and saying, 'I can't believe you're excluding me as a blind person.' That doesn't serve anything.

So I went to them and told them, 'I'm a customer of yours and wanted to try the new airline. Unfortunately, when I got to this step, because of my disability...' I explained I wasn't able to solve the CAPTCHA etc. 'I'd like to be able to use your site again. Do you have any plans to deal with this?'

I got an email two days later. It took a little bit of time, because as we all know, as much as we'd like to put fixes into production yesterday, that's not the way things work. You need to schedule things, talk to the product manager, explain to them what the problem is. They need to size the effort, find developers and resources for testing, schedule...

I think that's what gives me an interesting perspective, because, separate and apart from being a consumer with a disability, as I'm working in the accessibility field I have that other insight. I'm actually seeing how challenging it can be to even put in a small fix. So they responded to me and then over time, once they put the fix in, they reached out to me. They said, 'Could you check it out for us?' It was great.

Jonathan: It's great that you were able to reach them. But shouldn't it have been easier?

Jennison: Thank goodness for LinkedIn.

Jonathan: BS 8878 would say you should provide an easy mechanism for people to feed back. It's great you were tenacious enough to get your point through. That you were aware enough about the development process to make it appeal to the people you were communicating with. Some of the emails that I got at the BBC were really challenging. Things like, 'Dear BBC, your website is inaccessible. You have 40 days to comply. Yours sincerely, X.' It's like, 'Well, sorry, who are you? What's the specific problem? On what part of the website? What access need do you have?' Thankfully if organizations are following BS 8878, they should get feedback which is like the feedback you would give them, because they asked for it correctly. Rather than the sort of...

Jennison: ...caustic?

Jonathan: I actually found that most people are generous, but they're also aware that they're likely not to be listened to. So invariably we would have people misquoting massive statistics at us, and making assumptions. They're scared that if it's just them, no one's going to pay any attention.

So they say, 'Your site is inaccessible. Not just to me; it's inaccessible to everybody with disabilities. You've got to sort this out now.'

It brings in a level of exaggeration, which isn't helpful. BS 8878's line is that if you can enable disabled people to be clear about their particular disability, the assistive technologies they're using, and their problem, they can rely on it being handled well, as the organization is used to making justifiable decisions about the cost-benefits of accessibility...

Jennison: And be aware, when people write those notes, they're coming from total frustration. 'Agh, no assistive technology's ever going to work. I'm never going to be able to use the web.'

Watch the complete video interview with Jennison Asuncion at: http://qrs.ly/rd49k5o

Read about Jennison's Global Accessibility Awareness Day at: http://www.globalaccessibilityawarenessday.org

Part 4 of the RuDDeR: Repeat – making sure a good start doesn't sour over time

The final part of the RuDDeR is often neglected in organizations' thinking about accessibility. Yet it is often where the most accessibility problems occur. I'm talking about what happens after launch, when your 'A team' have moved on to a new project and the maintenance of the product gets given to your 'B team'.

One of the most critical periods of the product's development for upholding the quality of its accessibility is after launch. In a product's history more time elapses after launch than before it, and much of the content on most websites has been created after the launch. So, this part of the RuDDeR is essential to ensure a great start with accessibility doesn't get ruined. Or, conversely, that a poor start gets remedied before too much reputational damage is done.

Part 4 only has one step – Step 16. But it is key, for it effectively sets in motion further iterations of the whole BS 8878 process when new versions of the product are created.

That's why it's called Repeat.

Step 16: Plan to assure accessibility in all post-launch updates to the product (including handling user feedback)

'We've created this product to be accessible. It's up to you now to make sure you don't screw that up.'

That was the first line one of my clients asked me to include in an accessibility maintenance manual I created for him. And the point and the tone are justified. After all the hard work done to make things accessible for launch, sloppy decisions made by content staff, who could easily have got them right, can leave a product's hard-won accessibility victory vulnerable to death by a thousand cuts.

So Step 16 is all about planning to assure accessibility in all post-launch versions and maintenance. These activities can be prompted by two sources:

1. *proactive activities*, that you initiate to freshen or improve your product;
2. *reactive activities*, that are forced on you by changes in the browsers, devices or contexts in which your audiences use your product.

Proactive activities – Upholding accessibility during site maintenance

Let's start with ensuring that the web product's accessibility doesn't degrade through its maintenance. This can be a challenge, because often the people in charge of maintaining a website are not the same people who were in charge of creating it.

So you need to transfer all of the awareness of the need for accessibility, and how to achieve it, from the product creation team to its maintenance team. This is challenging, especially as it may often be the case that the number of people maintaining content on a website or mobile app is many times more than the number of the people on the team who created it. Moreover, for organizations that need to create versions of their products for different territories, one set of site or app templates could be localized, tweaked and reused by many content teams spread all over the world.

You have three options for helping your maintenance team to get things right:

1. to assume that they will get things wrong unless you spend money putting in place continuous accessibility auditing tools to *police bad practice*;

2. to spend that money training your maintenance team in content accessibility, embedding motivation and best practice in the team so *they want to get things right* and are able to do so;
3. to spend that money embedding that best practice in the content management system they will use to maintain and create content, *so they can't get things wrong.*

As the third of these is the most scalable solution, let's start with understanding that.

Embedding accessibility constraints within your content management system

Chances are, your project will have delivered a content management system (CMS) to maintain the product's content, as well as the product itself.

This CMS will ideally embed accessibility best practice by preventing authors from adversely affecting the accessibility coding of page templates by mistake, and requiring them to create accessible content.

The best standards after all are not ones that you have to read but ones that are embedded in tools to such an extent that you cannot but follow them.

So it is with authoring tools and content management systems – the best way of ensuring a web product's continued high level of accessibility is to make sure its content management system automates, requires and facilitates various accessibility cues to be included by content authors. For example, the CMS can:

*   *automatically* mark-up text formatting (like heading, bullets, bold and italics) entered into its rich-text editor with the correct semantics;
*   *require* authors to include alt-text with images, or else the 'add image' widget won't allow the image to be included in a web page;
*   *facilitate* the creation of captions for video, by providing non-mandatory tools that content authors may use to create them efficiently – for example, embedding access to YouTube's ability to automatically create captions from transcripts[207], or Amara's workflows that help you commission people anywhere in the world to create the captions for you cheaply.[208]

The WAI Authoring Tool Accessibility Guidelines (ATAG)[209] are a great resource to help you create the accessibility specification your CMS needs

---

[207] https://support.google.com/youtube/answer/2734799?hl=en-GB
[208] http://amara.org/en/
[209] http://www.w3.org/WAI/intro/atag.php

to have to facilitate content accessibility before and after launch, whether you will be creating it yourself, or procuring it from a supplier.

With such a CMS in place, content staff only need to be trained in how to create and publish content on the site in a way that makes use of all of its accessibility settings and features.

Embedding accessibility constraints within your content authoring teams

If you are not planning to include delivering a CMS as part of the back-end of your web product, you should provide specific accessibility guidelines and training for content authors maintaining the site, so they understand their responsibility easily, without needing to wade through guidance directed at development staff (see the Appendix for a summary of what should be in such guidance).

You should also train your content authors in the justifiable reasoning practices that you've applied while developing the web product. These will help them deal with situations when it may not be possible or reasonable to ensure that each piece of new or edited content is accessible to everyone (see the 'captioning of live streaming' example from the previous step, and the following interview with Brian Kelly).

Interview with Brian Kelly, author of the UK Web Focus Blog and Innovation Advocate based at CETIS, University of Bolton, UK

Brian: When the WCAG guidelines were actually first produced in 1997, we had a view that web resources were just being created by small groups of people. Back then, the web was a scarce resource, and effort could be put into ensuring that all resources created conformed to particular guidelines. Suddenly, there are millions/billions of resources. Now we've got the issue of not scarcity but abundance.

So the guideline which says every individual resource must conform to a particular set of guidelines is not a scalable solution. I think there's the need to acknowledge the things that we can do and the things that we can't do. Things that are appropriate and things that aren't appropriate. So with my mobile phone, every day I'm curating digital resources. I'm taking a photo, I'm uploading it to Flickr, I'm tweeting it. Some of these times I don't think about the accessibility, because it's not really relevant. Or it might be a title but not the full description of the photo I'm taking that means something for me and people who access this who I share it with. But I'm not making it universally accessible for everybody. It's not appropriate to do this.

When I'm writing a blog post, I have a large audience, so I do describe my images, provide alt-tags on my images in my blog posts. Or you may get your word processor out, and you write a paper and it's published. In our sphere, that's likely to be available on the web. So should you have ensured the Word or PDF resource conforms with accessibility guidelines?

So there's eternal processes and decision-making that we are going through, or should be going through. BS 8878 I think has value because it makes those decisions concrete.

Jonathan: That's a really interesting point, because I think one of the biggest challenges for accessibility, and one of the things that I talk about quite a lot, is user-generated content. For video, if I were to take the video that we're recording of us right now and pop it up on YouTube, then whose problem would it be that I've just made YouTube less accessible by doing that than it was previously? It can't be YouTube's responsibility because there's too much going up on there. But if it's my responsibility, why hasn't anyone told me?

Brian: I'm saying that the individual author should just ensure there are some best practices for the creation of digital resources. Those aren't just accessibility best practices.

Privacy issues. You take a photo and publish it on Facebook, and it's an embarrassing photo – should you do this? You see an embarrassing photo of somebody else; should you tag them?

These are the considerations that as an individual we need to think about in our environment as a 'responsible digital citizen'.

Watch the video interview with Brian Kelly at:
http://qrs.ly/4d4a6by

Read Brian's blogs on Accessibility and Web 2.0 at:
http://ukwebfocus.wordpress.com/author/ukwebfocus/

Embedding continuous accessibility audit tools to police bad practice

The types of accessibility error that may be made before launch and in post-launch maintenance are quite different:

- *accessibility errors before launch* are invariably to do with the architectural design and coding of page templates, including navigation, branding, interactive elements like forms and transactional workflows;
- *accessibility errors in post-launch maintenance* are invariably to do with the accessibility of content, such as images, videos or text.

So, the types of testing that are effective differ too:

- *before launch*, task-based user-testing of key pages, page elements and user journeys are the most reliable form of testing to ensure disabled people can use the website.
- *after launch*, accessibility errors introduced through content maintenance – an image missing alt-text or an article missing headings – are likely to be less severe, more localized in impact, and more distributed across the content of the site. For this reason automated accessibility testing, especially for large sites with hundreds of people creating content, can be appropriate. This should be able to identify where any errors have been introduced on a day-by-day basis, highlighting these errors to the product owner in a high-level dashboard view, and automatically generating requests for content owners to fix accessibility errors in the content they have created.

Proactive activities – managing the user experience when making major version updates

New versions of products are created to add new functionality, restructure creaking information hierarchies, respond to changes in the context in which the product is used (see later in this step), or just to 'keep them fresh'. At the BBC, for example, most web products were refreshed into a major new version every 18 months.

Your aim should always be that accessibility quality is upheld or improved when you are creating new versions of a web product. This will help keep your disabled and older users loyal to your product.

However, if you manage this, it is still possible, if you're not careful, that changing the product too often could lose you as many users as it attracts.

One of the qualities that marks out an experienced product manager is how they plan for, and handle, large product updates. For, while product updates always aim to deliver a better product than the previous version, whenever you change a product in any big way there will be a period in which your users may feel uncomfortable as they have to *relearn* how to use your product. You may recall my example of this in Chapter 2.

It is not uncommon for the number of people using your product immediately after its relaunch to go through a dip, as existing users decide whether to go to the bother of relearning how to use your product, and the new users that your redesign aims to reach have yet to establish a relationship with your product that makes them return to it day by day.

I mention this here because, while these new version 'audience dips' are common for most web products and most web audiences, they are most marked for disabled and older people who find learning, and relearning, how to use a website more of a challenge. This 'relearning inertia' is normally useful for website owners – if your website can attract disabled users, and they can learn how to use it, they are much less likely than your other users to switch from your site to your competitor's on a whim. However, when you launch a new version of your site, it may be as easy for them to learn to use another site as it is to relearn your new version.

So, to retain your users' loyalty, you need to make sure that you actively support all of your users, especially disabled and older users, in easily relearning how to use your new product. Do this by providing guidance for how they can do what they used to do in the old version, and any new things that they can now do that they couldn't before. You also need to make sure you don't change the page structure or navigation of your site or app too often, as changes that might be obvious for sighted users who are confident in the use of technology may not be as easy to handle for disabled and older users (as Jennison Asuncion highlights in our interview).

Finally, when you update a major version, make sure that your product's accessibility policy and statement are updated, detailing any existing accessibility deficiencies fixed, and any deficiencies introduced in any of the new features. An out-of-date statement is rarely any use to anyone, which is why accessibility statements should include a 'last updated' date.

Interview with Jennison Asuncion, IT Accessibility Consultant, Royal Bank of Canada; now Senior Staff Technical Program Manager, LinkedIn

Jennison: There's something that keeps me up at night. We have the standards, the WCAG 2.0 AA and 2.0 AAA. We have ARIA specifications that allow for some of the richer internet experiences to be more accessible to people using screen readers. You can make a website completely accessible.

But if Joe or Joanne has older technology and they only go online to check their email, to look up a recipe here and there online, maybe to check on sports scores and they understand those sites.

But then they go to another website, say an e-commerce site that is a fully rich internet experience and it's been coded to be accessible, but they have never experienced that before. They might think that website's totally inaccessible, because they have not been trained on how to use the modern web.

That is something that is a concern to me; that we are doing everything we can as accessibility people to make stuff accessible. But then out there in the main, the average adaptive technology or assistive technology user doesn't know a carousel from a tab panel or a modal window.

All they want to do is to be able to get information. It's not their fault they might have JAWS version 10 or they're using one of the free screen readers that are out there on the market with an earlier version of Firefox. That's all they might be able to afford, or all they might have access to. They might not be comfortable downloading a new version of a browser, because frankly they're comfortable with what they have.

I know there was a survey or some research done that showed people with disabilities... In particular, change is something that a lot of people have challenge with.

So if you can imagine changing them to the latest technology if they've been using something that's worked for them for years.

So learning how to use the actual assistive technology and then learning how to interact with the modern web is a lot to learn, for someone who just wants to be able to, every once in a while, get online to read their email.

Jonathan: One aspect of that learnability that we coded into BS 8878 is the whole issue of websites keeping on improving, keeping on going through versions. We had situations where a website was not only accessible but also we tested it so we were sure it was usable by disabled people.

Jennison: And there is a difference, as you and I both know, between being accessible... You could be completely accessible but it might not be that usable.

Jonathan: Absolutely. But even when you get to there, the idea of how easy it is to learn a website I think goes to what you're talking about. Especially where you have become accustomed to using a website and then you decide to move it from one version to the next.

Jennison: One thing around that – and I think it's very unique to blind and low vision folks in particular. Because as fully seeing people, even if your website changes, if you go to a website and it was one way before and it's another now... Because you can see, you can get a full screen's view. You can eyeball the entire screen quickly and see how everything is laid out.

Whereas a screen reader is very linear. It's left to right, top to bottom. So if things have moved around, like if you've moved a link from the top left to the bottom right, for a sighted person, sure it might take you a second but you'll see.

You'll look down, because of the way your eyes will dart around a screen, you'll see it. But for the average blind person who's going to your site, it may take them a bit of time or they might not even see that the new link is buried somewhere else on the site.

It's almost like if you've rearranged a house. You've decided to move the coffee table to another part of the living room, for example. When I walk in, I'm used to it being on the left-hand side.

You as a sighted person are walking into the room and you see the coffee table has moved. I walk into the room, and if no one else is with me, I'll whack myself right into the coffee table. From then on, I'll know it's there, but it's one of those things I don't think people think about from that perspective. When you're totally blind like myself, you definitely notice.

Jonathan: BS 8878 suggests how to handle that. How you ensure that as a website goes through its versions you provide some help. If you have to move the coffee table, if it's imperative to do that as part of the redesign, then you need to give people a map between how things used to be and how things are.

Jennison: Yes, the learnability is important. I'm not saying people can't change around their sites, because that's important to do; you want to keep things fresh. But as you were saying, Jonathan, to provide even a 'What's new?' link where people can activate that link and there might be some information that says: 'For screen reader users or for assistive technology users or for people with disabilities, just so you know, we've redesigned the site in this way.' Then just put that information there. I bet you that information would be useful to people without disabilities, too.

It's interesting because internally – and I know this because in my previous life helping do large technology implementations in-house in an organization – we spent a lot of time on change management and communication, because we needed people to buy into using that application, whatever it is or was, on day one.

It's interesting that from a customer or e-commerce or just an outside facing thing, we need to have a step in their process when they're doing the enhancements or maintenance releases that is a change management and communications piece.

It's a step in there to say, 'Is there anything we need to communicate?' 'What's new?' first of all, 'How is that going to impact the customers? Do we need to create any change management or communication pieces to go with it?' So maybe three months ahead of time, before those changes go into the website, you might start having little banners or little things that are just saying to people, 'Coming soon, a new website, a new look and feel.' Maybe they can click on a link or activate a link and maybe there's a video or some text there that says, 'This is what we're planning to do.'

Jonathan: For internal facing stuff, you're not going to lose those users. Whereas for your external sites, you may lose your customers.

Watch the complete video interview with Jennison Asuncion at: http://qrs.ly/rd49k5o

Read about Jennison's Global Accessibility Awareness Day at: http://www.globalaccessibilityawarenessday.org

Reactive activities – responding to changes in technology, post-launch

One thing that is often overlooked after launch is that the *context* in which your users use your product changes over time.

It is important to revisit the research steps in your accessibility policy as time goes on to check that the findings are still true. In the same way that your product will go through versions, so will the assistive technologies that disabled people will access it through, and the types of device they use it on.

It is not always the case that disabled people keep up to date with the newest version of the assistive technology that they use (for example, they may not be able to afford to do so). However, it is worth keeping an eye on any new versions of the assistive technologies that you support because, like new browsers or operating systems, new ATs versions may potentially break the existing good user experience of your site because they use a new underlying technology. Or they may simply just have bugs.

While none of these situations are the fault of the product manager, if enough assistive technology users upgrade to the new version and it doesn't work well with your web product, then you may have to make a difficult decision – whether or not to divert team resources from delivering your product's roadmap of updates to re-establish the good user experience people used to have, with the new AT version.

While having to deal with such unplanned sources of work may be frustrating, they are a common factor of web product development. Dealing with new assistive technology updates is not much more onerous than having to deal with new versions of browsers, operating systems or plug-ins when they are released.

Reactive activities – responding to accessibility feedback

Finally, make sure that all audience feedback about the web product's accessibility, which is likely to come through your organization's accessibility email address (or some other accessibility communication channels specified in your product's accessibility statement), is consistently handled well.

As I often say to my clients: 'all feedback is a gift...that might blow up in your face if you don't treat it correctly'. Each accessibility lawsuit started out with an accessibility complaint from a user about an accessibility deficiency of a web product. If complaints are handled correctly from the start it's likely that most potential legal threats can be avoided.

So how should you correctly deal with accessibility feedback from your users?

Well, firstly you need to check whether the feedback is a comment or a complaint.

If it's a comment, you should send a standardized response thanking the user for their feedback, and keep the comment in your log, as it may just help you work out how to improve the product, when you're planning the next version.

If it is a complaint, you need to be able to get to the bottom of the issue as quickly and efficiently as possible. So it is essential to:

- understand what the problem is; and

- verify whether the problem has been caused by an accessibility deficiency in your web product or is due to user error.

This is why BS 8878 recommends that sites include advice on how to make a complaint about accessibility in their site's accessibility statement via a link to WAI's 'Contacting Organizations about Inaccessible Websites' (see Step 15). This document advises disabled people on the information they need to provide to website owners:

- what type of disability they have;
- what assistive technology, browser and operating system they are using;
- what page or pages they experienced the problem on;
- what exactly the problem is; and
- how serious they regard it to be.

This information will give you a chance of understanding and replicating the problem the user is having, as long as your help centre and support staff know who on your maintenance team to pass the call to, and that person has some expertise in understanding how disabled people use the web, and has the assistive technologies available that the person is using.

However, for most organizations it does not make sense to train maintenance staff to become experts in using assistive technologies, just so that they can replicate and investigate accessibility problems users report concerning your web product. So a second option is for organizations to enter into an arrangement with an accessibility support supplier to provide advice in these circumstances (see the following interview with Cam Nicholl and Gavin Evans).

One final option is to invite the user to demonstrate their problem to you, either by coming to your offices, or you going to the place where they normally use your product. For those product teams that have not been able to afford to do user-testing of their product with disabled people, such a demonstration can be a real eye-opener, and does not require the expense of recruiting or incentivizing disabled people to take part in research.

The only potential negative in dealing with accessibility complaints in this personal way is where you cannot fix the problem because of some technical issue. But even in this case, with the right expectation management from the beginning, you are better placed to explain to the user the justifiable reasons why you cannot fix their problem, and mitigate the accessibility risk caused by not being able to meet their needs.

Now it's your turn

Use the web product accessibility policy template to guide you in planning for how you will maintain the accessibility of your product after launch. Review the content author accessibility guidelines in the Appendix, and work out how to socialize these with the content authors in your organization.

Interview with Cam Nicholl and Gavin Evans, Digital Accessibility Centre, UK

Gavin: We've had some great feedback from our clients, to say that someone has emailed or telephoned in and said that they can now use the product after our testing and remediation work.

Jonathan: It's rare that you get that kind of positive feedback. Most peoples' experience is that the only time they hear from a disabled user is when there is something wrong. You have a new product AccessIN (www.accessin.org) that looks at that whole kind of post-launch angle and handling feedback...

Cam: The idea came because I am not technical, it came through frustration. I was driving down the motorway coming home one day. Something somebody had said to me was bugging me. I thought, 'Wouldn't it be great if there was a button that somebody could push to say, 'I'm having a really bad time, can somebody help me?' When I got back, I asked Gavin, 'Could we create that button and help them on the client's sites?'

That's how the idea was born. AccessIN is a real-time accessibility maintenance and support tool. It's a little button that sits, ideally, in the header of the site. If a user is having a difficulty, they can activate the button. It generates a short form that asks them what was the issue they were having in that particular area? Do they use assistive technology, if they do would they mind telling us which one? They can leave their email address in case they need additional support, or we may need to ask them a question. They click submit and an email is generated; one comes to us and the other one goes through to the client – identical emails.

Gavin: Actually it's not quite just a form. Any screen reader user, Dragon NaturallySpeaking user, voice activation user or keyboard user interacts with the page via the browser document object model or DOM. So any time a person clicks our button, everything is collected from the DOM, and gets sent with the email. That allows us to analyse the mark-up to say whether or not there's an issue with the page itself or whether or not it is a learning issue for the user.

Cam: When we get the email we first of all take a look at what the person's written, the issue they're having. I'll give you an easy example, somebody who's blind cannot navigate around a form. The first thing we do is go out to one of the test team, Carly or Jamie or maybe Ziad and say, 'Can you just see if you can complete this task?'

If they can and it's a user error, with the client's permission. Carly, Jamie or Ziad will go back to the user and say, 'I also am blind, I use this screen reader, if you try using these commands you should be able to complete your task.' That's all the user wants to do – complete their task. If, on the other hand, whoever we asked can't complete the task, we know that there's an issue.

And, because we've got a developer on board, we've got all the tools that we need here [to suggest a solution]. So basically we sell the button complete with anything from 10 plus hours per year of support directly from the team.

Jonathan: I can see two great things about AccessIN. Firstly, BS 8878's Step 15 says you've got to provide that feedback loop. It also says that it would be really good for people to advise the site owner of what information they would need. Your button is a good way of doing that without the user needing to do much work.

The other great thing is the support for the client. I remember at the BBC someone coming through and saying they'd had a problem with iPlayer. One of my team spent a couple of weeks trying to work out what the problem was and it turned out it wasn't due to our product, it wasn't even the user's browser, it was a browser plug-in that turned off pop-ups that wasn't working properly. It took us about two weeks to work that out.

Cam: What does that translate to in monetary terms?

Jonathan: It was considerable expense. And that was analysis by somebody who knew and understood accessibility issues, like one of the members of your team. Most of my clients haven't got that level of understanding. I provide them with some training in what you should do when people send you a complaint, how you should try to reproduce it. I generally resort to telling people, 'This is your big chance to meet a disabled user of your site. Invite them into the building and get them to demonstrate their issue to you there and then.'

Gavin: Our solution's more immediate. It provides 24/7 support straight back to the user, on the client's behalf. The market's responding to it great.

Watch the complete video interview with Cam and Gavin at:http://qrs.ly/8r4a6bu

Read DAC's blogs on accessibility
at:http://www.digitalaccessibilitycentre.org/index.php/news

Chapter 6

EFFECTS – how to measure the effects of your accessibility strategy

> 'Clients do not care about features, benefits or solutions. It is the outcome that matters. Does the outcome help achieve their goal?'[210]

Unless you're an organization with the ability to 'print money', like Google or Facebook, the continued success and prosperity of your accessibility programme will be massively enhanced if you can prove that it provides a reasonable return on investment (ROI) to the organization for which you work or are consulting.

But, unfortunately, the tools we have for proving this ROI are currently letting us down. To illustrate the current situation, let's compare the business case for search engine optimization (SEO) with accessibility, from an ROI perspective.

> If I were an SEO consultant, this is how I would sell my services to clients:
>
> The monetary value to a website of ranking high on a Google search for their most important keywords is very well-established[211].
>
> We can benchmark your current ranking within seconds by just typing your keywords into Google and finding your ranking on screen, right now.
>
> So tell me where you want to rank, and I'll get you there.
>
> I can quite precisely tell you how much it will cost to get you there.
>
> And I can even give you a 'you don't need to pay me unless I can prove I got you there...' because it only takes a matter of seconds to check my proof by just typing your keywords into Google and finding your ranking.

This sort of business case is compelling to many organizations, which is why SEO is such a big industry.

---

[210] https://twitter.com/JayBrokamp/status/451479083268833280
[211] see http://training.seobook.com/google-ranking-value for a start

So compare this with how I would sell my services to clients as an accessibility consultant:

> The monetary value of making your website accessible is still in debate – we have an idea of the number of disabled customers in every country, but figures of their buying power often clash with figures of their relative lack of employment and their age.
>
> We can't benchmark the current number or frequency of disabled people using your site as we currently don't know when a disabled person uses your site. And if you'd like us to benchmark your current level of accessibility, it will take us a couple of days, and cost you...
>
> So tell me how many disabled customers you'd like to reach, and I'll get you there.
>
> The cost of doing this will depend on the purpose of your site, the technology it's built in, how often you maintain it, the size and prior accessibility knowledge of your team, and how you will promote it to disabled people once it's created. This could vary immensely from team to team, and product to product.
>
> I can't give you a 'you don't need to pay me unless I can prove I got you there...' because I have no way of proving how many disabled people are using your site, and even proving the site is now more accessible is going to cost you – the more proof you want, the higher the price.

If you had to choose to prioritize between SEO and accessibility, where would you put your time and money?

This is why accessibility consultants currently have to spend so much time educating their clients on the value of the other business cases for accessibility before starting to create an accessibility strategy for them, as they cannot provide benchmark information to support the 'reach' business case. We want to let our clients know how much they are 'winning' because of their commitment to accessibility, but our current accessibility benchmarking tools are just not up to the job of giving us sufficient reliable proof.

Capturing accessibility ROI

So it's very important that you do everything possible to enumerate and put a value on the benefits that your accessibility programme is creating, as well as capturing its costs.

In the Governance section of Chapter 4 we outlined some of the benefits you can capture, but it's worth reminding ourselves of them here:

- The risk mitigation value of not being sued: the value of the 'accessibility insurance policy'.
- The value of minimizing the cost of handling accessibility complaints after launch: especially where you can compare the costs of making your product accessible (and communicating that accessibility well) against the resource costs of dealing with accessibility complaints the last time you launched a web product (for example, when you deployed a new 'Software as a Service' application to your workforce).
- The PR value of any awards for your web product: either specifically for the accessibility and usability of the product; or for the product in general, where accessibility was an aspect of the product that the awards committee considered in their deliberations.
- The impact of your product's level of accessibility on the value of your brand: this is difficult to quantify, but where you or your audience already do surveys of how your audience feel about your product – either your own customer loyalty surveys on the website itself (like Net Promoter[212]), or through 'rate this app' comments in iTunes/Google Play app stores – you could include and monitor response to questions around the accessibility/inclusiveness of your product.

Counting the reach of accessible websites

The most compelling evidence for accessibility ROI is to count the number of people with impairments who use your product, and the extent of their use of your product's features, over time.

The most compelling case study for the ROI of accessibility that I know of is Tesco's case study of the benefits of their separate Tesco Access website back in 2001.[213] In that case study, as they had created a separate website for disabled people to use – something frowned upon then and hardly ever done now – Tesco was able to count the exact cost and revenue it enjoyed from having created that accessible site.

As inclusively designed sites have taken over from inefficient separate 'accessible sites', it has unfortunately become harder to differentiate the benefits arising from considering disabled people's needs, from benefits arising from more general usability (see, for example, the benefits arising from accessibility experienced by Legal & General Group[214], which are mixed in with general benefits from usability testing and market research into customer behaviour).

---

[212] http://www.netpromoter.com

[213] http://www.w3.org/WAI/bcase/tesco-case-study

[214] http://www.w3.org/WAI/bcase/legal-and-general-case-study

In an age of ubiquitous Google analytics, where product owners are used to being able to count any number of different things about how people are using their web products, and filter them against inferred customer demographics, there has been no way of including disability as one of the demographics that analytics solutions provide for this audience segmentation.

So we've looked for this data wherever we can. We've tried counting the views to the site's accessibility statement. But this is a flawed method of gaining some level of understanding of accessibility ROI. If disabled people only visit your accessibility statement when they find an accessibility defect on your site, counting the number of people who visit that page is actually measuring the number of disabled people who found your site 'inaccessible', not the number of disabled people who used your site. If that is your measure for accessibility ROI, then it will actually go down as your accessibility programme improves the accessibility of the site.

More successful has been counting the usage of the disparate accessibility features like signed, captioned or audio-described video on your site. It's no coincidence that the other published case study for the benefits of accessibility is for video-captioning and transcripts – CNET's 30% increase in SEO referral traffic from Google when they launched an HTML version of their site in 2009 with transcripts[215] Closed captions are a *user preference*, so you can count the number of people who view your videos with them turned on. Although you cannot rely on this figure giving you 'the number of people who are hard of hearing who are using your site', as many people use captions who don't have a hearing difficulty, it's the start of some useful data.

If you also provide the transcript of the captions on the same page as the video (so deaf-blind people can use their Braille displays to access the video's content) then you can use standard SEO tools to count whether this has increased the keyword density on the page and rated it higher for SEO. And you can use this information to partly explain any increase in traffic to those pages that you experience. While it's difficult to run a full scientifically controlled study to see the exact SEO referral impact of putting transcripts on one page, the anecdotal evidence is already compelling.

The CNET case study gives us a clue to the best way ahead for measuring accessibility ROI. Encouraging users to share their preferences with you so that you can monitor their journeys through your site, is the best chance you have of enabling their needs to be considered alongside those of other users in the product manager's understandable preoccupation with web analytics.

---

[215] http://www.w3.org/WAI/bcase/resources.html

What product managers want is to be able to use disability as a demographic filter on top of all the other things their analytics counts for them, such as how many people with a particular preference use a section of the site (so that they can start to understand statistically the most important parts of the product to different types of user).

It would be useful to show, for example, how many people with a particular disability fall out of the web product's conversion funnels and don't complete the key transactions you wish them to achieve on your site (fully purchasing the items in their basket on an e-commerce site, or signing up for a newsletter on a blog). This would allow you to start putting a monetary value on the loss of revenue caused when a particular group of disabled users is not able to complete a transaction due to its lack of accessibility/usability.

How to get disabled users to share their preferences with you

So how do you go about encouraging people with disabilities to share their preference information with you?

The problem is that disabled people are currently not incentivized to give you any information on their impairments.

In some ways disabled users are just like the general population with regard to their privacy online. We all use the same (conscious or unconscious) cost-benefits calculation whenever a site asks us to tell it something about ourselves, or create a login – if there is something in it for me, some sort of benefit, I'll give you my details. For example, Facebook wants you to disclose lots of your personal information and publish it on your page, which it can use to drive advertising to you in increasingly targeted ways (the 'cost' of membership); but you agree to make that bargain because it also allows you to communicate with your friends in ways that would be a lot more time-consuming otherwise (the 'benefit' of membership).

However, while disabled users may enter into that bargain with you regarding many aspects of their preferences and lives, they can be very private about their needs – in data-protection terms their needs are 'sensitive personal information', the highest category of information security.

Many people with disabilities have a history of being discriminated against because of their disability, so they may be reluctant to give out this information to a website if, for example, they are using that website to apply for a job. If they aren't assured that the information will be stored anonymously and only used for their benefit, they won't give it out.

So the data you need is locked behind two requirements for disclosure that you need to carefully handle:

1. enabling the disabled user to understand what's in it for them – how disclosing that information will give them a better user experience of your web product; and
2. enabling the disabled user to understand that you can be trusted to store this information in a way that is anonymous, and that you will only use it to benefit them.

Until recently, accessibility advocates seem to have not been able to get past the second of these requirements, acting as if there is no good reason why a web product should try and work out whether the person using it has any disabilities.

However, I was delighted to see that WebAIM's 2014 screen reader survey asked a couple of very useful questions to screen reader users about this issue[216]:

1. 'How comfortable would you be with allowing websites to detect whether you are using a screen reader?' and
2. 'How comfortable would you be with allowing websites to detect whether you are using a screen reader if doing so resulted in a more accessible experience?'

The results were fascinating:

- 'The vast majority (78.4%) of screen reader users are very or somewhat comfortable with allowing screen reader detection.'
- '86.5% of respondents were very or somewhat comfortable with allowing screen reader detection if it resulted in better accessibility.'

As WebAIM themselves conclude:

'Historically, there has generally been resistance to web technologies that would detect assistive technologies – primarily due to privacy concerns and fear of discrimination. These responses clearly indicate that the vast majority of users are comfortable with revealing their usage of assistive technologies, especially if it results in a more accessible experience'.

This information provides some quantitative support to findings of qualitative research that I did at the BBC – that disabled users might not be as reserved about disclosing their accessibility preference information, or having it detected by websites, as accessibility specialists think.

The subsequent discussion about the WebAIM findings that raged on accessibility blogs and mailing lists still has advocates arguing on both

---

[216] http://webaim.org/projects/screenreadersurvey5/#srdetection

sides. But I think the path ahead should be clear. We should draw out all of the sensible arguments against detecting[217], or asking for, accessibility preference information from users. Then we should work hard to find solutions that solve those issues, so everyone can get the benefits they wish for. Because the prize is worth it.

What analytics information is available today?

While we wait for that to happen, let's look at the one place we already seem comfortable in asking for this information – as part of 'style switchers', which gain information about the user's preferences in order to provide them with a better user experience. These are just one example of the user-personalized 'additional support measures' discussed in Step 8.

These additional support measures are an obvious gift to analytics – you should be able to count the number of people with certain preferences who use your product. The data has been provided directly by the user. So it should be accurate, and they will have given you permission to use it. And yet, most style switchers don't make it easy for this data to be collected, and organizations rarely use it to enrich their analytics. This is one of the reasons why these tools have never been particularly valued by site owners. Most site owners put these tools on their sites because they can. But if you don't count analytics on any aspect of your site's usage, you're saying you don't care enough to check whether or not it's an important part of your site.

This is one of the reasons why it's essential for any accessibility personalization solution you create or procure to include analytics. For example, the personalization tool I created – *restylethis*[218] – includes usage analytics as a core part of its functionality. Just by adding *restylethis* to your website your analytics is immediately enriched with the ability to track some disabled peoples' use of your site, in an anonymous way that they consent to.

'If you build it, then they'll come' – don't forget to promote your accessibility

One final thing is essential for your ROI figures, should you manage to reliably capture them, to show that your accessibility programme is helping you 'win'.

It's something that is still badly understood or researched.

---

[217] google 'screenreader detection 2014' and you'll find at least six, mostly well considered, views at the top of the search results
[218] http://restylethis.com

Yet it's essential for all of your hard work to have been worth it.

I'm talking about promoting the results of your accessibility work to the audiences who need it. And, as an industry, I don't think we're very good at it.

If you make your web product beautifully accessible, it doesn't guarantee you visits or downloads from people in the disabled or older communities. They may become loyal customers if you've made a great user experience for them. But they can't do this unless you find a way of letting them know what you've created for them in the first place.

You need to *market* it to them like you would to any other audience with common interests. But unfortunately, it's still difficult to easily market products to disabled and elderly communities, mostly because the communities are rarely communities; they are often disparate, isolated people.

This is another constraint on ROI which urgently needs attention, as Debra Ruh highlights in our interview.

While few people are publishing useful articles in the field of marketing successfully to disabled people, Michael Janger's drumbeat blogs[219] are a good starting point to highlight some of the issues and directions – they come highly recommended.

> **Interview with Debra Ruh, Director of Ruh Global, USA**
>
> **Jonathan:** A couple of years ago you merged your company TecAccess into SSB Bart Group. You took on the role of the chief marketing officer for them. Handling marketing, communications, all of those sorts of things for one of the largest American accessibility companies. That must have given you a lot of insight into the organizations you were working for, what they thought about accessibility, why it was important for them...

---

[219] http://drumbeatconsulting.com/blog/2012/06/06/marketing-roi-advertising-effectively-to-consumers-with-disabilities/

Debra: It was interesting to take on that role and get engaged not only with multinational corporations and Fortune 500 companies here in the US, but also foreign governments that were trying to implement the UN Convention on the Rights of People With Disabilities, or were thinking about it or ratifying it. I think the marketing of accessibility has maybe been a bit lacking in the past. That people have kind of assumed that the legal imperatives are sufficient for people to just get in line. To me that's always felt like the worst reason for organizations to get into accessibility.

When Target got sued and it went into a class action lawsuit, I got multiple large companies that came to me. I remember one company that I had been courting for years came to me specifically because of it because they said, 'We know we're a target.' The reality in the United States is that large corporations get sued all the time – we are a very litigious society. We put our laws on books and then we pound our laws out by suing each other. It's become very fear based, 'You'd better be compliant, you'd better be accessible or the community of people with disabilities are going to get you.' It's a sort of 'who wants to be a millionaire?' let me pick which corporation I'm going to sue.

But the problem with the fear-based approach is that it creates an 'us against them' thing, and people don't change behaviours because of fear, or if they do it'll be temporary. What's worse is that we, the accessibility community, have often complicated things, and have not always spoken with one voice. So a lot of corporations feel like they do not know what to do and they don't know how to place this community. They're terrified of the disabled community.

Jonathan: That's a reasonable reaction on their part. More recently you left SSB Bart to concentrate on your work at *Ruh Global*. Can you tell me what the main emphasis of that work is?

Debra: It's very important that we look at [accessibility] from an international perspective, it's the only way that we're going to be successful. It's really about marketing, communications and strategy: how do we make sure we're including people with disabilities in every aspect [of our businesses], in the most appropriate way for those people. I believe that this community of people with disabilities, all the stakeholders that are part of it, need to have a better voice, a more active voice, a less silent voice. We need to do a better job of actually documenting consumer behaviour.

The United States, like other countries, is very economics-driven and we will say in the US to corporations, 'There are 54 million Americans and we control $ billions and one in three households are impacted.'

But what we can't prove is that a family that has a person with a disability, like my family – my husband, myself, my daughter (who has a disability) and my son, we're a perfect family for corporations to pursue to buy their hamburgers, their cars, whatever...What we cannot currently prove to corporations is that I will make buying decisions to buy from them as opposed to somebody else because they did or did not include people with disabilities. Because they did or did not make their website accessible. Until we can define that consumer behaviour and get the data out there, even if it's by telling one story at a time, we're going to have a hard time really executing as a community of people with disabilities.

We've got to track that data!

Watch the complete video interview with Debra Ruh at: http://qrs.ly/tq4a6c6

Read Debra's blogs on accessibility and disability at: http://www.ruhglobal.com/category/blog/

Now it's your turn

Use the web product accessibility policy template to guide you in brainstorming how you will promote the accessibility of your web products to the disabled and older communities, and what mechanisms you can embed in your practices and products to capture the ROI of your accessibility programme.

Chapter 7

The future of web accessibility and inclusion

'Welcome to the Gold Rush!'

The importance of web accessibility is growing.

The demand for people who understand how to make web products inclusive to everyone is going up and up – you only have to look on accessible job boards on Twitter[220] or LinkedIn[221] to see the world's top companies advertising large numbers of accessibility-related roles, from accessibility unit testers to strategic accessibility programme managers.

And accessibility is becoming more mainstream – just look at the race between Apple and Google to add more accessibility features, as standard, to their mobile operating systems. Large firms like Facebook, LinkedIn and twitter are now really engaging with accessibility. Google even went to the trouble of inviting 40 experts like myself from all over the world to a global accessibility summit to advise them on the work they're doing to make all of their products consistently accessible.

This demand is also being fuelled by a global move towards inclusion. At least 158 nation states have signed up to the United Nations Convention on the Rights of Persons with Disabilities[222]. This is the first step towards them creating anti-discrimination laws that include access to websites and apps, which creates demand for accessibility guidelines and services so that website creators are able to live up to those laws.

While the creation of WCAG 2.0 was mostly a 'push' from accessibility evangelists to get industry to take web accessibility more seriously, the 'push' is slowly turning into a 'pull', evidenced by a growing clamour for clearer guidelines for handling the accessibility of mobile web and app user experiences. The industry is increasingly buying in to the evangelists' message on the importance of accessibility. But the accessibility community needs to keep up with industry's rate of innovation, or accessibility will continue to lag behind.

---

[220] https://twitter.com/a11yjobs
[221] https://www.linkedin.com/
[222] http://www.un.org/disabilities/documents/maps/enablemap.jpg

As the demand for accessibility grows, we need to train more web and mobile professionals in web accessibility, by embedding it in University curricula[223] and freely available Massive Open Online Courses (MOOCs) like Google's 'Introduction to Web Accessibility' training course[224].

There are signs that the accessibility community is maturing – see my CSUN 14 SlideShare '7 Signs of maturing in accessibility & inclusion',[225] and the creation of the International Association of Accessibility Professionals.[226]

But we also need to make 'doing' accessibility more embedded and more efficient. There is no other way we are going to be able to require more, or all, of our technologies to be accessible.

And make no mistake – this is absolutely necessary. 'Digital by Default' is not just the slogan of the UK Government Digital Service, but the direction in which most businesses are going. So it is imperative for society that we make sure no one is left behind.

'Including your missing 20%' is not just about maximizing the web's potential to make money, it's about ensuring no one is excluded from the future of products and services.

While much of the Western world is still paying lip service to the particular needs of older people in using the web, companies like NTT DoCoMo in Japan are not alone in their far-sighted desire to see 'universal design' become common practice in product design.[227] This needs to happen in advance of us reaching a tipping point in demographics arising from an ageing population.

The clock is ticking...

Including your missing 20%

The web, and computers in general, have done much over the last 20 years to benefit disabled and older people – see my accessibility innovation heroes gallery for some of the people who should be thanked[228].

---

[223] http://www.slideshare.net/sloandr/inclusive-design-and-accessibility-education-at-the-university-of-dundee

[224] https://webaccessibility.withgoogle.com/course

[225] http://www.slideshare.net/jonathanhassell/7-signs-of-maturing-in-accessibility-and-inclusion

[226] http://www.accessibilityassociation.org/content.asp?contentid=1

[227] See: https://www.nttdocomo.co.jp/english/corporate/csr/ud/ and http://accessinghigherground.org/handouts/ephox/G3ict_Ephox_Web_Accessibility_for_Better_Business_Results.pdf

[228] http://www.slideshare.net/jonathanhassell/accessibility-innovation-through-gestural-and-signlanguage-interfaces-32684441

And there are many more interesting technologies coming along that will continue to transform our lives.

Computers are becoming more and more *personal*: from the gesture technologies I've been working with in uKinect[229]; and wearable techs that continually monitor our well-being[230], and place screens closer to our eyes than ever before[231]; to brain–machine interfaces and nano-machines that work around or inside us, integrating technology with our biology[232].

Computers are becoming more and more *pervasive*: our personal devices put the vast power of the cloud at our fingertips, augmenting our personal processing power capabilities as well as our entertainment opportunities; and intelligent web-bots may soon perform tasks for us as increasing numbers of everyday physical objects become more and more networked through 'the internet of things'.[233]

All of these technological marvels have the potential to enable or disable people with impairments; to be a threat to their continued ability to be informed and engaged members of society, or to be the opportunity that they've been hoping for to engage more fully than they'd ever dreamed possible.

The future can be a more enabling place for everyone. It's up to all of us who create the web, whether we're running a multi-million dollar cloud service, or are posting funny photos of our cats, to 'include our missing 20%'. Otherwise, many people will be disabled from living in the same brave new world as the rest of us.

Why embedding web accessibility is critical to our future

Unsurprisingly, my view is that the only way we can handle the growing demand for accessibility is via embedding the sorts of competence in this book in all our organizations. The time has gone when we could get away with web accessibility being an 'add-on' or 'niche'. It cannot be as effective as it needs to be even if it becomes a more appreciated professional ghetto.

No, for us all to ensure we design for our future selves, we must make accessibility a key value at the heart of every web product we create – alongside privacy, security, stability and availability.

---

[229] http://www.slideshare.net/jonathanhassell/accessibility-innovation-through-gestural-and-signlanguage-interfaces-32684441/42

[230] https://www.apple.com/ios/ios8/health/

[231] www.google.com/glass/

[232] http://www.huffingtonpost.com/2013/06/18/mind-uploading-2045-futurists_n_3458961.html

[233] http://en.wikipedia.org/wiki/Internet_of_Things and http://mashable.com/2014/01/13/what-is-nest/

We must make it 'just the way we do things' for each person to play their part, consistently, repeatedly, in making products accessible.

Or else the technology the generation after us create may exclude us too.

Opportunities/threats for the future of accessibility and how BS 8878 helps

That's how I see things.

But I wanted to give the last word to my contributors. So I ended each of my interviews with the contributors to this book with the same question:

'Is there one opportunity or threat to the accessibility of websites, apps and digital products in general, for disabled and older people, that you see coming along?'

This is a brief compilation of the themes from their responses. The full video is available from:

http://qrs.ly/214a6cc

'Concentrate on helping authoring tools embed accessibility'
– Brian Kelly

'For me, I think the future would be that we stop talking about accessibility; it just becomes part of the best practices that we adopt in developing digital resources in order to support their intended purposes. So there's nothing special about it; it becomes part of those processes. Becomes embedded in everything we do. One thing that could really help that would be a focus on authoring tool accessibility, rather than WCAG. If you make one website accessible, you've done something good. If you make an authoring tool or theme accessible, and enable lots of websites to be made accessible, you've done something better.'

'Enable authoring tools to be used by disabled people too'
– Graham Armfield

> 'I'd not only like to see accessibility baked in to WordPress themes and plug-ins so it's easier for people to get accessibility 'for free' when they quickly create new websites, but I'd also like disabled people to be able to create sites as easily as everyone else. I'm a member of the Make WordPress Accessible team who are a group of volunteers who are trying to make the situation better. In the past, one of the frustrating things that would happen is when a new version of WordPress comes out, sometimes the new functionality pushes accessibility backwards, because the people who built it haven't thought about accessibility at all. We're working to ensure that sort of thing doesn't happen in the future.'

'Be careful with using technology naively that has accessibility 'baked in''
– Steve Green

> 'The problem that has been growing, really, I think since 2007/2008 is the increased use of JavaScript libraries. A lot of our accessibility problems now stem from the use of those libraries. Before we had *jQuery* and all the other libraries like it, if you wanted JavaScript you had to write it yourself. So a lot of websites just didn't have that – drop-down menus were as complex as things got. If someone did write some JavaScript themselves, they were generally skilled enough to make it accessible, once we told them there was an accessibility issue. Then, six or seven years ago, all the libraries started to come out, and anybody could throw in all this dynamic content, all the hide-reveal and tabbed interfaces, and light boxes. You didn't need to understand any code at all. You just call a function, pass it some parameters and hey presto, there it is.

> But none of those libraries are accessible out of the box. Even with those that claim to be, there is massive variation from function to function. I keep hearing developers talking about accessibility being 'baked in' to *jQuery* or some other library, as if they don't need to even consider it, it's just going to be accessible. But, unlike 'baking in' accessibility checks into a CMS for content authors, which works great because it's fairly simple, there will always be a certain amount of additional work the developer needs to do to make their usage of a function with accessibility 'baked in' truly accessible. Unfortunately, a lot of people are relying on work done by others, just picking up libraries or code modules, and not really understanding what they do.'

'Require governance and policy or the technology gap will only widen' – Jeff Kline

'The worry is that something that comes along and the accessibility community hasn't really foreseen it, and so we have no solutions to the problem. Suddenly a technology becomes incredibly popular, without there being any way of making it accessible. That's this technology gap that we've talked about a few times. But if you can really drive the technology through governance at the regulatory level and through policy of the different organizations, I think you have a better chance of coming up with technologies that are accessible, because that becomes a primary constraint of the development of the product.'

'Encourage those funding start-ups to care about accessibility' – Jennison Asuncion

'I'd love to see venture capitalists and angel investors start thinking about funding IT start-ups based in part on digital accessibility being a criterion.

A lot of the stuff we're dealing with is coming out of the labs of these amazing start-ups. Where you have brilliant people who are building all this new technology we're going to be consuming now and into the future. There are some that are thinking of accessibility, but there are a lot that are not. I appeal to all of these stakeholders to ask the people who are coming to them for funding whether they're even thinking about people with disabilities when they're building their technologies. I have a feeling accessibility is going to become less and less a priority unless we really, really start thinking about it early and actually put it physically on these agendas as a topic for discussion. I could see BS 8878 becoming a standard that could help organizations worldwide do that.'

'Keep assistive technologies up to speed with technology because 'we'll all need them one day' – Cam Nicholl and Gavin Evans

'We're constrained by the assistive technology keeping up to speed sometimes and also the browser vendors as well. They're obviously trying to do good, to work to ensure they're all interoperable. Because at the end of the day as a person, as a person with a disability or a person without a disability, I don't care whether they're all fighting with each other about whose fault it is, I just want to do what I came to do.

We need to keep this level of attentiveness to accessibility because we're all living longer. In five years, ten years' time the three of us could sit together – I will probably have to use a magnifier, you may not be able to use a mouse. But our expectations don't change. If I did internet banking today, my expectation is that I will do internet banking tomorrow. We need to make sure just out of common courtesy for each other that everybody has got that and not just the majority.'.

'Take assistive technology mainstream through mobile' – Andrew Arch

'The thing that I find exciting is the convergence that's happening in the hardware: in-car devices, talking televisions, you can gesture at your television now. You can talk to your computer with your smartphone… This convergence where assistive technology is becoming mainstream. I think that given a little bit longer we're just going to see this stuff, everybody is going to expect to use it because of their situational disabilities. That's going to make life a whole lot easier for many. Not everyone, but many, many people with disabilities.'

'Ensure copyright laws don't get in the way of accessibility' – Axel Leblois

'The big opportunities are in the mobile platform. I think that a person's mobile will become their universal interface to all sorts of things: fans or the heating system in their homes, the ATM at the bank, maybe watching captions at the cinema. On the negative side I would say that the proliferation of user-generated content that is inaccessible is creating a massive barrier for persons with disabilities. There are still copyright legal issues around the world that are creating invisible barriers. There are many tensions in the legal system that must be addressed.'

'Raise awareness to ensure accessibility doesn't lag behind the technology advance curve' – David Banes

'We need to explain how disabled people access and make use of technology. Awareness raising is key. Teaching 7 year-olds about universal design. What works for disabled people is easier for everyone.

We've found that once people are aware that what they offer can make the difference to lives of people with a disability, and once they realize that 'my actions can have social good', they're quite committed to it.

This is particularly important with technologies changing so quickly. So BS 8878's emphasis on 'actually we don't care which technologies you're using; these processes can be applied to all of them' hopefully should provide a framework at least for preventing accessibility lagging behind the technology advance curve.'

'Make accessibility more easily understood and embedded' – Debra Ruh

'I think the problem is we've made it too complicated. We've made it too, 'Oh let the experts handle this, move back little lady.' The biggest threat is that we continue to do that and create a bigger digital divide. As the accessibility experts and gurus and thought leaders openly fight with each other about this it broadens that digital divide more and more. We need to embed this at the process level and it's really not that complicated to do that. The British Standard is a wonderful example. Just get everybody a copy of that and let's do it. Part of the process...'

Now it's your turn

So those are their thoughts... What do you think?

Are you going to create threats or opportunities to including your missing 20%?

Now that you've read this book, I hope that you wish to join the increasing number of organizations, product creators and accessibility advocates who are working towards a future of more inclusive web products.

This book has aimed to teach you the theory behind setting up an accessibility strategy for the products you're creating, in the organizations you're creating them.

I hope you now feel motivated, empowered, competent and confident that you can start doing that.

I'd encourage you to resolve to become a master at implementing that theory, like some of the people I've interviewed for this book. Seek out opportunities to implement BS 8878 across many different projects (and organizations, if you're inclined towards consultancy). Seek out mentoring from people who have been there before you, in how to deal with the specific challenges of each project, product and organization. And keep up to date with these accessibility thought leaders, as the nature of the web is that there's always something new happening, and accessibility is no different from that.

Accessibility is a journey.

Thanks for coming with me a few more steps along that path.

Here's to your next steps!

Get help for the rest of your journey from:

http://qrs.ly/3a4a6bm

And please let me know if I can help you further.

Jonathan Hassell
www.hassellinclusion.com

A note on how I wrote this book

I believe that the best way of understanding how someone uses technology is to put myself in their shoes.

So I have written most of this book using Dragon Dictate speech recognition software[234] – the same sort of speech recognition technology that people with motor difficulties and low literacy use to help them enter text into computers.

If you haven't tried speech recognition yourself – and, with Apple's Siri bringing it to the mainstream, many of you may already have – I'd recommend it. You may find it deepens your creativity while enabling you to understand the highs and lows of the alternative interfaces that disabled people use every time they interact with a digital device.

---

[234] http://www.nuance.co.uk/dragon/index.htm

Appendix

Index – ordered by job role

This Appendix notes the key things that people with different job roles need to do to play their part in achieving your organization's accessibility goals.

Annex F of BS 8878 expands this list of responsibilities to cover other departments of the organization: governance, internal communications, external marketing and communication, training, procurement and HR.

Accessibility guidance for information architects

Information architects set strategies that simplify how people navigate and use information across websites and mobile apps. They break down and categorize information in ways that should make sense to the user, allowing the user to understand where to find information on a page or across the site or app.

Information architects need to take into account the needs of all your users, including those with impairments due to ageing or disability, to make sure their work is truly user-centred. Key to this is ensuring that disabled people, like everyone else, are able to understand the words used on the site to structure information into sections – navigation menu headings, page section headings etc.

In this book, I recommend they particularly read:

- the 'Accessibility testing of initial wireframes and visual designs' section of Step 14 in Chapter 5, as this will be their key contribution to a project's accessibility success.

Accessibility guidance for interaction designers

Interaction designers specify the interactive feel and structure of websites and mobile apps, aiming to achieve a balance between users' needs, business goals and technological capabilities.

Interaction designers need to take into account the needs of all your users, including those with impairments due to ageing or disability, to make sure their work is truly user-centred. Key to this is structuring user journeys through the website or mobile app that are easy to follow for all users, and choosing navigational and interaction paradigms and widgets that can be used by all (for example, using 'click and stick' rather than 'drag and drop').

In this book, I recommend they particularly read:

- 'Step 6: Define the user goals and tasks the product needs to provide' and the 'Accessibility testing of initial wireframes and visual designs' section of Step 14 in Chapter 5, as these will be their key contribution to a project's accessibility success.

Accessibility guidance for visual designers

While interaction designers specify the interactive feel and structure of websites and mobile apps, visual designers specify the look of websites and mobile apps, in accordance with your organization's branding and style guides.

Visual designers need to make sure their visuals can be appreciated and understood by all your users, including those with impairments due to ageing or disability. Key to this is the choice of the colour palette for the site – background colours, body text, link text and highlight text colours. The range of shades used to differentiate areas of the page or site from each other should be chosen so that all users are comfortable with them, and other non-colour-based cues should be included to help some users who are unable to differentiate coloured elements from each other. This sort of thinking we call 'inclusive design'.

In this book, I recommend they particularly read:

- the 'Accessibility testing of initial wireframes and visual designs' section of Step 14 in Chapter 5, as this will be their key contribution to a project's accessibility success.

Accessibility guidance for client-side developers

While visual designers specify the look of websites and mobile apps, and interaction designers specify the interactive feel of websites and mobile apps, developers use technical code to create working products that deliver that look and feel across the range of browsers and operating systems the product needs to support. Developers are also in a key position to decide which technologies they will implement that look and feel in.

Developers need to make sure their code reflects the semantics of the interaction design they are given, as well as the required visual design. For example: a button should be coded as a button and then styled to reflect the required visual design, not be coded as a graphic with a link; a heading should be coded as a heading and then styled to reflect the required visual design, not just coded with a div.

In this book, I recommend they particularly read:

- Steps 9 (delivery platform support), 10 (browsers, OSes and assistive technology support), 12 (choice of web technologies) and 13 (choice of tactical guidelines) of Chapter 5, as these will be their key contribution to a project's accessibility *specification*; and
- the 'Unit and integration testing of code accessibility' section of Step 14 and 'Embedding accessibility constraints within your content management system' section of Step 15 in Chapter 5, as these will be their key contribution to the success of a project's accessibility *implementation*.

Accessibility guidance for content authors

While designers and developers create the navigational frame for websites and mobile apps, content authors are responsible for filling that frame with content, often on a day-to-day basis, both before and after launch.

Content authors need to make sure the content they create is understandable to all your users, including those with impairments due to ageing or disability, to achieve your organization's accessibility goals for the product's launch, and maintain it in all content updates after launch.

In this book, I recommend they particularly read:

- the 'Testing of content accessibility' section of Step 14 in Chapter 5, as this will be their key contribution to a project's accessibility success; and
- the 'Upholding accessibility during site maintenance' section of Step 15 in Chapter 5, as this will give them the bigger picture.

Accessibility guidance for quality assurance and usability testers

While the designers, developers and content authors of sites and apps may use WCAG 2.0's success criteria to advise them on how to create each aspect of the product to be accessible, testers need to understand how to test that they have done their work correctly. And they need to be able to test that the combined effect of the whole team's work has resulted in user journeys that can be achieved by the groups of disabled and older users using the assistive technologies, browsers and operating systems defined in your organization's accessibility goals.

QA and usability testers need to know which testing methodologies should be best employed, at which times in a site or app's creation, and how to best integrate testing of a product's accessibility alongside its usability, learnability, functional completeness, stability and security.

In this book, I recommend they particularly read:

- the user research steps (3 and 4) and testing (14) steps of Chapter 5, as these will be their key contribution to a project's accessibility success.

Accessibility guidance for product managers

Product managers need to be able to balance the sometimes competing needs of the product's different users, including disabled and older users, and the business requirements for the product, throughout its conception, specification, development, delivery, maintenance and versioning.

Product managers should have a clear understanding of the product they wish to be created, to satisfy the needs and preferences of the target audiences – including those with impairments due to ageing or disability – they have defined for the product, and set the tone for decision-making in their project teams to drive towards that product. It's their job to own the accessibility of the products they manage.

In this book, I recommend they particularly read:

- the 'Overview of the four parts of the RuDDeR – to keep you on course for success' and 'Integrating the BS 8878 process into your organization' sections of Chapter 5;
- the 'Documenting your decisions' section of Chapter 5, to understand the purpose and value of documenting accessibility decisions;

- the 'How to report test results to aid prioritization of accessibility defect fixes – the Accessibility Issue Prioritization Matrix' section of Step 14 in Chapter 5, to learn more about the Accessibility Issue Prioritization Matrix; and
- Steps 1 (purpose), 2 (audiences), 5 and 8 (personalization), 6 (user goals), 7 (accessibility aims), 9 (delivery platform support), 11 (outsourcing and procurement), 13 (choice of tactical guidelines) and 15 (communicate accessibility decisions at launch) of Chapter 5, as they will be the key decision maker in those steps.

Accessibility guidance for project managers

For the activities of the different people working on a project to come together to deliver a product that achieves your organization's accessibility goals, the project manager needs to know how to plan accessibility work across the length of the project.

Project managers need to use BS 8878's process to identify all the research, strategic and tactical accessibility decisions that need to be made in each web development project, and to drive the team through each of BS 8878's steps. They are responsible for planning accessibility work across the project's sprints and test plans – separating which aspects of the product's accessibility should be a testable quality of all the user stories/functionality being created, and which aspects of the product's accessibility should be captured in backlogs as separate user stories. They need to estimate the time needed to deliver accessibility on the project – both in development overhead on all sprints, development time for accessibility functionality sprints, planned testing, and planned time for fixing deficiencies.

In this book, I recommend they particularly read:

- the 'Overview of the four parts of the RuDDeR – to keep you on course for success' and 'Integrating the BS 8878 process into your organization' sections of Chapter 5;
- the 'Documenting your decisions' section of Chapter 5, to understand the purpose and value of documenting accessibility decisions;
- the 'Using your product's tactical accessibility guidelines for planning accessibility' section of Step 13 and 'Putting accessibility into the project's test plan' section of Step 14 in Chapter 5;
- the 'How to report test results to aid prioritization of accessibility defect fixes – the Accessibility Issue Prioritization Matrix' section of Step 14 in Chapter 5, to learn more about the Accessibility Issue Prioritization Matrix; and
- all the other steps of Chapter 5, as they will be the key driver in ensuring the product team have considered each one.

Accessibility guidance for procurement managers

Many organizations outsource more of their web products than they create with internal web development teams. Consequently, procurement managers are increasingly key to ensuring that web products whose development is outsourced to external agencies, and web components that are procured, modified and mashed together to create web products, have had accessibility assured in their selection.

Procurement managers need to be able to: clearly specify the accessibility requirements of any product or competent they wish to procure; confidently score shortlisted products on their alignment with those accessibility requirements; know how to handle situations when no product is available that satisfies the accessibility requirements and the other procurement requirements; negotiate costing, commissioning and testing of accessibility improvements with product suppliers; and communicate the resulting accessibility delivered to IT staff who will integrate the component into the larger product being delivered, and to the product manager.

In this book, I recommend they particularly read:

* 'Step 11: Choose whether to develop or procure the product in-house or outsource its creation' in Chapter 5, as they will be one of the key decision makers in it.

Accessibility guidance for legal and compliance / risk managers

Legal and compliance, or business risk, managers need to assess the legal case behind accessibility, to advise the organization on the risks it may pose to the organization.

In this book, I recommend they particularly read:

* the 'Threat – the legal business case' and 'Threat – the regulatory business case' sections of Chapter 3; and
* the 'How good does the accessibility in a 'version 1' product have to be?' section of Step 15 in Chapter 5.

Accessibility guidance for sales managers

If your organization sells web products to clients, your sales managers need to assess how accessibility conformation information should be presented in the sales information for your products, so clients who care about or require this can easily find it. They also need to find ways of marketing the accessibility of your products to disabled and older people, to gain ROI on your accessibility investment.

In this book, I recommend they particularly read:

- the 'Opportunity – the commercial business case (selling tools to clients)' section of Chapter 3; and
- the "If you build it, then they'll come' – don't forget to promote your accessibility' section of Chapter 6.

Accessibility guidance for customer support managers

If your organization has a customer support team, this team need to understand: how to handle support calls from disabled and older users; how best to communicate with them to understand their issue; and where best in the organization they should refer that issue.

In this book, I recommend they particularly read:

- the 'Opportunity – the commercial business case (minimizing complaints)' section of Chapter 3; and
- the 'Reactive activities: Responding to accessibility feedback' section of Step 15 in Chapter 5.

Accessibility guidance for research & development / Innovation managers

If your organization has a Research & Development or Innovation department, this team need to understand the innovation potential in accessibility, and what they can do to harness the challenging questions of disabled and older people to suggest new innovation opportunities.

In this book, I recommend they particularly read:

- the 'Opportunity – the commercial business case (creativity and innovation)' section of Chapter 3.

Accessibility guidance for HR managers

HR managers need to be able to work with the accessibility programme manager and executive accessibility champion to audit the accessibility skills of the current staff, compare them with the skills that are needed, and commission prioritized training to upskill staff, starting with those that need it most. They also need to be able to embed appropriate accessibility competence responsibilities into the job descriptions of all staff that impact accessibility.

In this book, I recommend they particularly read:

* the 'Which job roles impact on the accessibility of products', 'Embedding motivation and responsibility', and 'Embedding competence and confidence' sections of Chapter 4.

Accessibility guidance for analytics managers

Analytics managers need to understand how to create sensible measures for counting disabled and older people's use of your web products, and how to embed these in your analytics solutions and standards.

In this book, I recommend they particularly read:

* the 'Opportunity – the commercial business case (reach)' section of Chapter 3; and
* the 'Capturing accessibility ROI' section of Chapter 6.

Accessibility guidance for brand managers

Brand managers need to understand the threats and opportunities to your organization's brand which will arise from the organization's decisions on how to support your disabled and older audiences. They particularly need to know how to ensure that brand guidelines take accessibility into account, to prevent situations occurring where you cannot be 'on brand' and accessible.

In this book, I recommend they particularly read:

* the 'Threat and opportunity – the ethical business case, and its link with brand values' section of Chapter 3.

Accessibility guidance for accessibility programme managers and executive accessibility champion

The accessibility programme manager and executive accessibility champion need to be able to generate compelling arguments for accessibility within the organization, and structure, finance and implement the organization's accessibility programme.

While the whole book is core for their responsibilities, I recommend they particularly read:

- the business cases for accessibility in Chapter 3; and
- the definition of their roles in the 'Embedding motivation and responsibility' section of Chapter 4, and all the other components of embedding accessibility throughout the rest of that chapter.

Accessibility guidance for governance managers

Governance managers need to understand how to establish and embed effective and efficient accessibility governance mechanisms within your organization, to monitor accessibility assurance across your organization's entire digital portfolio.

In this book, I recommend they particularly read:

- the 'Embedding governance' section of Chapter 4, which details everything needed to set up and regularly benchmark your organization's progress against its inclusion goals.

Accessibility guidance for social-media managers

Social-media managers need to understand the accessibility challenges of using multiple social-media channels to communicate with your organization's audiences, as each social-media platform has different accessibility strengths and weaknesses that you are unlikely to be in control of.

In this book, I recommend they particularly read:

- Step 1 (for a case study), and the 'Why create a website at all when you can use a social media platform?' section of Step 12 (for a discussion of choosing and using social-media channels) in Chapter 5; and
- the 'Reactive activities: Responding to accessibility feedback' section of Step 15 in Chapter 5 (for dealing with customer feedback from disabled people via social-media).